Diego Bonilla

Making Sense of Tracking Data

Diego Bonilla

Making Sense of Tracking Data

Connecting Interactive Storytelling, Computer Use, and Cognitive Processing

VDM Verlag Dr. Müller

Impressum/Imprint (nur für Deutschland/ only for Germany)
Bibliografische Information der Deutschen Nationalbibliothek: Die Deutsche Nationalbibliothek
verzeichnet diese Publikation in der Deutschen Nationalbibliografie; detaillierte bibliografische
Daten sind im Internet über http://dnb.d-nb.de abrufbar.
Alle in diesem Buch genannten Marken und Produktnamen unterliegen warenzeichen-, marken-
oder patentrechtlichem Schutz bzw. sind Warenzeichen oder eingetragene Warenzeichen der
jeweiligen Inhaber. Die Wiedergabe von Marken, Produktnamen, Gebrauchsnamen,
Handelsnamen, Warenbezeichnungen u.s.w. in diesem Werk berechtigt auch ohne besondere
Kennzeichnung nicht zu der Annahme, dass solche Namen im Sinne der Warenzeichen- und
Markenschutzgesetzgebung als frei zu betrachten wären und daher von jedermann benutzt
werden dürften.

Coverbild: www.purestockx.com

Verlag: VDM Verlag Dr. Müller Aktiengesellschaft & Co. KG
Dudweiler Landstr. 125 a, 66123 Saarbrücken, Deutschland
Telefon +49 681 9100-698, Telefax +49 681 9100-988, Email: info@vdm-verlag.de
Zugl.: Syracuse, Syracuse University, Diss., 2003

Herstellung in Deutschland:
Schaltungsdienst Lange o.H.G., Zehrensdorfer Str. 11, D-12277 Berlin
Books on Demand GmbH, Gutenbergring 53, D-22848 Norderstedt
Reha GmbH, Dudweiler Landstr. 99, D- 66123 Saarbrücken
ISBN: 978-3-639-06370-7

Imprint (only for USA, GB)
Bibliographic information published by the Deutsche Nationalbibliothek: The Deutsche
Nationalbibliothek lists this publication in the Deutsche Nationalbibliografie; detailed
bibliographic data are available in the Internet at http://dnb.d-nb.de.
Any brand names and product names mentioned in this book are subject to trademark, brand or
patent protection and are trademarks or registered trademarks of their respective holders. The use
of brand names, product names, common names, trade names, product descriptions etc. even
without
a particular marking in this works is in no way to be construed to mean that such names may be
regarded as unrestricted in respect of trademark and brand protection legislation and could thus
be used by anyone.

Cover image: www.purestockx.com

Publisher:
VDM Verlag Dr. Müller Aktiengesellschaft & Co. KG
Dudweiler Landstr. 125 a, 66123 Saarbrücken, Germany
Phone +49 681 9100-698, Fax +49 681 9100-988, Email: info@vdm-verlag.de

Copyright © 2008 VDM Verlag Dr. Müller Aktiengesellschaft & Co. KG and licensors
All rights reserved. Saarbrücken 2008

Produced in USA and UK by:
Lightning Source Inc., 1246 Heil Quaker Blvd., La Vergne, TN 37086, USA
Lightning Source UK Ltd., Chapter House, Pitfield, Kiln Farm, Milton Keynes, MK11 3LW, GB
BookSurge, 7290 B. Investment Drive, North Charleston, SC 29418, USA
ISBN: 978-3-639-06370-7

TABLE OF CONTENTS

4

5

7

Writing, producing, and experimenting
wouldn't have been possible without the help of many friends and colleagues.
Thank you all for supporting me in this long journey
of honest inquiry and discovery,
part of it fictional, part of it scientific.

FIGURES

9

11

TABLES

INTRODUCTION

The promises of the Internet as a communication medium are starting to consolidate. No more than a decade ago the Internet, even though functional, appeared to be dormant when compared to current communication technologies. The impact of these changes has already altered organizational and interpersonal communications, it has re-channeled money spending in the advertising industry, it has taken a dominant role in the planning of future endeavors of mass media providers, it has rebalanced the overall consumption of media to allow time for Internet related activities, and it has redefined interpretation of standing laws to accommodate new practices derived from the use of the World Wide Web.

In relationship to the entertainment industry, the Internet and the characteristics of the medium are also developing to support new forms of storytelling. The Internet is a communications medium that allows not only new forms for the transmission of meaning but also new means to evaluate and learn how audiences receive entertainment content.

The power of the medium for entertainment purposes can be envisioned if the following hypothetical scenario is taken into consideration: Let's consider a film producer who is able to wire a movie theater in a way that would unobtrusively gather data on the thoughts of each individual in the audience as the film is shown. This would empower a producer not only to assess how absorbed or how impatient the audience is at different moments of the film but also to determine what is the impact of each one of the parts on the overall enjoyment of the experience. If a scene has a detrimental effect on the overall enjoyment of the piece, the scene can be manipulated or extracted from the whole.

No current technology can record thoughts, even if we "wire" a movie theater. Nevertheless, interactive media allows us to have some access to the understanding of cognitive processes that occur while a person is receiving content. If a person is browsing different web pages on the Internet and suddenly decides to stop giving input to the computer (clicking with the mouse or typing on the keyboard) the browser will stay idle with the same content on the screen. To obtain more content, the person not only has to use an input device, indicating the computer what content to provide, but also has to engage in a certain amount of cognitive processing to make a selection regarding what content the person wants to receive. Simply, interactive behavior is the result of a communication and decision making process. It is not possible to record thoughts but it is possible to record behavior based on cognitive processing of information.

This window to understand how interactive content is being experienced is an incredible resource in itself, but if it is combined with other user information (like traditional media use data) it could also direct producers and artists into a better construction of content depending on individual user's profile. People with different media use patterns could receive alternate versions of the same experience to emphasize meaning, communication objectives and ultimately enjoyment of interactive content.

The interactive content used for the book is a non-linear story entitled *A space of time*. *A space of time* is based on a virtual environment in which user navigates and from which different units of content related to the story must be retrieved. The virtual environment is a 5 floor building constructed with QuickTime Virtual Reality (QTVR) technology and contains links to QuickTime videos and Flash animations with the narrative elements of the experience.

The research methodology applied in this book acknowledges that there are several connecting steps between traditional media use and enjoyment of a non-linear interactive story. Different browsing behavior has a direct effect on the experiencing of the multimedia non-linear story; while some browsing might allow time to experience the entire content of a node in the story's structure, other type of browsing might just grab instances from many different nodes. User's interaction with the non-linear story structure will make the medium communicate content in dissimilar ways.

In order to determine how previous media use affects behavior, an unobtrusive tracking device was embedded within the programming structure of the non-linear experience. The device keeps track of the subjects' interaction with the medium while being exposed to the different multimedia elements of the non-linear story. All of the interactions are time-stamped and registered on an internal database until the experience culminates. At that moment a database file is created and sent via email and FTP to two different servers located in the United States (one in New Jersey and one in California).

Before digital communications, research regarding the use and the effects of media were commonly broken in two steps: the experiencing of content and, then, the research effort to measure the effects of the content in individuals. This book seeks to take advantage of the fact that the medium that provides the content is at the same time part of the research effort. In other words, interactive media gives communication researchers the unique opportunity to obtain detailed information about how the content was experienced. For research purposes, when it comes to any interactive medium, the medium can become a measurement of itself.

This book also seeks to find a relationship between previous media use and user's sense of control. Sense of control encompasses the degree to which the user believes that the structure of the non-linear story and the navigation through the virtual environment that delivers the story affected negatively his or her ability to concentrate on the story's plot. A sense of disorientation in hypertext and hypermedia has been empirically supported by research, and it is believed to have an impact on users' performance. If disorientation is present at the time of browsing, the user invests more cognitive processes on finding content structure rather than in understanding the plot. If the user feels comfortable with the medium and the content structure, then the user will be able to devote more cognitive processes to the understanding of the story per se and would be in a better position to enjoy the non-linear multimedia experience. This indicates that enjoyment of a non-linear interactive piece could be related to the amount of time spent with media similar to the one that the user experiences (content connected through links or hyperlinked content).

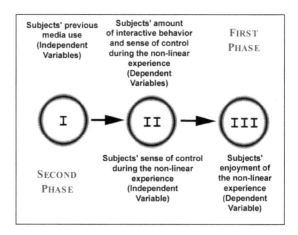

Figure 1. Research Model

Schema theory supports the idea that the human brain reduces cognitive overload through a process of encoding repetitive tasks. Within the scope of Schema theory, it is possible to justify an optimization of resources to make cognitive processing more efficient. Schemata help individuals perform better on every type of tasks, from obtaining solutions to mathematical problems, playing chess, typing a memo, or writing short stories, to selective exposure during a news broadcast. Any activity that is done regularly creates a schema to facilitate cognitive processes related to that activity.

Schema theory explains why an individual, when confronted with a new form of content structure, in this case a multimedia non-linear story that utilizes a virtual reality tour of a building as a narrative device, would retrieve schemata from other media to make sense of it. Because the non-linear story contains video-intensive segments, text-intensive segments, audio clips that are triggered while the user is browsing the virtual environment, it is expected that schemata coming from film, television, radio, text-based media (newspapers, books, magazines,) and others will be activated and combined. For example, if the user has used a computer video game in which units of content are retrieved from the video game structure based on interaction, most probably those users will feel less disoriented experiencing the non-linear story than a person who has never used a computer before. Furthermore, if any of the subjects for the current research project has experienced the non-linear story before, it would be expected that he or she will have already started developing a schema to facilitate its viewing.

The model outlined in Figure 1 has the potential to guide multimedia content producers and creators to consider changes that will augment the probability of digital media enjoyment. In order to achieve this, the operationalization of enjoyment is crucial and it is based on research coming from several different disciplines in addition to mass communications theories. Even though in mass communications research the constructs of "satisfaction" and "gratification" have a long, well-documented history as dependent variables, their operationalization often is more functional (i.e., functions of mass media: how individuals use news programs to inform themselves about current events, or how individuals use media to escape) than the enjoyment of the media content as an objective in itself. Users and Gratifications theory also carries the assumption that individuals know the content and the medium before deciding to make purposeful use of it; a premise difficult to sustain in the case of the non-linear story used for this book because the probability that the subjects have experienced such a similar story structure is small if not negligible.

Even though we might have schemata to process every repetitive task in life, previous media use is posited to be the best candidate to influence browsing behavior, sense of control and possible enjoyment of the multimedia non-linear story.

Finally, the project not only seeks to understand the impact of memory in the use of an interactive experience through a deductive method but also seeks to find behavior patterns using an inductive approach to analyze the bulk of the data captured. The amount of data that a tracking device can obtain is very large and it can be studied in several different ways to understand behavioral patterns. For example, data obtained with the tracking device can be graphed on top of the floor maps of the virtual environment to visualize behavioral patterns within the experience. An inductive approach to the data provided by the delivery medium could help understand how memory affects behavior and could facilitate future creative endeavors and augment enjoyment.

Non-linear content

A crucial difference between traditional media and digital media is *random access*.
Random access (see Figure 2) refers to the ability to jump from one unit of content to other
non-sequential units of content in a negligible amount of time. Current hard drives can
locate data anywhere in their surface within a few milliseconds (see Table 1). If a unit of
content within a larger body of content can be accessed "instantaneously," then the
sequential structure of the content is blurred. In terms of the chronological display of the
information contained in a digital medium, the beginning equals the end, and both
beginning and end are equal to any of the parts.

ATA	Performance SCSI	High-End SCSI
8.0-9.5 milliseconds	5.3-8.5 milliseconds	3.9-5.2 milliseconds

Table 1. Access speeds on different types of hard drives. Source: Seagate, 2001.

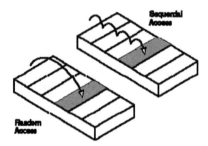

Figure 2. Random Access vs. Sequential Access. Source: Webopedia (2001)

Traditional media have linear or sequential displays of information. A common
example of such media is television, which does not provide immediate access to the end

or to any of the parts of the program being watched[1]. The same happens with films: At the time of experiencing a film in a theater, the audience does not have the ability to disrupt the chronological presentation of the content. The so-called non-linear films are productions that contain elements that are misplaced in the chronological order of the story (for example, using narrative devices such as flashbacks and flash forwards); however, these events happen at the same moment during the experiencing of the film, making it a linear experience.

In analog media like audio cassettes and video tapes, content is also displayed continuously but they offer a limited degree of control; the only way to access the end of a body of content is by advancing through the rest of it. It can be argued that books, magazines and newspapers can provide fast access to different units of content; the reader simply has to flip several pages to find new information. Nevertheless, even if we consider flipping through pages a form of "fast-accessing" new information, the logical continuation of content is questionable. A news article that appears on the front page and continues somewhere else in the newspaper is considered linear content that has two physical locations within the publication. The newspaper does not give any other means of linking information except for the use of internal references, the main purpose of which is to distribute the information within the physical body of the publication. Therefore, a second crucial difference between traditional media and digital media is that in the latter information is broken into *many discrete addressable* units. Any unit can be accessed from any other part in the body of content through code, creating a "web-like" structure of linked units of information.

The prefix "hyper-" found in the word "hypermedia" and "hypertext" comes from the Greek word *ηψπερ (hyper)*, which means "over, above, beyond." As explained in the introduction of "Hypertext and Hypermedia" (Woodhead, 1990), hypermedia is a "subset

---

[1] At the time of writing this book one of the commercial first fiber optic networks is being deployed in the cities of Sacramento and Carmichael in the State of California. Fiber optic networks bring to television Point-to-Point communications, a feature previously found only on the Internet. A 10 Mbps allows subscribers to have "video on demand," disrupting the scheduling of television programs and giving the subscribers the ability to pause, rewind, and fast forward movies on the television.

of the more general class of interactive multimedia –not all implementations of which support 'hyper' functionality" and hypertext is a subset of hypermedia. Hypermedia is constructed through of units of contents called "nodes" and the "nodes are connected by links, in a variety of possible structures such as webs and hierarchies" (Woodhead, 1990). Therefore, the constructs *hyper*-text and *hyper*-media refer to text and different types of media composed of independent addressable units linked to each other through code. The result is not only a form of media in which content can be broken into many parts but also a set of units of content that do not have to be finished before switching to other parts of the corpus with logical connections to the preceding content.

The structural flexibility of hypermedia and its interactivity transfer the control of the sequence, the pace, and most importantly, what to look at and what to ignore from the designer to the user (Kristof & Satran, 1995). Therefore, the assumption that the physical attributes of a medium are a strong determinant of the type of content that the medium provides resides at the core of my research.

The breaking up of messages and parts of the content into multiple non-sequential units of content affect the way a message is conveyed. Such fragmentation has different impacts on different types of content. While meaning might not suffer in the case of non-linear news bites, meaning might suffer when it comes to non-linear chapters in a full-length story; that is, units of content that are small and independent are different from large units of content meant to be read sequentially. Furthermore, the amount of time destined to the experience of the non-linear pieces should also be important to the overall understanding of the content; half an hour devoted to the reading of small news bites, that each can be read in 30 or less seconds, provides a more flexible structure than the same amount of time devoted to the non-linear watching of 7 minute video segments.

Linear content is defined by a series of rules that frame our understanding of reality; for example, in almost all storytelling –fictional or non-fictional, the plot is presented as a set of events that converge into a conclusion in a sequential order. The typical layout of linear content might have an effect on the human psyche by setting a causal linear relationship among events. Therefore, another assumption of this project is that non-linear content requires a different frame of mind than that created by linear storytelling. Based in an environment of interlinked units of content, storytelling changes –

and those changes go from an absence of closure in a story to the integration of a multiplicity of *lexias*[2] that could be part or not of the corpus, or to the integration of randomized events that will have certain level of chance of being incorporated into the story.

Even though a rhetorical analysis could also be implemented to find in what way the sequencing of the units of content might have on the understanding of the story itself, the main emphasis of the project is to find first if the content structure has an impact on the experiencing of *A space of time*; the theoretical approach for this project is based on psychology and the study of human memory.

---

[2] Lexias are independent units of text that integrate the whole. (Landow, 1992)

THEORETICAL BACKGROUND

This section delineates the theoretical framework utilized for the derivation of theoretical linkages and operationalization of constructs. This chapter starts with a broad view of the external and internal factors that affect computer use in order to recognize users and not external factors as the focus of the project. Schema theory and other approaches to the understanding of memory structures are introduced as the main theoretical framework to understand how human memory works and how it aids cognitive processing while experiencing interactive media. Lack of memory structures regarding interactive communications is then associated with disorientation and cognitive overload. Subsequently, a theoretical framework regarding disorientation and lack of control is introduced with the purpose of creating a theoretical linkage between disorientation and enjoyment. Flow theory and other research on leisure is analyzed as a means to provide a construct for the enjoyment of a non-linear experience such as *A space of time*.

A space of time is a non-linear multimedia story that must be experienced on a computer to maintain all of its interactive and random features. As a starting point for the theoretical background it is important to delineate the elements that might affect the joint performance of the computer and the user. It is possible to divide the factors that affect a person's use of a computer into five parts (Rumpradit, 1999, pp. 2-11):

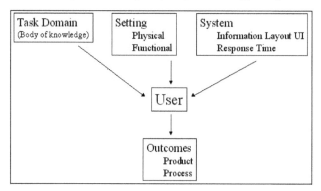

Figure 3. Factors that affect a person's use of a computer. Source: Rumpradit, 1999 (chap. 2 p. 11)

23

Task Domain: Mainly the body of knowledge composed of entities and relationships (i.e., entries in a bank account, items in an online newspaper, a catalogue of products that can be ordered via the Internet).

Setting: Encompasses the physical environment in which the user is performing a computer-based task and the functional characteristics of that task (for example, the time allotted to such activity, motivation, purpose, etc.).

System The medium itself. Relevant studies are common in Information Studies, where User Interface (UI), response time, information search, and database structure are frequent subjects of research.

User: Studies related to the user extend into the realm of psychology, where constructs of recall, disorientation, and mental models, among many others, are frequently studied with regard to computer or Internet use.

Outcomes: Behaviors that result from internal information-seeking strategies in combination with the task domain, setting characteristics, system and user.

User Interface studies shows that navigation patterns are affected by the way in which menu layout is displayed. Norman (1991) created a simple set of structured menus conveying the same information but having a different structural layout: a computerized shopping menu guide for the purpose of buying gifts. Subjects to the experiment were given two types of targets: 1) Specific targets: the actual name of the gift, or 2) Scenario targets: a description of the person who is going to receive the gift.

A visual representation of the menu styles and a main results chart are shown in Figure 4:

24

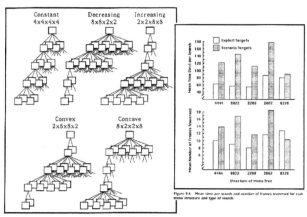

Figure 9.1. Menu structures having the same number of items and depth but
varying the breadth with depth.

Figure 4. Source: Norman (1991), p.217, 222

The form in which information is presented with the Interface has an effect on how
a person is able to complete determined tasks on the computer. Following Figure 3 and
focusing only on the user part of the diagram, we can break the influential browsing-
determinant factors into several parts. One of the most important factors that affect the
browsing of information is the user's memory, more specifically, the user's mental model
of how the system works.

In *A space of time*, the task domain is the overall integration of all the information
contained in the experience: Pandora's Flash animations that show her deep discontent of
the alienation and apathy of citizens; the video segments in which she appears that tell a
part of the story on the last years of her life; the video segments that show contextual
information of why Pandora dies, and the virtual environment that holds all the links to the
multimedia elements of the story. The setting for the regular Internet user is the location
where the computer is placed, for example, at home, the office or a university cluster and
the time that the user assigns to the experiencing of *A space of time*. The system is
composed of multimedia elements with which the user interacts: the QTVRs, QT movies,
Flash animations, and the buttons at the bottom of the screen. In terms of the user interface,
A space of time does not have many screen variations; most of the experience is displayed

in three main interfaces: 1) one that forms part of the virtual tour showing a QTVR and a series of 7 buttons displayed in a bar at the bottom of the screen, 2) one that displays the QT movies and the animations with a single small representation of the button bar that takes you back to the QTVR tour, and 3) one that shows Pandora's Flash animations and the same button bar to return to the tour. The user is a complex entity that can be fragmented, for research purposes, in many ways. The user brings a set of previous experiences, cognitive resources, and motor differences, among many others, that may or may not have an impact on the outcome. Finally, all the elements converge to influence the outcome, which in the case of *A space of time* is the enjoyment or lack of enjoyment of the non-linear experience that tells the story of Pandora Hamilton.

Pertaining to the user part in Rumpradit's (1999) illustration, "mental models" are frequently used for examining the impact of human memory on the way in which computerized systems are operated and the outcome obtained from the system. However, the study of memory in psychology is very broad and may have several applications to the understanding of media use in mass communications studies (DeFleur, 1999).

SCHEMA THEORY

Developing a schema is a process of encoding. This means putting together a kind of mental organization that will be used to remember ideas and events. Schemas are structures of organized knowledge acquired through experience; these structures help people confront the same or similar situations in the future more effectively. The concept of a cognitive structure appears in several different disciplines under various names, for example: *prototypes* (Cantor and Mischel, 1977, 1979), *frames* (Minsky, 1975), *stereotypes* (Lippmann, 1922), social *scripts* (Shank & Abelson, 1977) and *cognitive maps* (Fauconnier, 1997). Within mass communication studies, most of the work related to schema theories is attributed to Doris Graber, who describes schema theories as a form for people to deal with an "information tide" (Graber, 1988). This vision takes into account a user, or audience, already overwhelmed by the amount of information available in the news media stream, who has to establish a cognitive structure to extract relevant information. This cognitive structure, for example, is applicable to common formats of TV news broadcast where the program follows an typical sequence: first a summary of news, display of major national news, major local news, the weather and, finally, a happy ending clip. People apply a personal schema, which will allocate different attention levels to the different segments of the TV news broadcast, to obtain the information that they care most about. This schema comes from many previous exposures to the same type of TV news broadcasting.

Economizing Information Processing and Social Schemas

Graber's work in mass communications starts from the assumption that there is already too much information in the environment and that the human brain is not capable of processing the entire news stream; therefore, a schema is a mental structure destined to economize cognitive processing (Crocker et. Al., 1984; O'Sullivan & Durso, 1984; Tesser & Leone, 1977.)

However, schema theories encompass the creation of schemata not only for the efficient processing of news broadcasts but also for every human activity, which leads to the work of Fiske & Taylor (1984, pp. 149) who divided schemata into:

- Person schemata: Cognitive structures that define the characteristics of other people ranging from usual behavior to an understanding of the psychology of typical or specific individuals.
- Self-schemata: General information that provides us with a structure of our own psychology, an easy to verbalize self-concept.
- Role schemata: Closely related to stereotyping, they give a structure in which we interpret and categorize the behavior of different types of individuals in terms of the role they play.
- Event schemata: Related to the typical sequencing of events, like the one mentioned before in which a person recognizes the pattern of a TV news broadcast and uses a mental structure to determine the time in which he/she will be allocating attention resources.

The categorization of social schemata, more than giving a specific solution to understanding browsing behavior, shows that a person creates schemata for every set of repetitive events in that person's life. They are applied not only to the interpretation of social cues but also when a person browses the Internet ritualistically, absorbing the medium's information layout.

Schema Processing Models

Schemata as cognitive structures have a role in the constant information processing of a person. Norman & Brobow (1976) developed a "data-pool" model that describes information processing from the moment physical signals are perceived to the moment in which data is interpreted under the influence of different schemata. An outline of the data-pool model is shown in Figure 5:

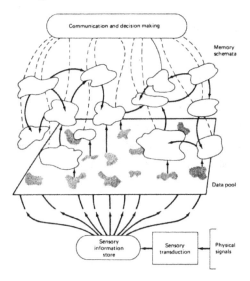

Figure 5. Source: Norman & Brobow (1976), p. 118

The main characteristics of the "data-pool" model can be extracted from Figure 5. Physical signals are received through our senses and translated into what Norman & Brobow call the data-pool. Schemata are memory structures that apply to the data-pool in order to facilitate information processing. This model works under several assumptions about information processing:

- There is only one data-pool, a limited resource pool from which the processes must draw.
- Memory is composed of active and fluid units (schemata) that use the information present in the data-pool. Then the brain performs computations on the information and sends it back to the data pool or modifies the schemata.
- Schemata tie together the information of any given concept.
- Schemata can be invoked and change in relevancy according to repeated experiences.
- There are no fixed memory locations in the brain; there are interrelated sets of concepts united by a schemata.

Schemata

The existence or the absence of a schema might be supported by empirical research; nevertheless, a description of actual parts that constitute schemata is hard to support by research and is not regularly found in the literature. Iran-Nejad (1989) defines two different kinds of schemata giving more "depth" to the regular use of the construct in social sciences:

- Biofunctional Schema Theory and
- Parallel Distributed Processing (PDP) schema.

The former is a one-unit-one-concept representational system as the one shown in Figure 6:

29

Figure 6. Source: Iran-Nejad (1989), p. 130

Two concepts are represented in Figure 6: One is a cube that seems to be laying in a surface and the other one is a cube that seems to be attached to an upper surface – or a ceiling. According to the Biofunctional Schema Theory, each of the cubes has a schema of its own; that is, a schema for each object. This converts the brain in an enormous "database" of more or less relevant schemas that are activated depending on the situation a person is confronting. The more frequently a person faces a situation, the bigger the relevance of a set of schemas over other; that is, schemas are treated as memories reinforced by repetition.

A PDP schema is based on a set of features that constitute the overall object –in this case, a cube. But the features can be broken into many types of attributes, making schemas resemble a set of networked features that activate at a deeper level.

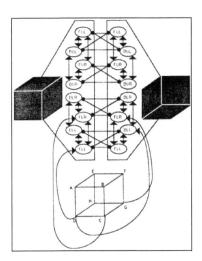

Figure 7. Source: Iran-Nejad (1989), p.130

Each one of the nodes represents each one of the vertices of the cube (i.e. FLL is Front Lower Left, BLL is Back Lower Left, BUR is Back Upper Right, etc.) This system creates a set of features that represent a cube that a person could extract in many different forms – making the process of schema-saving and schema-retrieving a more efficient system. If the cube has one of its corners broken, instead of retrieving a schema of a cube with a broken corner, Parallel Distributed Processing assumes that all of the remainder features of the cube will activate in the same way as if the cube was complete and the broken corner will activate other schemata.

Even though the presence or absence of schemata can be empirically supported, there is no experimental evidence that supports the hypothesis that schemata are actually constructed in a specific way, leaving them as nothing more than important constructs or metaphors to understand memory and cognition.

Coincidentally, the Parallel Distributed Process actually resembles a hypertext or hypermedia system in which a set of independent features is interconnected to create the whole. It is quite common to find computer metaphors in the study of memory, attention and cognition; from the most elementary assumption that the human brain receives an input, processes the information and then provides an output, to more complicated metaphors in which the structure of hypertext documents function in the same way that memory or the brain does (Ayersman, 1995; Ayersman & Reed, 1995; Liu, Ayersman & Reed, 1995; Weller, 1995; Hailey & Hailey, 1998).

Schema rotation or schema adaptation

The idea of a schema with independent parts that is not stored in an infinite capacity brain brings the idea of schemata as independent memory units that are replaced for other independent memory units when needed or as independent units that are modified accordingly to/from every situation. The literature on schema replacement is scarce; however, three models can be extracted from three major interdisciplinary studies (Fiske & Taylor, 1984; Rothbart, 1981; Taylor, 1981):

- The bookkeeping model: Establishes gradual changes in a schema depending on each discrepant encounter –a fine-tuning approach to schema building and preservation.
- The conversion model: States that schemas are changed on their entirety when a discrepant encounter occurs.
- The subtyping model: Incongruence creates adjustments in the form of subcategories in a hierarchical set of schemas.

The rotation and adaptation of schemata is important because it supports the idea that the more people experience non-linear content the more they will adapt to its content structure. Non-linearity in the display of information is the medium's constant feature, the linking between nodes can change in terms of their visual attributes – from blue-colored underlined text, static images, animated images, image maps, to video[3]. In the last decade we have been experiencing a change in the type of content on the Internet; from a display of information that was mostly hypertext to information that is starting to be true hypermedia. Explained by schema replacement theories, these changes in the type of visuals that users see when browsing the Internet should convey changes in the users' schemata too. The bookkeeping model supports the idea of fine-tuning a schema to reflect changes in the visuals but not changes in the non-linear nature of the medium, while the conversion model would suggest a total replacement. The subtyping model adds the disruptive elements of an experience to a set of hierarchical set of schemata; it differs from the booking model not by fine-tuning a schema but by adding a layer to a hierarchical structure. Under the subtyping model, constant use of non-linear documents on the web would add a schema to understand logical connections among links instead of replacing previous schemata by conversion or bookkeeping.

---

[3] An example of a hyper linked video development endeavor can be found at:
http://www.media.mit.edu/hypersoap/

COGNITIVE FLEXIBILITY THEORY

Cognitive Flexibility theory addresses the process undertaken by the human brain and its memory structures to make sense of knowledge domains that are "ill-structured." An "ill-structured" knowledge domain is defined as: "one in which the following properties hold: (1) each case or example of knowledge application typically involves the simultaneous interactive involvement of multiple, wide-application conceptual structures (multiple schemas, perspectives, organizational principles, and so on), each of which is individually complex […] and (2) the pattern of conceptual incidence and interaction varies substantially across cases nominally of the same type" (Spiro, Feltovich, Jacobson, & Coulson, 1992, p. 3). According to Lawless & Brown (1997), physics and mathematics (algorithmic in nature) are well-structured domains, and history and literature are ill-structured domains (heuristic in nature).

Cognitive Flexibility theory, instead of promoting a system of education in which ideas are oversimplified, builds on the notion that multiple connections among knowledge domains enhance understanding and learning. Inherently, the theory assumes a Parallel Distributed Process that retrieves features of different knowledge domains to improve efficiency.

Translated to the experiencing of *A space of time*, Cognitive Flexibility supports the idea of retrieving other media schemata to make sense of the non-linear experience. A QTVR panorama looks like as a still image on the screen. First, probably the fact that it is displayed statically on the computer — while the cursor changes shape when placed on it — would indicate to a person who has used computers in the past that some interaction could occur; and if the user opts not to interact, the image will remain static in the screen indefinitely. However, when the user interacts with the QTVR panorama, it becomes a moving photographic quality image that is not a photograph, and even though now and then sounds are heard while moving the image, it is not a TV show. When the first video sequence is launched, the video looks like a normal film clip where all the rules of cinematography apply, but it stops suddenly and then goes back to another QTVR panorama. To make meaning of a spinning image and short video sequence that brings you back to the same spinning image, the user should bring schemata from other media.

Even though the schemata activated to understand what is happening in *A space of time* would integrate text-based, audio-based, and video-based media, the schema that more closely resembles the information structure of the non-linear story is the World Wide Web. Furthermore, the best schema that can be brought to the understanding of *A space of time* is the schema coming from the experience of *A space of time* itself. In this case, the navigational structure, interface design and pieces of the story will be retrieved from memory to free cognitive resources and the schemata related to the experience will be reinforced.

DISORIENTATION AND COGNITIVE OVERLOAD

Text, audio and video are common in mass media; nevertheless, units of content linked to other units of content in a web-like structure had not been common to the public until the growth and acceptance of the World Wide Web. This type of structural difference makes disorientation one of the major usability problems while browsing hypertext (Nielsen, 1990). According to Boechler (2001), scholars in the field have suggested that "unless disorientation and cognitive overhead can be effectively reduced the ultimate usefulness of hypertext will be severely limited" (p. 28), and another source states that it has been estimated that 60% of hypertext-related research has been devoted to disorientation (Dvorak and Summerville, 1996).

The literature review for this book concurs with the opinion of McDonald & Stevenson (1996) that most experimental investigations regarding disorientation are based around a question-answer task. The usefulness of hypertext and hypermedia for teaching and learning or for information retrieval is normally found in Instructional Design or Information Systems literature. Consequently, the lines of inquiry revolve around the use of hypertext/hypermedia to improve recall or to achieve faster and more accurate information searches.

Measurements normally involve two different categories (Boechler, 2001, p. 37):

Efficiency measures: Number of nodes visited in the context of the overall amount of nodes in the information structure, number of nodes visited that were not needed in the information retrieval task, number of nodes revisited, time spent on each node and total task time.

Effectiveness measures: Search accuracy (number of correct answers in an information search task), recall of the information contained to which the user was exposed (number of node titles remembered), or comprehension of the document structure (accurate sketch map of a document).

This leaves a yet undeveloped space for research regarding disorientation in hypermedia systems for which the main purpose is, as in the case of *A space of time*, to entertain. Several of these measurements lack purpose in the experiencing of a non-linear story. For example, in the efficiency category: The number of nodes visited does not necessarily indicate efficient behavior, instead it suggests an individual approach to the experiencing of content that can be truncated and reorganized; also, revisiting nodes might not represent unproductive behavior but an individual desire to re-experience the content found in that specific node. In the effectiveness category: The construct "accuracy" lacks meaning for entertainment because it is not a search-and-retrieve information task..

TYPES OF DISORIENTATION

In a research experiment designed to assess the relationship between data structure and disorientation in a question-answer task with a recall component, Edwards & Hardman (1989) tested three different "forms of being lost" outlined previously by Elm & Woods (1985):

Not knowing where to go next.

Knowing where to go, but not knowing how to get there.

- Not knowing where they were in relation to the overall structure of the document.

The independent variable in this case is data structure with three categorical values: 1) Hierarchy condition, 2) mixed condition and 3) index condition. The hierarchy condition interface would present the information in a hierarchical structure that could only be navigated from the first page down, the index condition would present a word index as the only means to find information, and the mixed condition would allow hierarchal as well as index browsing. The results are summarized in the next table:

Form of being "lost"	Hierarchy condition	Mixed condition	Index condition
Not knowing where to go next	2	7	3
Knowing where to go, but not knowing how to get there.	-	3	-
Not knowing where they were in relation to the overall structure of the document.	1	4	1

Table 2.Forms of being "lost" reported. Source: Edwards & Hardman (1989), p. 121.

From Table 2, it can be inferred that users felt more disoriented in the mixed condition, which raises the question about how the number of "navigation paths" in a given task is related to disorientation. Foss (1989, p. 972) classified the problem of "feeling lost" into three categories depending on the user's symptoms:

1) The navigational disorientation problem
   a. Causes
      i. Lack of knowledge of the topological organization.
      ii. Unfamiliarity with the access tools.
      iii. Lack of knowledge of the extent of the document.
   b. Symptoms
      i. Looping.
      ii. Inefficient paths.
      iii. Query failures.

2) The embedded digression problem

    a. Causes: Difficulties in the planning, managing and executing of digressions.

    b. Symptoms

        i. Screen layouts with multiple windows.

        ii. Repeated retracking.

3) "Art museum" problem

    a. Causes: High cognitive demands. The title of the problem comes from an analogy related to the feeling of being "overwhelmed" that museum visitors experience after a period of time browsing vast collections of art; this includes the inability to remember details or to summarize the contents of the museum.

    b. Symptoms

        i. Short reading time on each node.

        ii. Restrictive paths.

Once again, this type of inquiry is related to the performance of specific tasks and not to the experiencing of non-linear entertainment. *A space of time*, as a non-linear experience, shares some of the causes for each one the categories even though the symptoms for each one of them cannot be directly applied. For example: "Looping" is not necessarily a construct related to inefficient means of experiencing the content; subjects might return to previous units of content for pure entertainment purposes. One of the biggest assets, for a non-linear story, is the experiencing of a story in many different ways, while in a question-answer task the most efficient path could be the shortest or fastest past to the right answer; therefore, the idea of an "inefficient path" is not applicable either.

Even though Foss (1989) and Elm & Woods (1985) establish that disorientation causes bad performance in the tasks assigned, during the experiencing of *A space of time*, the problems of lack of knowledge of the structure and the structure's length or size, unfamiliarity with the access tools, and high cognitive demands could translate into frustration and therefore lack of enjoyment.

THE LINK BETWEEN DISORIENTATION AND COGNITIVE LOAD

Browsing a computer document that is fragmented into multiple interlinked nodes requires carrying several tasks simultaneously, and these tasks are divided into three categories (Kim & Hirtle, 1995, p.241):

- Navigational tasks: The planning and execution of "routes" in a network of interlinked content.
- Informational tasks: Understanding of the information contained in each node and its relationship to other nodes.
- Task management: The coordination of both navigational tasks and informational tasks.

Each one of these tasks draws cognitive resources from the user and has an impact on the user's performance. In the case of *A space of time*, the navigational task will draw cognitive resources from the user to understand how to operate QTVR files, how to navigate in the virtual environment (concerning decisions related to where the user wants to move next), how to activate video scenes and how to skip them, and how to interact with the main interface buttons; interface design by itself has been studied for its impact on cognitive load (Harmon, 1995).

Informational tasks have a cognitive load because the user has to understand the information contained in the nodes; in the case of *A space of time*, the story of the Pandora Hamilton. Even though there are parts of the story that are less complex than others (for example, the short film clips that are located throughout the inner walls of the building), a good portion of the dialog involves complex relationships regarding the pervasiveness of the advertising industry, the threats of fast technological advance and "detailed" explanations of the inconsistencies between the idea of democracy and free market capitalism.

Task management combines both navigational tasks and informational tasks: Would the user be able to understand how everything fits together? The building and

Pandora's life are interrelated in the story; she dies inside the building. The characters of the movie are floating around in the building because they represent a "limbo-like" environment after the death of Pandora where she has access to many of her memories. The figure of the tramp represents a broken link in the rationale of the story and suggests a different reason for the characters floating inside the building: The tramp suffers from Temporal Lobe Epilepsy, a mental condition that normally carries visual and auditory hallucinations. This "condition" of the tramp is hinted throughout the diner discussions and explained thoroughly in a scene where the doctor lectures in an academic environment about his research on Temporal Lobe Epilepsy.

The navigational task is related to previous research by Gygi (1990), who addresses the act of deciding where to go next as part of a "literary contract" that the reader and the author establish in a hypertext document. The "literary contract" is the transferring of some of the traditional author decisions to the reader, specifically, the order in which the units are accessed. In traditional paper-based media the authors are expected to establish the order in the presentation of ideas; in hypertext this becomes part of the user's responsibility.

In relation to the finding that disorientation is related to degradation in user performance (Foss 1989; Elm & Woods, 1985), degradation in performance also "occurs when a hypertext user's cognitive resources are overwhelmed." (Boechler, 2001, p. 27)

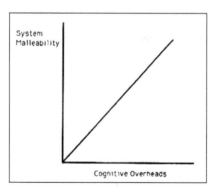

Figure 8. System Malleability vs. System Overheads. Source: Woodhead, 1991, p. 138.

Furthermore, it has been hypothesized (see Figure 8) that an increase in the hypertext malleability (like the Mixed condition between Hierarchical and Index conditions, see above) would increase the cognitive overhead (defined as the cognitive resources implemented in a hypertext-related task) (Woodhead, 1991). Kim & Hirtle (1995) made the same connection citing a tradeoff between flexibility, cognitive loads and disorientation: "The price of the increased flexibility of access by browsing is an increased cognitive load on the user, which results in disorientation problems." (p. 240) This relationship is summarized in Figure 9:

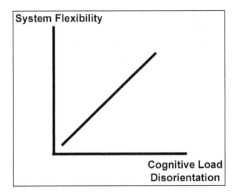

Figure 9. System Flexibility vs Cognitive Load/Disorientation

Chou, Lin & Sun (2000) refer to both cognitive overload and disorientation as the "twin problems" that "can become even more serious if the hypertext system has a large number of nodes and links," which can be related to the "Art museum problem" described above. A theoretical link between disorientation and frustration could be drawn from the literature review regarding disorientation. "One of the most frustrating usability problems faced by users is becoming lost or disorientated." (Otter & Johnson, 2000, p. 3) If enjoyment is most probably absent at a time of frustration, as a logical extension of the findings regarding disorientation, it could be deduced that disorientation does not bring enjoyment but lack of it.

All of the above points towards the conclusion that, having a limited cognitive processing capability, the more cognitive resources are placed on the navigational task, the fewer cognitive resources can be applied to the informational task and to task management.

ENJOYMENT

As explained in the "Disorientation and Cognitive Overload" section of the book, most of the research regarding disorientation and cognitive overload relate these two factors to a decrease in user performance. In the case of a non-linear story meant to entertain, enjoyment is an important dimension to evaluate. Nevertheless, at the time of writing this book, searches for research involving the pure enjoyment of non-linear entertainment have been fruitless.

Uses and gratifications theory "has always provided a cutting-edge theoretical approach in the initial stages of each new mass media communications medium: newspapers, radio, television, and now the Internet" (Ruggiero, 2000, p. 26). "Satisfaction" and "gratification" have a long and well-documented history as dependent variables in mass communications theories.

Uses and gratifications theory could offer a venue to understand enjoyment; nevertheless, the "gratifications" construct assumes some sort of pre-exposure to specific media because exposure derives from personal selection based on psychological and social needs. In the case of *A space of time*, this approach would violate this assumption because the probability of exposure to the non-linear story, or any non-linear story told with a virtual tour and random video scenes, is very small[4]. Furthermore, in a research environment where subjects participate in exchange of monetary or academic rewards, the gratification sought is not the experience per se but the compensation for participating in the scientific study. From a uses and gratifications approach, media selection is initiated by

---

[4] Hopefully this will be a reasonable assumption in the future, when other non-linear video experiences become more common.

the individual and not by a third person. To this matter, Rayburn & Palmgreen (1984) explain the gratifications as a function of expectancy theory and offer a mathematical model where media consumption is preceded by gratifications sought and followed by perceived gratifications.

One theory helps to explain the relationship between schema, disorientation and enjoyment: Flow theory. This theory seems to be derived from Maslow's definition of "peak experiences": "sudden feelings of intense happiness and well-being, and possibly the awareness of 'ultimate truth' and the unity of all things. Accompanying these experiences is a heightened sense of control over the body and emotions, and a wider sense of awareness, as though one was standing upon a mountaintop" (cited in Guiley, 1991, p. 438). Flow theory's main goal is to reach an understanding of human optimal experiences and enjoyment. These optimal experiences, as described by Csikszentmihalyi (1990) in his conceptualization of Flow Theory, are elicited when a series of factors are present during an activity:

1. There are clear goals every step of the way. When people are in flow, they know exactly what has to be done at every moment. This sets the creator's and the athlete's mind to be focused on each task, and the focus is not only in the task itself but also in the goals to be accomplished at that specific point.

2. There is immediate feedback to one's action. This can be easily translated into knowing how well we are doing. If there is no feedback, there is no chance to monitor self-performance.

3. There is a balance between challenges and skills. If the challenges overcome the skills, the person fills anxious and the state of flow is more difficult to achieve. Similarly, if the skills overcome the challenges there is a feeling of boredom that inhibits the state of flow.

4. Action and awareness are merged. In the state of flow a person feels enjoyment when he or she is totally engaged in an activity, a moment in which the mind and the body are working in parallel all the time

5. Distractions are excluded from consciousness. Maintaining focus in the task at hand is one of the typical characteristics of the moment of flow.

6. There is no worry of failure. In the middle of a state of flow, a state of enjoyment, there is no worry of failure. For example: Athletes in a state of flow acknowledge that during a competition they do not think about winning or losing.

7. Self-consciousness disappears. Self-consciousness makes us aware of how people perceive us. In a state of flow self-awareness disappears and sometimes this feeling is accompanied by a feeling of union with the environment.

8. The sense of time becomes distorted.

9. The activity becomes autotelic. Autotelic means in Greek: an end in itself. In the state of flow, when all the above factors are present, the experience surpasses what we are, where we live, the weather, or anything that is not related to the experience itself.

The balance between challenges and skills that is proposed by Flow Theory could be explained also with schema theory and the proposed linkage between disorientation and enjoyment. According to Csikszentmihalyi (1990), the two most important dimensions of an experience are challenges and skills, and they interact in the following way:

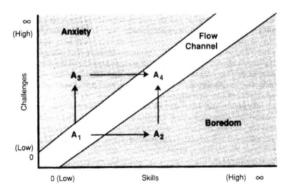

Figure 10. Challenges vs. Skills. Source: Csikszentmihalyi, 1990, p. 74

The interpretation of such interaction is not only intuitive but also it has been supported by Csikszentmihalyi's findings. If a person confronts an activity in which the challenges are far greater than his or her skills, the person will feel anxiety (A3). To the contrary, if a person's skills are far greater than the challenges, the person will feel boredom (A2). Finally, if a person has a balance between challenges and skills the person will get involved in the activity and would experience a state of flow and enjoyment (A1 and A4).

Let's create a hypothetical scenario based on a chess tournament in which a novice player is confronting an expert player. Within the context of schema theory, the novice chess player is still creating schemata that help him understand the basic movements for each one of the pieces, while the expert chess player already has those schemata and is able to concentrate on strategy. In order to beat the expert player, the novice will have to process information regarding basic movement of the pieces and strategy at the same time. If the novice tries to do so, he will have a cognitive overload that entails a decrease in performance and eventually leads to a feeling of frustration. After his defeat, the more time the novice spends playing chess the more chess schemata he will be able to bring to the next competition. Finally, when the novice skills improve (by developing mental schemata necessary for competitive chess-playing), he will be in a better position to engage into a flow experience and feel enjoyment.

As the theory of Flow evolved and started to be refined, several other models with more dimensions have surfaced in academic literature. The following two figures, extracted from Massimi & Carli (1988), show the addition of dimensions to the original constructs (p.270):

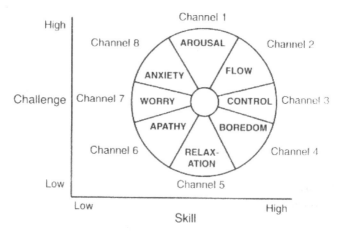

Figure 11. Eight Dimension Flow Model. Source: Massimi & Carli (1988) p. 270

As can be seen in Figure 11, apathy occurs if an activity brings low challenges for which low skills are needed. Consequently, anxiety occurs if the challenges are high and the skills are low, boredom occurs when the skills are high and the challenges low, and flow occurs if the challenges are high and the set of skills is high too. This relationship between challenges and skills is self explanatory in the chess example given above: If the experienced chess player competes against a beginner, the experienced player will feel boredom due to the perception that the challenge is lower in relationship to the skills. On the side of the beginner player, the challenge is far greater than present skills leading most probably to anxiety.

This relationship is also found in video games like Pac-Man: "Pac-man's addictiveness would be explained as follows: It is an action system where skills and challenges are progressively balanced, goals are clear, feedback is immediate and unambiguous, and relevant stimuli can be differentiated from irrelevant stimuli" (Bowman, 1982, p. 15) . If understood within this context, raising the level of difficulty on a video game is nothing more than providing an extra level of challenges to a changing skills level in order to endure the state of flow. Figure 12 shows a more flexible theoretical background where the beginner player (chess or Pac-man) will move from a state of anxiety to arousal if the player's skills increase and the challenges remain constant. If the player's skills increase more, flow, control and ultimately boredom will occur (a good moment to raise the challenge level to start the cycle again).

Nevertheless, Flow Theory has many methodological problems. The method applied by Csikszentmihalyi is called Experience Sampling Method. Participants carry a pager and every time they receive a notice they have to register their emotional and cognitive state. This method allowed Csikszentmihalyi to investigate the concept of flow in a day-by-day basis.

The first complication is theoretical in nature. If flow is an emotional and cognitive state which is described, among other dimensions, by merged action and awareness, exclusion of distractions, non-self-consciousness and no sense of time[5], sending a page to the participant is to momentarily stop all of the above: Action and awareness are stopped, the participant engages in a distraction, the participant is self-conscious of his or her actions by analyzing and registering them and, finally, time becomes stamped by the pager making the participant aware of it. By definition, if the above dimensions are not present, the chances of an autotelic experience are reduced. In short: The measurement of the dimensions of flow interrupts the state of flow itself.

In a more practical issue, the method employed has a large and unexplained error variance (Ellis, Voelkl & Morris, 1994). Furthermore, in order to investigate each one of the 9 dimensions in a single controlled experiment would entail a 9-way factorial design which makes the experimental design impractical (Chan, 1998). Chan (1998) suggest that an alternative approach is to categorize the dimensions into "super-flow" construct in order to reduce the number of variables and make the experimental design feasible. This approach was taken by Chen, Wigand and Nilan (1999) in a research project to assess the validity of the flow construct to World Wide Web experiences. The authors modified the 9 dimensions from the original model and categorized into three categories or stages:

---

[5] Flow theory dimensions 4, 5, 7 and 8.

1) Antecedents: Clear goals, immediate feedback, and matched skills and challenges.

2) Experiences: Merging action and awareness, and a sense of potential control.

3) Effects: Loss of self-consciousness, time distortion, autotelic experience. (p. 589)

Furthermore, Chen, Wigand and Nilan (1999) question the validity of the flow construct based on its applicability, making a major distinction between flow-related research in leisure activities or work and flow on the web, which is a multi-activity medium. The web should not be understood as a single-dimension activity due to its versatility and multifunctionality; typical uses include, but are not limited to, chat, email, browsing for information, work, shopping, etc., in a computer-mediated environment. The literature review presented here supports this finding and suggests that many different cognitive skills are needed in order to use the medium. They also suggest another methodological concern by assessing that the measurement of perceived challenges and skills is subjective and very complex, making the operationalization of these constructs critical to the success of a research project regarding flow.

Following this rationale, Chen, Wigand and Nilan (1999) used content analysis to narrow the definition of the factors that facilitate the occurrence of flow and gain face validity in their operationalization. In the same way that Chen, Wigand and Nilan (1999) establish that the use of the World Wide Web is not monolithic but instead promotes many different uses (making the study of flow situational), Webster and Martocchio (1992) build on Csikszentmihalyi's findings and consider that human personality differences also are determinants of the amount of "playfulness" exerted while using a computer. Considering that a flow state is dependent on personality traits and situational activities, the model becomes richer and more complex but less suitable for making generalizations. Novak & Hoffman (1996) added two more dimensions to the construct of flow in a study about marketing in hypermedia computer-mediated environments:

47

1) Control characteristics: Skills and Challenges.

2) Content characteristics: Interactivity and Vividness.

3) Process characteristics:

    a. Goal-directed: Extrinsic motivation, instrumental orientation, situational involvement, utilitarian benefits, directed search and directed choice.

    b. Experiential: Intrinsic motivation, ritualistic orientation, enduring involvement, hedonic benefits, non-directed search and navigational choice. (p. 62)

Ghani & Deshpande (1993) also propose another dimension important to the study of flow in computer-mediated experiences. Following Hackman and Oldham's (1976)[6] job characteristic theory, Ghani & Deshpande divided computer task in two, finding statistically significant differences in both regarding motivation and enjoyment:

1) High-scope: Greater autonomy in selecting the specific ways of carrying out work.

2) Low-scope: Lesser autonomy in selecting the specific ways of carrying out work.

High scope entails more motivation and low scope entails less motivation.

The literature points towards a complex relationship between several variables and the experiencing of flow; nevertheless, not only Csikszentmihalyi's Flow Theory but also the previous literature review on schemata produces a sound theoretical linkage between disorientation and enjoyment in the context of a hypermedia system. Therefore, even though flow could provide a theoretical frame to explain a connection between previous media use and the enjoyment of the experience, it poses several methodological challenges. For example, there is no goal in *A space of time*; it is not a quest for information or a task with specific objectives. The goal in any case is just to entertain. In *A space of time* there is immediate feedback because it is an interactive product, but it doesn't provide the users

---

[6] Authors not covered in the book literature review but mentioned in Ghani & Deshpande (1993).

with any idea of "how well they are doing." *A space of time* does not behave like Pac-man and does not change level of difficulty; part of the purpose of the study is to provide a similar level of challenge to understand what type of skills are brought into play. Schema Theory provides a better theoretical frame that helps explain the level of skills in individuals in comparison to their perception of the non-linear experience. Schema Theory addresses the first premise of Flow Theory: How the creation of schemata enhances a person's skills in order to overcome challenges. In summary: If there is no schema that would help the experiencing of a non-linear story that involves a navigational task, an informational task and a management task, then a person will not have enough cognitive resources and will experience disorientation, frustration, and a lack of enjoyment. Therefore, a construct of enjoyment derived from leisure activities and flow theory is better suited to understand perceived enjoyment at the time of experiencing a non-linear story like *A space of time*.

A SPACE OF TIME

A space of time, as a creative project, seeks to break the boundaries of linear narrative and let audiences explore and, to a certain extent, find story versions that may vary from individual to individual and from one experience with the story to the next. To do this, *A space of time* makes full use of the possibilities offered by new communication technologies, especially the way that digital content can be fragmented. A digitized page of text can be fragmented easily into paragraphs, sentences, words, letters and eventually a collection of eight or more successive ones and zeros organized in a limited number of permutations. Digital images can be decomposed into millions of individual units called pixels. Videos can be broken into segments, frames per second, and eventually every frame into the pixels of a digital image. Videos can also be fragmented into a visual track and an auditory track.

Of course, fragmentation per se is normally irrelevant for digitized content. Its significance comes when it is rearranged in meaningful ways in a matter of milliseconds. *A space of time* benefits from this medium characteristic, not only by the speed with which fragments can be called from the Web or a DVD, but also by giving audiences a richer experience not only by presenting non-sequential units of content without losing coherence, but also by providing random multimedia elements that reinforce the experience thematically. These random elements can be presented in any order and still form part of a whole but are not indispensable to the understanding of the plot, instead they provide "richness" or "depth" to the story.

Stories that lend themselves to non-linearity can justify a disruption of time and, in some cases, of various "realities." Devices such as "flashbacks" and foreshadowing have helped audiences explore narratives in non-linear fashion, but only as the storyteller determined. So even though the author of a book or the scriptwriter for a movie may offer the narrative in fragments, the audience experiences the story within pre-established boundaries.

In order to do so, without losing coherence, each one of the units has to be a whole in itself and a part of the whole. However, it is important to address the possible benefits of reorganizing the same units of contents in different order –what can be gained from doing so? One example might help clarify what impact the presentation order of a story might have on its interpretation. The making of *A space of time* was preceded by one project that displayed information in a non-sequential way: "Girando Bajo"[7] the story of a skydiver that suffers an accident in the skydiving zone of Tequestitengo, Morelos (Bonilla, 1993). "Girando Bajo" starts at the moment in which one of two brothers arrives at a hospital in Mexico City with many broken bones and internal bleeding from a skydiving accident. While the skydiver is battling between life and death in the Intensive Care Unit, his brother and other members of the family devise a system to have always someone present in the hospital in case of an emergency. The brother, who has the ability to switch his sleeping schedule with relative ease, is selected to cover the midnight to 7 a.m. shift. The way the brother stays awake throughout the nights is by writing in his laptop a diary of what occurred during the day. The text of the diary is the core of the non-linear story. The diary is broken in several types of entries: Real life (including medical data, visitors, complications, etc.), dreams about skydiving (the few moments in which the brother sleeps he dreams about actual jumps), and hallucinations told by the heavily sedated skydiver to the brother during the night visits.

---

[7] "Girando bajo" means literally "Low turning." The title addresses a general recommendation to inexperienced and intermediate skydivers: When a skydiver is close to the ground with the parachute open, he should not make any more turns because it is difficult to measure the descending speed in relationship to the altitude.

51

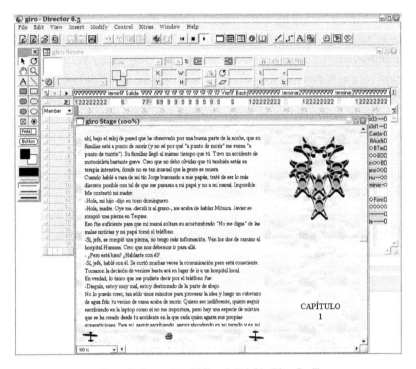

Figure 12. Screen shot of "Girando Bajo" by Diego Bonilla

The part with real life is pretty much linear; however, the dreams and the hallucinations are non-linear and their presentation time in the story is shuffled every time it is experienced. One single instance stands out from the others for its chronological importance in relation to the rest of the story. When the skydiver arrives at the hospital, life-threatening wounds are prioritized and treated immediately. Due to this, the next most serious injury is discovered after two weeks in the Intensive Care Unit. The sacrum[8] is broken into five different pieces. This turns out to be one of the most damaging aspects of the accident. Even though the revelation about the sacrum in the story happens always at

---

[8] The sacrum is the final bone of the spine. Lower body nerves pass through holes in the sacrum.

the same time chronologically, there is a random (shuffled) element that talks about the sacrum. In one of the dreams, both brothers step onto the platform attached to the wing of the airplane, look into each others eyes and jump simultaneously. During the fall everything goes as planned, but at the time of opening the parachute, the brother who is writing about the dream opens the canopy successfully but the brother who suffered the accident does not. With the parachute open, the writer starts screaming to his brother to open the parachute immediately. Nothing happens. He screams again and again while he watches how an ever tinier human figure gets closer and closer to the ground. When apparently there are no more options and the body of the brother is about to impact, the brother in the open parachute says gravely: "Oh no, the sacrum."

This dream can occur before or after the moment in which the doctors assess that the sacrum is broken into five pieces. The same unit of content placed in different moments will yield different meanings:

1) Before: The brother who is writing a diary has a premonition in his dream and will later find out that what he dreamt has become a reality.

2) After: The brother who is writing the diary responds subconsciously to what the doctors say about the injuries of his brother.

This enriches the plot with alternate meanings by randomly shuffling parts of a story with the help of a computer, fragmented units of content, addressable units and seamless speed. Furthermore, the story can be written in such a way that it can benefit from this re-accommodation of content. By the end of the skydiving story, the skydiver who suffered the accident is released from Intensive Care after 21 days, and the brother who is writing the diary has another dream in which something else happens that is quite ambiguous. If the person experiences the story in a way that premonitions seem a regular narrative element of the story, most probably the watcher will interpret it as an omen. In addition, if the dream is experienced before the disclosure of the fractured sacrum, any dream has the potential of a forewarning – that is, the occurrence of the dream before the fact would influence the rest of the story.

As explained above, the purpose of *A space of time* is to further explore non-linearity as an element that can enrich a story and provide a background for the understanding of new narrative possibilities. As was the case in "Girando Bajo," two story lines in which time (or the perception of time) can be bent are implemented. The story of *A space of time* is about David and Pandora. David is a homeless person who has found temporary shelter inside the building –which he normally refers to as "the container." Pandora Hamilton is an undergraduate who decides to study advertising because she hates the advertising industry, and in order to fight it she is trying to understand it from "the inside." David and Pandora never meet, but the story relates to the two of them.

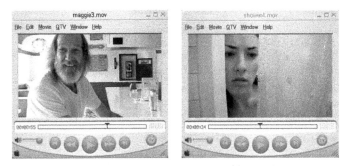

Figure 13. David and Pandora. (Apple's viewer does not appear during the experience.)

There are two elements present in the story that justify the non-linear construction of the story. Pandora dies inside the building, and the tramp believes that after her death the most important moments of her life were trapped inside the rooms – this is the reason why the tramp calls it a "container." This is similar to the concept of "all of your life flashes before you eyes when you die" or to the concept of a limbo state in which a deceased person wanders before "passing on." This idea of death gives ample room for rearranging units of content in a random fashion and simulating the close-to-death moment in which the most important moments of life are re-experienced or remembered. The second element "natural" to non-linear storytelling is mental illness. David, the homeless person, suffers from a disease called Temporal Lobe Epilepsy. This epilepsy, far different from the grand mal type of epilepsy in which the human body is subject to convulsions, is a series of electrical discharges in the temporal lobe area of the brain. These discharges cause strong auditory and visual hallucinations (among many other symptoms), which normally are a combination of two elements: current perception and memories stored in the brain. The disease is quite spectacular from storytelling point of view and experienced by several real life artists (among them: Vincent Van Gogh, Fiodor Dostoyevsky, Lewis Carroll, Jonathan Swift, Søren Kierkegaard and many others). So it is possible, even though it is never mentioned in the story of *A space of time*, that Pandora and all of her life is just something that the tramp "sees" inside the building due to his mental illness. This suspicion is re-enforced by the fact that the tramp "agrees" with all of Pandora's theories (maybe the theories are his and not Pandora's) and the fact that the tramp talks about "using" the container and its ability to trap time to recover memories of his lost daughter.

Most of the scenes related to Ira (Janitor of the building) and Jeremiah (nephew of the janitor) are related to the tramp and the building. One of Pandora's friends has a connection to Jeremiah and that is why Pandora enters the building. Others of Pandora's friends (Rogan and Jess) do not meet Jeremiah or Ira, but they go to the building after Pandora's death. The characters of the doctor, the historian and the detectives appear mostly in the diner, and they are constantly interchanged throughout a single scene, hinting that the tramp is hallucinating but never resolving the issue. The doctor's appearance in a lecture room talking about the tramp and temporal lobe epilepsy, because it is a scene extracted from the container, could just be a tramp hallucination, too. The same caveat can be applied to the detectives entering the building to investigate the death of Pandora.

This flexible environment of reality and imagination filled with connections is what enriches a non-linear experience; hence, it was assumed that the greater the number of scenes and the greater the number of connections among the characters the richer the experience. In terms of its length and depth, *A space of time* resembles more a novel than a regular movie.

The most important elements in *A space of time* are units of digital video with scenes that follow traditional film techniques, fragments of 8-millimeter film showing the childhood of the main character, text-intensive animations that represent the work that the main character uploads to the World Wide Web and an ample set of QuickTime Virtual

Reality (QTVR) files[9] linked through programming to create an immersive experience in an empty 100-year-old-building in Syracuse, NY. The rest of the elements present in *A space of time* are random video sequences that are thematically related to the scenes and random sounds that occur while the user is experiencing the immersive virtual environment.

The way *A space of time* provides non-linear elements is twofold: First, people who experience *A space of time* have to decide where to "walk" once that they are inside the virtual environment. Depending on the direction that they take, different scenes will be accessible. Second, the scenes are broken into fixed discrete units that are shuffled on the fly by the computer; therefore, the final plot presented to the user varies every time it is experienced. *A space of time* incorporates a random process to choose which fragment will be seen next, but it is a "controlled" randomness. If pure randomness were applied, as was tried at one point, the display of the sequence loses its narrative coherence. Therefore, as part of the development of *A space of time*, a "formula" was incorporated to give a minimum direction, a minimum necessary order, for the scenes to make sense. This formula contains random processes applied to a set of probability distributions that contain information about the segments.

The non-linearity, hence, is based on behavior (where the viewer goes next in the building) and random processes integrated into the video scenes. The first type of non-linearity is present in both the World Wide Web version of the experience and the DVDROM version of the experience. The algorithm to disrupt meaningfully the sequence of the segments that create a scene applies only to the DVDROM version of the project.

The process of running the algorithm is very fast and the selection of a new segment for a scene can be made in milliseconds; however, the speed of retrieval of the video differs significantly from a DVDROM (which retrieves the video from an optical device attached to the computer that is running the experience) and the World Wide Web (which retrieves the video from a remote location in the World Wide Web and it is subject

---

[9] QuickTime Virtual Reality is an Apple technology that runs in both Windows and Apple computers. Described in detail in subsequent sections.

not only to slowdowns but also physical constraints coming from the user's system or the server that delivers the content).

MULTIMEDIA ELEMENTS IN A SPACE OF TIME

A space of time Digital Video

The most prominent type of multimedia element used in *A space of time* is digital video. Digital video is divided into several categories depending on their type of content: 1) Scenes related to its central story; 2) fragments of 8-millimeter film transferred to digital video that show the main character when she was young; and 3) random video scenes (extracted from the shooting of the experience, but not included in the final editing of the video scene in which it may or may not appear) or related to the life of the characters (time-lapse videos of the building, Pandora's house, etc.).

While *A space of time* has several storylines that intersect in different ways, probably the most important ones are those of the tramp and Pandora. *A space of time* contains 57 scenes that use traditional film techniques to tell the story; more than 6 hours of edited content. The story, even though it goes in-depth in many different directions, contains a few scenes that are crucial to its understanding. The first two scenes are necessary to contextualize the experience and to give as much information as possible to the user about what he or she will experience after entering the virtual environment. These two scenes are the only two that are forced at the beginning of the experience; nonetheless, they can be skipped if the user decides to do so. After those two first scenes, the user can choose whether to experience the rest of the movie scenes.

The first scene is about Jeremiah, the janitor's nephew, arriving at the building for the rehearsal of a performance in what he calls his "playground." The movie starts on the day that Pandora dies. The building, some of the fantastic imagery that takes place inside the building and some of the main characters related to the building (including the tramp) are introduced. The second scene introduces fully the main narrator of the story: The tramp. It also introduces the doctor, the historian, the detectives and Maggie, the waitress.

The shortest way to understand *A space of time* is by experiencing the first two scenes and the scene in which Pandora dies . So, if a user is disinclined to discover why she dies, the story of *A space of time* could last less than 20 minutes. Every segment beyond those three scenes adds complexity and richness to the overall plot, the mind of every character and the work of Pandora on the World Wide Web.

For example: One of the longest scenes is about Jeremiah and a friend taking drugs inside the empty building. The scene introduces the context, rises to a climax, decreases, and finally ends with a climax when Jeremiah bumps into an "apparition" inside the building.

Figure 14. Jeremiah's hallucination. (Apple's viewer does not appear during the experience.)

The apparition is that of two Pandoras floating in the air and turning in opposite direction, but because of the drugs the nephew cannot be sure if it is the building or his own mind that is making all of it happen. This scene reinforces the tramp's idea of the building as a "container of time," makes a link between Jeremiah and Pandora, enriches Phil's character, and shows the size of the building (potential "walking" path). As it is the case with "Girando Bajo," *A space of time* leaves this scene "floating" in time. If it is experienced before Pandora dies, it might be considered as a premonition, if it is experienced after Pandora's death, then it becomes a natural psychological product to the traumatic memory of her death and the drugs that Jeremiah took.

58

The more *A space of time* is experienced the easier it is to understand the different storylines and their contribution to the main plot. Among the several storylines: 1) The tramp experiences incredible events in the building that are tied up with Pandora but he doesn't know why; 2) Pandora fights the advertising industry by ranting on the web; 3) Pandora's two best friends, Jess and Rogan, attack current capitalistic structures for promoting uneven distribution of wealth and the concentration of technological knowledge in a very small percentage of the population; 4) Ira, the janitor, is revealed as a dangerous, evil man; and 5) Claudia unintentionally leads her platonic love (Pandora) to her death. Other story lines also develop but they only have one scene or two.

Video shorts of Pandora's past.

The virtual environment contains on its hallway walls images of Pandora when she was a girl. These images link to 58 short scenes transferred from 8-mm film to digital video. The quality, color and flickering of the 8-mm film provides a tone of nostalgia to the story and suggests the possibility that the tramp is thinking of Pandora as his daughter. In one of the diner scenes, David confesses: "Part of what we remember is not what happened, but what we think happened. The older the memory the more it has patches here and there of what we want to remember. So our memory is a mix of what really happened with how we make sense of it." Later on, towards the end of the scene, he adds: "I lost my daughter at some point in my life. I loved her. She appears every now and then inside the building, and when I see her... I know that the container is also starting to extract pieces of my own head. But I see it as a necessary marriage, I receive if I give [...] I don't know why I have blocked a lot from my memory. If the container is an active memory, my own memory is an empty building sometimes."

59

Figure 15. 8mm videos of Pandora as a little girl. (Apple's viewer does not appear during the experience.)

If the user experiences the 8-mm segments distributed along the building's inner walls, probably he or she will attach a feeling of nostalgia to the tramp's words and will understand more of the rationale behind his decision to stay inside and "study" the container.

Random video scenes

A space of time contains approximately 700 individual random videos related to the story. In order to create a flexible flux of multimedia elements, the number of scenes had to be increased considerably. The bigger the number of random videos, the bigger the combinatorial possibilities. Therefore, *A space of time* contains a large number of videos divided in several categories:

60

1) Building: Shadows moving, doors closing by themselves, "flying camera views," slow pans along the rooms, outside shots of the building in each of the four seasons, shots of the tramp inspecting the building before he enters it, and time lapse sequences in which the sun appears (sunrise) and disappears (sunset) at incredible speed (reinforcing with production techniques part of the psychological profile of Pandora and her feeling that time is speeding up).

2) The place that Pandora house-sits: Shadows moving, outside shots in each of the four seasons, the clock of the lower floor advancing at irregular intervals and, also, time-lapse videos inside and outside the house.

3) Pandora: Video sequences in which Pandora appears sleeping, laughing, resting (very short, probably 7 seconds maximum); Pandora's face being illuminated by the projection of a kaleidoscope (similar to the description that the tramp gives of Pandora when he "experienced" the container for the first time); and images of Pandora in a white limbo-like space.

4) Tramp: Video sequences of David staring at a fixed point inside many of the rooms in the building. This could be interpreted as the tramp "experiencing" the container but it never resolves if he actually sees things or if he is in the middle of a temporal lobe epileptic attack.

5) Surrealistic scenes: Many other scenes showing varied elements of surrealistic nature (a ray of light floating over the shell of an egg lying somewhere inside the building, a bird trying over and over to escape the container by crashing into the windows, etc.)

These videos remain on a database inside the experience and are shown until they are randomly invoked by the program. Furthermore, to increase the sense of flux and randomness, the program can grab a fragment of any of the video scenes in the entire experience and present it backwards for a random number of seconds (between 2 and 4).

The program determines which videos will be played during the scene at the beginning of each sequence, enabling the computer to fade out and fade in the individual pieces resembling a pre-made edition of the experience, even if the experience unrolls differently every time. Considering that the experience has more than 900 video clips to choose from, the possible number of permutations is large and most probably not worth calculating.

FLASH ANIMATIONS: WORK OF PANDORA DISPLAYED ON THE WEB

Pandora expresses her opinions and views (what the character constantly refers to as "rants") through animated poetry that she publishes on her WWW site (http://www.hypergraphia.com/panda/). *A space of time,* the DVD experience, contains also the 18 Pandora's rants that appear on her website. Even though the video sequences show a concerned, thoughtful, measured and sweet character, her rants are quite the opposite. Pandora's rationale for creating bitter and direct messages is related to her thoughts that the public, the masses, are already dulled by the deluge of messages that they receive on a daily basis and their inherently persuasive tone. In one of the scenes, Pandora explains her underlying principle for creating the animations with an "insulting" tenor: "I think the problem with my rants is that they are too textual. I'm targeting people who spend more time watching ads than reading, so I've got to make them look like ads even if they say something totally different." In Pandora's mind, this will create a memorable cognitive dissonance. All of the poetry is narrated but it also appears written in the screen throughout the animation.

Figure 16. Pandora's flash animation. (Flash viewer does not appear during the experience.)

The purpose of the website is twofold: 1) Create a real environment for the expression of a character's opinion in a public space and 2) Promote the experience of *A space of time*. The user might find the experience by watching any of Pandora's rants on the web because at the end of all the animations a few lines of code open the main website for the experience (http://www.aspaceoftime.net). Also the main page of the rants has a small icon stating that "This is just a small part of a bigger story"; by clicking it they launch the main experience website.

The rants are also located inside the building room walls; sometimes they appear by themselves, sometimes they complement one of the scenes, indicating that probably Pandora decided to write the rant based on the scene that the user just experienced. Also, one of the video scenes shows Pandora at the actual moment of writing one of the rants at her house. Each of the 18 rants is on average 4 minutes long and was created in Macromedia's Flash, a technology compatible with the programming environment of the experience (Macromedia's Director). The rants are the most important textual element of the story; even though there is music, voice-over and graphics while they are playing, most of the spoken words appear as writing on the screen.

RANDOM SOUNDS AND AUDIO CLIPS

Even though audio is a common feature of video, the experience contains approximately 200 audio clips that are triggered at random moments while the user "walks" in the virtual environment. The sounds vary in nature:

Building sounds: Sounds of doors closing, objects being dragged on the floor, dripping of water. The building sounds complement the tramp's belief that things constantly "shift" within the container.

Dialog fragments: These fragments are extracted from their context; they do not include the ambient sound of the scene itself, just the recording of the voice with an echo effect. The sound of the dialog is intended to introduce the user to multiple parts of the experience story just by "walking" in the virtual environment and to provide a sense of variation and flux by extracting them from their own ambient sounds.

A SPACE OF TIME'S STRUCTURE

The structure of the building was constructed with QuickTime Virtual Reality panoramas. The technology is based on stitching photographs together in order to create a 360 degree views. The number of images varies depending of the field of view of the lens used for photographing the environment; the wider the view, the smaller the number. In the case of *A space of time*, each one of the rooms was created from 18 photographs, each one of them separated from the previous one by 20 degrees (20 degrees times 18 equals 360 degrees).

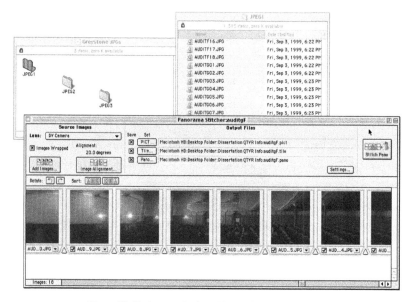

Figure 17. 18 photographs times 20 degrees for a full 360 view.

The project includes 187 QTVRs to recreate the building structure and 13 QTVRs to recreate the house where Pandora lives for a total of 200 panoramas (200 panoramas times 18 photographs equals 3,600 photographs). Once the panoramas are created, the independent images were extracted and single long image (in PICT format) for each room was used for the rest of the project (See Figure 19.)

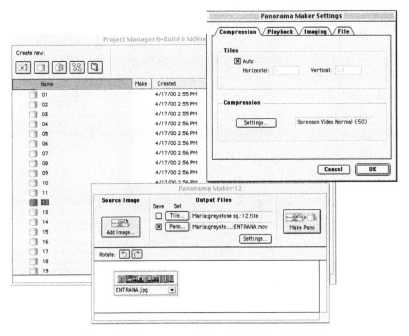

Figure 18. Project manager for the main level floor ("b" floor)

Once a single image for a single panorama has been created, the 360 degree field can be modified with any image editing software[10]. In this way, lighting problems can be fixed, errors at the time of shooting can be retouched (for example, the power cable for the camera was removed from the floor in 80% of the rooms), and objects can be added.

Both the building and the house are located in Syracuse, NY, and both of them were constructed over a century ago (1902). The building used to be a high school but it had been closed for more than a decade at the time the movie was made. A couple of reconstruction projects had taken place to adapt the building for other purposes but hadn't been finished. The reconstruction can be easily noticed in the QTVR structure because the

[10] In the case of A space of time, Adobe Photoshop.

66

stage of the auditorium is covered by a wall, and the backstage area was adapted to be office space[11].

Once the photographs were taken and the panoramas were constructed using QTVR Authoring Studio 1.0, they had to be internally coded to create the linked structure. This linking is created through "blobs," pieces of information that Macromedia Director retrieves as an ID number for that specific blob (See Figure 20). The average number of hot spot areas in each QTVR is around 4, with a minimum of 1 in some cases and a maximum of 14 in one room.

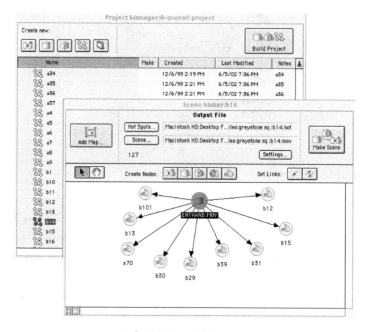

Figure 19. Blobs with ID numbers.

---

[11] As a special note about the building: It is quite unfortunate that the theater was disabled. The "Central High School" or "Greystone Square" building was the stage for famous operas and plays and used to be one of the largest auditoriums in the United States East Coast. Directors as important as Herbert von Karajan performed in the building's theater.

67

The color of each area depends on the 256 colors of the 8-bit default Apple palette. In this way it is possible to indicate what panorama should appear on the screen depending on a specific code, establish the area considered to be "hot" and color it within the image for fast visual reference (See Figure 21). In this figure it can be seen that the doors and thresholds of the rooms were used consistently as "hot spots"; the purpose of doing so was to create a uniform structural logic that the user could understand to move from one room to the other.

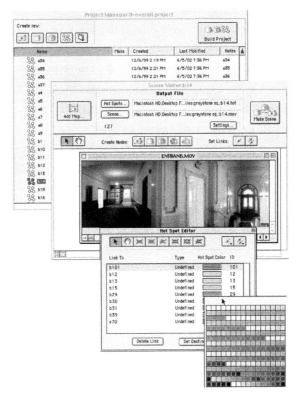

Figure 20. Colorized "hot spot" areas.

Nevertheless, throughout the initial testing of the experience with the production staff of the experience, disorientation occurred because the movement from one room to the other did not establish a "walking" direction. For example, if the user was facing north in "b13" and clicked on "b14," the default orientation for that room was southeast, making navigation confusing. To avoid this problem, all of the panoramas were integrated into a database containing the position of the North Pole. At the time of departing a panorama, the computer calculates the amount of difference between its original position and the coded north position, and then it adjusts the next panorama to reflect this difference. The overall effect is that of "walking" from one room to the other because the user's point of view does not change at the time of changing panorama (changing their position) within the building. This also allows the user to know that if they turn 180 degrees after the arrival to in any panorama, they would see their departing point in the building's structure.

In the same way that coding was used to navigate the building, the linking to the multimedia elements had to have also a code (and therefore a "hotspot"). Every floating character depicted in the rooms, as well as all of the "rants" imagery located on the inside walls of the rooms and the 8-mm sequences located on the inside walls of the hallways, also needed a code that would indicate to the programming environment which multimedia element is requested. (See upper left green hotspot covering the image of Jess in Figure 22.)

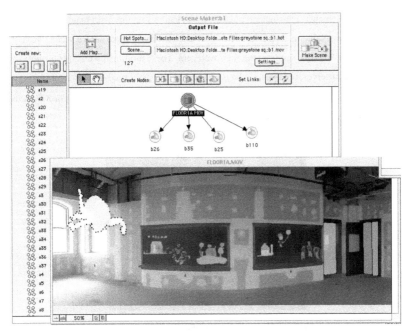

Figure 21. Assigning hotspots to multimedia elements.

200 QTVRs, 57 scenes that tell the story of David and Pandora, 58 shorts of 8mm film and, 18 rants add up to a total of 333 unique nodes, exceeding the programs limitation of 256 codes. To avoid this problem, the building was divided by zones: Floors, staircases and multimedia content. The code for each floor contains two values: a prefix that indicates the floor level (from "a" to "e") and a suffix which is the code number starting always with one. By doing so, the codes for each floor were the following: a1 to a37 (basement), b1 to b47 (main level), c1 to c26 (second floor), d1 to d32 (third floor) and, e1 to e15 (attic.) The stairway cases, instead of having a horizontal plane, as was the case with the floors, have a vertical plane, each stairway QTVR with a unique code: s50 to s68. Finally, the multimedia elements received a prefix depending the floor level and a suffix starting with code 100 (so just by inspection it can be known that the code b104 will link to

a multimedia element). This method of coding provided a structure with hundreds of hotspot codes available in each floor. The experience invites users to send a video commentary of Pandora's rants using their web cam. These multimedia units, contributions of the users themselves, are meant to be incorporated into the virtual environment.

The overall coding for the all of the floors in the building can be found in Appendix 5. The following are screen shots from A space of time's interface:

Figure 22. Screenshot of *A space of time* with floating elements (link to scene) in QTVR

Figure 23. Screenshot of *A space of time* with floating elements and image on the wall (link to Pandora's rant)

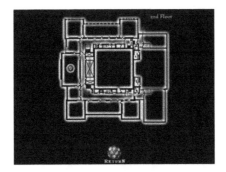

Figure 24. Screenshot of map location within building

Figure 25. Screenshot of help screen

Figure 26. Screenshot of credits

INTEGRATION OF THEORETICAL BACKGROUNDS AND DERIVATION OF HYPOTHESES

SCHEMA, DISORIENTATION AND ENJOYMENT

The literature review shows a working theoretical linkage between previous media use and behavior while experiencing *A space of time*. According to Landow (1992, p. 134) "if hypertext's greatest educational strength as well as its most characteristic feature is its connectivity, then tests and other evaluative exercises must measure the results of using that connectivity to develop the ability to make connections."

If there are different ways of watching the same content in a digital medium, then it is possible to test if digital media use creates an information-processing schema that will enable us to make "connections" while watching content in a non-linear fashion.

The type of schemata proposed in this project differs from person, self, role, and event schemata. If there are many different ways of accessing information depending on the type of media, then it is possible to assume that there is a schema or schemata that relate to the way a person normally receives such information. Different texts have different schemata and one should not expect a single schema to apply to all texts or to text in general (Mandler, 1984). For example: A volume of the yellow pages will be read differently from a Garcia Marquez novel. A person who is handed both volumes, would not read the yellow pages from beginning to end or to find an alphabetical order in the words of the novel that appear on the pages. If he or she is handed a textbook, it is probable that the person will review the index or table of contents before starting to read. They contain guides to the information structure of the book and can be used as aids to locate information in different ways than in the case of the novel or the yellow pages.

Schema theory explains also a relationship between disorientation depending on previous media use, especially if previous media use includes the regular interaction with non-linear documents on the Internet, playing with video games or previous experiences

73

with *A space of time*; all of which have interactivity and non-linearity as core characteristics. This is also speculated in Otter & Johnson's (2000) literature review: "Experienced hypertext users have a schema for hypertext structures, and that might affect how lost they become." (p. 12)

Schema theory also explains a decrease in cognitive resources if the user has prior knowledge or a cognitive map of the system structure (Woodhead, 1991; Gamberini & Bussolon, 2001; Boechler, 2001; Nielsen, 1990; Ayersman, 1995) or knowledge about the information that the system contains (Lawless & Brown, 1997; Liu, 1995; Reed & Giessler, 1995). Following the type of tasks presented by Kim & Hirtle (1995), users' knowledge about the structure (structure schema) frees cognitive resources for the informational task and users' knowledge about the information contained in the system frees cognitive resources for the navigational task.

The theoretical linkage between disorientation and enjoyment comes from one of the most important dimensions needed to find flow during an experience: A balance between challenges and skills. The acquisition of schemata equates the acquisition of skills to confront challenges; if the challenges are bigger than the skills, the subjects will feel anxiety (Csikszentmihalyi, 1990) and frustration (Otter & Johnson, 2000).

DERIVATION OF HYPOTHESES

For schema related to each medium categorized as "traditional" there are two hypotheses, each one of them related to the use of the medium itself (i.e., hour watching television) and: 1) amount of interactive behavior in the non-linear movie, and 2) sense of control in the non-linear movie.

Media Use, interactive behavior and sense of control set of hypotheses

Hypothesis 1

Independent Variable: TV watching.

Dependent Variables: Amount of interactive behavior, sense of control.

Hypothesis 1.1: The more hours of television watching, the greater the amount of interactive behavior.

Hypothesis 1.2: The more hours of television watching, the higher the sense of control.

Hypothesis 2

Independent Variable: Magazine reading.

Dependent Variables: Amount of interactive behavior, sense of control.

Hypothesis 2.1: The more hours of magazine reading, the greater the amount of interactive behavior.

Hypothesis 2.2: The more hours of magazine reading, the higher the sense of control.

Hypothesis 3

Independent Variable: Newspaper reading.

Dependent Variables: Amount of interactive behavior, sense of control.

Hypothesis 3.1: The more hours of newspaper reading, the greater the amount of interactive behavior.

Hypothesis 3.2: The more hours of newspaper reading, the higher the sense of control.

Hypothesis 4

Independent Variable: Book reading (fiction).

Dependent Variables: Amount of interactive behavior, sense of control.

Hypothesis 4.1: The more hours of book reading, the greater the amount of interactive behavior.

Hypothesis 4.2: The more hours of book reading, the higher the sense of control.

Hypothesis 5

Independent Variable: Radio listening.

Dependent Variables: Amount of interactive behavior, sense of control.

Hypothesis 5.1: The more hours of radio listening, the greater the amount of interactive behavior.

Hypothesis 5.2: The more hours of radio listening, the higher the sense of control.

Hypothesis 6

Independent Variable: Internet browsing.

Dependent Variables: Amount of interactive behavior, sense of control.

Hypothesis 6.1: The more hours of Internet browsing, the greater the amount of interactive behavior.

Hypothesis 6.2: The more hours of Internet browsing, the higher the sense of control.

Hypothesis 7

Independent Variable: Videogame playing.

Dependent Variables: Amount of interactive behavior, sense of control.

Hypothesis 7.1: The more hours of videogame playing, the greater the amount of interactive behavior.

Hypothesis 7.2: The more hours of videogame playing, the higher the sense of control.

Hypothesis 8

Independent Variable: Computer playing.

Dependent Variables: Amount of interactive behavior, sense of control.

Hypothesis 8.1: The more hours of computer playing, the greater the amount of interactive behavior.

Hypothesis 8.2: The more hours of computer playing, the higher the sense of control.

Hypothesis 9

Independent Variable: Computer work.

Dependent Variables: Amount of interactive behavior, sense of control.

Hypothesis 9.1: The more hours of computer work, the greater the amount of interactive behavior.

Hypothesis 9.2: The more hours of computer work, the higher the sense of control.

Hypothesis 10

Independent Variable: Book reading (non-fiction).

Dependent Variables: Amount of interactive behavior, sense of control.

Hypothesis 10.1: The more hours of book reading, the greater the amount of interactive behavior.

Hypothesis 10.2: The more hours of book reading, the higher the sense of control.

Hypothesis 11

Independent Variable: Movie watching (at the theater).

Dependent Variables: Amount of interactive behavior, sense of control.

Hypothesis 11.1: The more hours of movie watching, the greater the amount of interactive behavior.

Hypothesis 11.2: The more hours of movie watching, the higher the sense of control.

Hypothesis 12

Independent Variable: Internet longevity.

Dependent Variables: Amount of interactive behavior, sense of control.

Hypothesis 12.1: The more Internet longevity, the greater the amount of interactive behavior.

Hypothesis 12.2: The more Internet longevity, the higher the sense of control.

Hypothesis 13

Independent Variable: *A space of time* experience.

Dependent Variables: Amount of interactive behavior, sense of control.

Hypothesis 13.1: The more *A space of time* experience, the greater the amount of interactive behavior.

Hypothesis 13.2: The more *A space of time* experience, the higher the sense of control.

Sense of control vs. Level of enjoyment hypothesis

Hypothesis 14:

    Independent Variable: Sense of control.

    Dependent variable: Level of enjoyment.

    Hypothesis 14: The higher the sense of control, the higher the level of enjoyment.

The above Hypothesis related to interactive behavior and media use are summarized in the following matrix:

	TV watching	Magazine reading	Newspaper reading	Book reading	Radio listening	Internet browsing	Videogame playing	Computer playing	Computer work	Book reading (non-fiction).	Movie watching	Internet longevity	*A space of time* experience
Interactive behavior	1.1	2.1	3.1	4.1	5.1	6.1	7.1	8.1	9.1	10.1	11.1	12.1	13.1
Sense of control	1.2	2.2	3.2	4.2	5.2	6.2	7.2	8.2	9.2	10.2	11.2	12.2	13.2

Table 3.Media use vs. interactive behavior and media use Hypotheses

METHODOLOGY

RESEARCH DESIGN

A controlled exposure experimental design is considered to be the most appropriate research design to find if subjects of the experiment behave differently during exposure to *A space of time* depending on their previous media use.

A schema is a mental form, or a mental structure, that develops with time and through repetition. In traditional experimentation, the simplest design has three steps: Pre-test, treatment and post-test. Experimentation with this design has the underlying assumption that the treatment will create meaningful differences that can be observed and quantified on a post-treatment test. Therefore, the treatment should be powerful enough as to convey a difference in the responses of the subjects between pre-test and post-test. When applied to medicine or biology, considering that the treatment is a drug or a physical procedure, it is possible to assume that the treatment has an impact on the subject and that the effect of the treatment is measurable. When that same rationale is brought to mass communication research, the idea of a treatment that will change the outcome of a response variable from a pre-test to post-test is normally considered dubious or non-lasting.

In the case of mass communications, the assumption that exposure to the content of any mass media would create a significant difference between pre-test and post-test revives an old theory of mass communication named "Magic Bullet Theory" or "Hypodermic Needle Theory." The "Magic Bullet Theory" originated around the 1920's assumed that passive audiences would show meaningful behavioral changes due to exposure to a mass communication medium. Therefore, imagining that there could be a treatment that could alter response variables in mass communications would also suggest that the content and the medium independently or combined might have a "hypodermic needle" effect on the subject.

In this type of experimentation, the independent variable is the treatment. The dependent variable is the variable that changes after the independent variable is administered. The logic of this experimental design justifies an independent dichotomous

variable that might be present or absent during the experiment and therefore the existence
of a control group as part of a multifaceted experimental design. In essence, the existence
of a control group is nothing more than the absence of the treatment or the independent
variable.

When a social science experimental design lacks a control group, lacks a pre-test or
lacks influence over the independent variable, normally it is considered to be a "quasi-
experimental" design. Campbell and Cook (1979) give a good explanation of the basic
forms of "quasi-experimental" design:

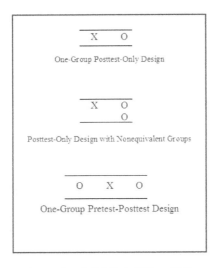

Source: Campbell & Cook, 1979, pp. 97-99

The quasi-experimental design that resembles the experimental design for this
research project is the One-Group Posttest-Only Design. This design assumes that the
independent variable (X) has already happened and the researcher only applies a posttest to
measure the dependent variable (O). Campbell & Cook (1979) state clearly the different
threats that a One-Group Posttest-Only Design conveys:

Lack of pretest observations from persons receiving the treatment. In most situations in social sciences, a lack of a pretest prevents researchers from inferring that the treatment is the cause of the dependent variable.

Lack of a control group. A control group helps to distinguish the relevant threats and a way to measure them individually.

Nevertheless, Campbell & Cook (1979) recognize that there might be individual instances in which proper scientific inquiry might take place under the One-Group Posttest-Only Design and that in some cases reasonable causal inference can be found. When a crime is committed, detectives look for clues that establish a relationship post-facto between the crime and the crime suspect. A methodology is established to rule out potential suspects because their usual "crime signature" is not observed. Using this method, detectives can narrow down the list of suspects to "one or two." The authors suggest that researchers can use a similar method to rule out alternative explanations in order to assess internal and external validities.

In the case of *A space of time*, subjects are asked to experience the non-linear multimedia story in a controlled environment and their behavior is registered in detail via a tracking device embedded in the programming of the experience. Because *A space of time* is an interactive story, the subjects are not passive; if the subjects stop interacting with the medium, the medium will stop providing content and this will be immediately reflected in the database that registers behavior and content delivered by the program.

It would be a mistake to consider that, because the experiencing of the non-linear story happens in a laboratory setting, the independent variable is the non-linear story per se. If this were the case, as a research project, differences in a hypothetical dependent variable due to the experiencing of the story would be expected.

Following the description of Quasi-experimental design in Campbell & Cook (1979), the experimental design for this project resembles the One-Group Posttest-Only Design. The independent variable (X) is the subjects' media schemata. The media use that creates schemata happens through long periods of time; that is, watching television for an hour or browsing the web for a week is insufficient to create a mental structure. It is the presence or absence of media use schemata that generates differences in the way people behave during exposure (O). The laboratory setting creates the controlled environment where the dependent variable (human behavior while interacting with a communications medium) occurs and is recorded.

Because the independent variable is media use schemata, the treatment has been already given, and there is no possible way of acquiring a pretest before the subjects start to use media. The possible methods to acquire the independent variable are 1) through a questionnaire that will ask subjects to report their media use (discussed in detail later) or 2) a longitudinal observational study where the subjects' exposure to media is registered (a very expensive proposition).

Cultivation Theory Research

Research related to Cultivation Theory has the same problems as the ones found in this research design. Cultivation Theory was developed by George Gerbner and explains that television watching influences viewers' ideas of what the world is like. Probably the most important part of Cultivation Theory, in relation to this book's research design, is that the effects of television in individuals are considered to be "small, gradual, indirect but cumulative and significant." (Chandler, 1995) It would be impossible to assess or measure any of these effects in an experiment, basically because the type of exposure that is needed for the type of effect sought happens through a long period of time, an event nonreplicable in a laboratory setting.

Most of the criticism related to the methodology in Cultivation Theory is summarized in "Cultivation Theory and Research. A Methodological Critique" (Potter, 1994). The measurement of media exposure (independent variable) is a common problem for Cultivation Theory researchers. Potter's meta-analysis starts by addressing the setback of having more cross-sectional studies than longitudinal studies. The norm in Cultivation Theory research is to have self-reported media usage data. In comparison to observational studies, self-reported media usage is far less expensive and logistically simpler than longitudinal observational designs.

The experimental design adopted for this research project has the same limitations. Nevertheless, some of these limitations are more of a theoretical mishap than a common mistake in the methodology of the research projects. Longitudinal observational methods

82

to obtain media usage data have also some validity and reliability threats. Unless subjects are held in a single place under constant observation, it is possible that media exposure might occur elsewhere. Also, the validity threats common to longitudinal research projects – such as history, maturation, mortality and selection effects — are to be considered and weighted.

Potter (1994) also describes 5 different forms of operationalization of television exposure: 1) Global assessment, 2) exposure to genres, 3) exposure to particular shows, 4) long-term exposure, and 5) exposure through attention. The types of operationalization that will be used for the evaluation of a presence of media schemata are: global assessment and long-term exposure. The former is an overall measurement of media exposure disregarding the type of content that subject is exposed to. In the case of media structure schemata, what is looked for will exist as part of the medium regardless of the message conveyed; this also explains why exposure to genres or exposure to particular shows is irrelevant. The latter, long-term exposure, is essential for both this research project and Cultivation Theory research because at the core of the examination is the creation of human memory structures that build with time. Finally, exposure through attention is a non-valid measure in interactive media because the subject has to interact with the medium in order to obtain content. A basic attention level is required at least to recognize the "clickable" elements on the interface.

Once again, the important distinction between the design of research projects related to Cultivation theory and the current research project is that the dependent variable is not perceptions, attitudes, values, or feelings (Potter, 1994), but behavior.

Establishing causality among variables

Another criticism that Cultivation Theory has had is that it uses mostly correlation analysis as a means to suggest causal relationship. One of the first things taught to doctoral students is that correlation does not imply causality and the use of correlation indicators is often discouraged. The purpose of finding causality in the social sciences is described in a book entitled "Correlation and Causality" (Kenny, 1979); even though observation, measurement, data reduction, and theory formulation are important for the social sciences, causality provides a stronger framework to solve social problems than just the indication of relationship among variables. If a relationship between a variable X and a variable Y is found this could mean one of three things (Shanahan & Morgan, 1999): 1) X caused Y, 2) Y caused X, 3) X and Y only appear to be correlated and another variable explains their relationship. This has been one of the major methodological battles of Cultivation Theory, where the existence of a "mean world syndrome" and heavy television use correlation does not have a causal direction; it could be that either heavy television use causes the "mean world syndrome" or vice versa.

Nevertheless, denying causality as a rule of thumb is not advisable; with other types of research constructs, causality can be found using only correlation analysis (Shanahan & Morgan, 1999): Without considering spurious relationships, if age (X) and political party membership (Y) are related, the direct causal relationship is that X causes Y; it would be difficult to find any sound logical statement that would say that party membership causes age (reverse causality). Also, Cultivation Theory has shown some of the limitations in social science research (Shanahan & Morgan, 1999): The list of possible spurious variables that could intervene is infinite, so the possibility of spuriousness can never be rejected.

The project seeks to establish a causal relationship between previous media use and behavior while experiencing *A space of time*. First, the means to obtain a possible positive or negative relationship among the variables is correlation analysis. Second, a careful evaluation of the meaning of the constructs has to be made in order to establish precedence in time. If a relationship among variables is found, it is understood that more Internet browsing or more television watching would create a mental structure that affects the way in which subjects behave while experiencing *A space of time* based on an impossible reverse causality: Can the behavior on *A space of time* cause how much subjects have used the Internet or watched television in the past? Could the sense of control that they had while experiencing *A space of time* explains subjects past media use? So, even though correlation analysis is going to be applied to find if there is a significant association, causality can be inferred by establishing logical and factual precedence among the media use variables, the behavior interactivity index and the sense of control.

The same precedence does not apply in the case of a possible relationship between the sense of control and the enjoyment of the non-linear story; therefore, causality cannot be assumed. The theoretical background supports the idea that if there is sense of lack of control (due to disorientation and cognitive overload), the possibility for enjoyment is scarce if not nil. However, is it possible that a lack of enjoyment could cause disorientation? Or, is it possible that a lack on enjoyment could cause cognitive overload? The reverse causality cannot be assessed or denied without further investigation.

Controlled Exposure Experiments

Some Controlled Exposure Experiments are a form of One-Group Posttest-Only designs and biggest similarity with the research design of this research project is that both are based on the observation of changes in behavior resulting from the exposure to an independent variable. One good example of such research design is the "Acoustic Response and detection of marine mammals using an advanced digital acoustic recording tag" (Tyack, 2000), where a tag is placed on a whale to measure the amount of noise in the environment coming from Naval active acoustics and the behavior and physiology of the whale. The underlying hypothesis of this study is that the noise coming from ships has a behavioral effect on whales. The tag is used to register not only the independent variable (noise) but also the dependent variable (behavior).

Another study that uses a similar method is "Monitoring Human-Virtual Reality Interaction: A Time Series Analysis Approach" (Stoermer, Mager, Roessler, Mueller-Sphan & Bullinger, 2000). The research project seeks to find physiological determinants for the optimization of Virtual Environments in the mental health field. While subjects are immersed into a virtual environment, continuous physiological data is recorded for later analysis. Among the different determinants sought are: Electrocardiographic (ECG) activity and oxygen saturation in combination with the kind of actions and the subject's velocity during exposure. In the case of this study, two physiological measurements were performed: one before exposure and one during exposure. Subjects showed increased heart rate and increased respiration rate during exposure. Some of the data obtained while monitoring the subjects in the virtual environment is summarized in the following graph:

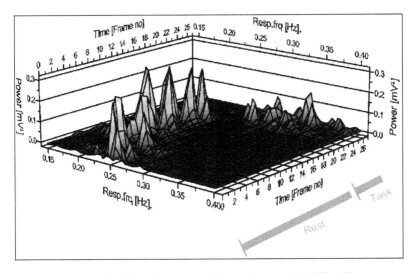

Figure 27. Physiological measurements Source: Stoermer et al., 2000, p.404

The physiological measurements taken before and during exposure show that there is an increase in respiratory frequency when the task (exposure to the virtual environment) occurs. In the case of the tracking behavior device embedded in the programming of *A space of time*, the same methodological principle is used to evaluate behavioral differences among subjects. Time is an important dimension for this type of methodology because it is used as a means to "time stamp" other measurements.

The tracking device in *A space of time*

The tracking "device" in *A space of time* is embedded directly into the programming code that controls the experience, and it registers the location and distances that the cursor covers throughout the entire experience. This amount of "behavior sensitivity" has a significant difference from similar methods used previously to capture the behavior users in hypermedia environments. Nielsen (1990) in an article that describes methods for usability testing of hypertext environments, explains some of the implementation problems of a tracking device made in HyperCard: "HyperTalk does not allow the programmer to define subclasses of objects such as buttons, and this led to problems in the code implementing the automatic checkmarking of anchors leading to previously visited nodes" (p. 304). The tracking device used in *A space of time* was programmed with the same programming language as the rest of the experience: Lingo (the programming code of the multimedia authoring software Director). The amount of user behavior that can be obtained depends only on the programmer's Lingo expertise. Furthermore, the amount of computer power (CPU, hard drive and monitor speed and capabilities) used for the rendering of the hypermedia environment is far greater now than it was in 1990.

However, such degree of sensitivity carries an inherent disadvantage: the amount of information that is delivered to the internal database and later on sent to the server could very large. Therefore, some of the information that is captured throughout the experience is processed while the program is running and what is captured on the internal database represents a summary of the user behavior.

Processing before transferring the behavior data to the database happens in the case of QTVRs and QT files. In a QTVR, the user can make endless number of pans to the left or to the right or make endless number of zoom-ins or zoom-outs. If the database registered each pan or each zoom, the size of the database could grow substantially and would not provide a lot of meaningful information. To avoid this, a process of counting the number of changes in panning direction and zooming direction and a process that registers the overall distance panned or zoomed reduces the amount of data considerably. Furthermore, it transfers some of the processing to the client computer instead of leaving all of the processing of information to the computer on the receiving end.

The Lingo that captures users' behavior is located in many different parts of *A space of time*'s code. All of the database-creating programming can be found in Appendix 3. The type of data that the tracking device provides is the following:

- IP address of the computer downloading the experience.
- Platform type (Windows, 32 or Macintosh)
- Date and time accessed.
- For QTVRs (QuickTime Virtual Reality panoramas): Name of the QTVR, amount of time spent on the QTVR, rotation distance covered to the left, rotation distance covered to the right, number of rotation changes (left to right, right to left), amount zoomed in, amount zoomed out, number of zoom changes.
- For movie scenes: Name of the scene, time spent watching the scene, number of fast forward instances, number of rewind instances, total amount of time fast forwarded, total amount of time rewound.
- For movie Flash animations: Name of the animation, time spent watching the animation.
- Order in which QTVRs, movie scenes and Flash animations were watched.
- Interaction with interface elements: Buttons and amount of time spent on the alternative interfaces of the non-linear experience.
- Overall time spent on the experience (which will be fixed to 90 minutes for the experiment).

Two full-length database files of actual *A space of time* experiencing sessions can be found in Appendix 4. The following is an extract of a database file:

```
20020309x216.51.190.254
Platform: Windows,32
Date: 3/9/02
Time: 9:02 PM
---

QT xopening 316 316 319*
QTVR b47 9 0 0 0 0 0 0 67*
QT xarrival 440 440 444*
QTVR b13 5 0 0 0 0 0 0 13*
QTVR b14 6 160 94 0 38 38 -1 48*
QTVR b12 8 0 0 0 0 0 0 8*
QTVR b7 4 0 152 0 0 0 0 22*
QTVR b30 6 0 0 0 0 0 0 4*
QT xpita46 38 38 41*
QTVR b30 0 0 0 0 0 0 0 51*
QTVR b6 6 0 56 0 0 0 0 10*
Flash flash2 0 2780 237*
QTVR b6 0 182 0 2 0 0 0 41*
QTVR b29 6 0 34 0 0 0 0 21*
QT xpita58 10 10 13*
QTVR b29 0 0 0 0 0 0 0 20*
QT xpita46 38 38 41*
QTVR b29 0 117 23 4 0 0 0 24*
QTVR b28 3 0 0 0 23 0 0 7*
QTVR b27 3 0 0 0 0 0 0 4*
QTVR b26 6 0 0 0 0 0 0 3*
QT xpita50 4 4 8*
QTVR b26 0 0 0 0 0 0 0 3*
QTVR b1 4 0 0 0 0 0 0 2*
QT xtvrona 258 258 262*
```

Figure 28.. *A space of time* behavior database

The data registered on the database can be easily read because it is already coded by type of media (QTVR, QT, Flash animation or screen) and because the amount of time is already converted to seconds and it is always displayed at the end of each line before the asterisk. This is not the case with the type of log files that are acquired with tracking devices that obtain the URLs of visited pages on the World Wide Web. In tracking websites navigation, the database files acquired provide no information on the type of media displayed on the screen, which contrasts with the detailed information recorded in *A space of time*'s database files. The log files or "dribble files" (Lawless & Brown, 1997) are not uncommon in research related to learning strategies using interactive multimedia. Nevertheless, tracking behavior is difficult because of the great variety in web page design and programming languages. Normally, the log files would have to be "cleaned" and interpreted because many different factors (i.e., use of multiple frames, the reloading of pages, Search Engine Robots) may affect the log entry (Brannen, 1998).

In *A space of time*, after the information is collected in the internal database (a field cast member enabled as a database within the *A space of time*'s executable file), it has to be sent back for analysis. In order to guarantee the delivery of the database files, two methods for retrieval are implemented: using a dedicated SMTP server that sends the data to an email account (movie@hypergraphia.com) and via a secure FTP upload of a text file identical to the database to a dedicated server. Both instances occur almost simultaneously when the user hits the "Quit" button. Because computer behavior tracking devices provide large amounts of information, a program independent of *A space of time* was created to analyze and summarize the data obtained from the subjects' use of the non-linear experience. This program was also made with Macromedia Director and its main purpose is to extract averages from the users' databases and the overall count of interactivity with the medium. The overall count of interactivity constitutes the amount of interactive behavior that took place during the experiencing of the non-linear story[12].

---

[12] These calculations will be explained in the operationalization of the variables.

CONCEPTUAL DEFINITION AND OPERATIONALIZATION OF VARIABLES

Data was acquired via an interactive on-screen questionnaire. Even though self-reported media use can lack validity, as expressed before, the alternative methodology would be a longitudinal study where subjects are observed and their media use registered – which not only involves high costs but also creates other sorts of validity problems. The data from the questionnaire are attached to the behavior database before transmission. The use of an interactive on screen questionnaire not only facilitated the process of entering data into the database but also eliminated data entry error. It allowed having a full screen per question, which provided enough space to separate answers and to provide information (i.e., the number of months using the internet screen contained a table to convert years and months into months).

Media Use

- TV watching (Average number of hours reading watching television): On average, how many hours per week do you watch television? (0 to 56 hours in 30-minute increments)
- Magazine reading (Average number of hours reading magazines per week): On average, how many hours per week do you read magazines? (0 to 56 hours in 30-minute increments)
- Newspaper reading (Average number of hours reading newspapers per week): On average, how many hours per week do you read newspapers? (0 to 56 hours in 30-minute increments)
- Book reading — fiction (Average number of hours reading fiction books per week): On average, how many hours per week do you read fiction books (for example: novels, short stories, etc.)? (0 to 56 hours in 30-minute increments)
- Book reading — non-fiction (Average number of hours reading non-fiction books per week): On average, how many hours per week do you read non-

fiction books (for example: textbooks, manuals, etc.)? (0 to 56 hours in 30-minute increments)

- Radio listening (Average number of hours listening to the radio per week): On average, how many hours per week do you listen to the radio? (0 to 56 hours in 30-minute increments)

- Internet browsing (Average number of hours browsing the Internet per week):On average, how many hours per week do you browse the World Wide Web (NOT email)? (0 to 56 hours in 30-minute increments)

- Videogame playing (Average number of hours playing videogames per week): On average, how many hours per week do you play videogames (for example: Nintendo, PlayStation, Xbox, etc.)? (0 to 56 hours in 30-minute increments)

- Computer work (Average number of hours using the computer for work per week): On average, how many hours per week do you use the computer for work? (0 to 56 hours in 30-minute increments)

- Computer playing (Average number of hours using the computer for playing per week): On average, how many hours per week do you use the computer for fun? (0 to 56 hours in 30-minute increments)

- Movie watching (Average number of hours watching movies at a theater per week): On average, how many hours per week do you spend watching movies at the movie theater? (0 to 56 hours in 30-minute increments)

- Internet longevity (Number of months using the Internet for browsing — not email): How long ago (in months) did you start browsing the World Wide Web (NOT email)? (0 to 99 in one month increments)

- *A space of time* experience (Number of hours experiencing *A space of time*): How many times have you experienced *A space of time* prior to this day? (0 to 9 in one unit increments). If more than 1, contingency question: For how long (in total) do you think you have experienced *A space of time*? (30 minutes to 10 hours in 30 minute increments)

Interactive behavior

Interactive behavior: Overall number of interactions with the program. An interaction is defined as a mouse-originated event that changes the content being provided by the medium. Therefore, "interactive behavior" is the sum of the number of QTVR hotspot clicks, plus the number of pans to the right or to the left in a QTVR, plus the number of fast forward, rewind or pause-play clicks in a QT, plus the number of clicks of any of the interface buttons.

This index provides an indication of the range of exploration undertaken and an indication of the users passivity/activity in controlling the content the medium provides.

Sense of Control

Sense of control: Lack of disorientation and cognitive overload while experiencing the non-linear experience. The following operationalization of the variables related to disorientation comes from a validated disorientation scale (Otter & Johnson, 2000) and it has been "stripped" of the questions that are intended to measure efficiency and effectiveness in a question-answer task. The first three elements come from the validated scale and will be used for hypothesis testing. The following two elements are my own operationalization of the disorientation and have been drawn from the literature review. They will only be included in the overall validated scale if all the measurements present a good Chronbach's Alpha.

- How lost or disoriented did you feel while experiencing *A space of time*? (1 = "Not lost at all" to 5 = "Very lost" in 1 step increments)
- How easy was the system to learn? (By system it is understood: *A space of time* as a whole.) (1 = "Very hard" to 5 = "Very easy" in 1 step increments)
- How frustrating was the system to use? (By system it is understood: *A space of time* as a whole.) (1 = "Very frustrating" to 5 = "Not frustrating at all" in 1 step increments)

- How clear is the connection among the pieces that you saw in *A space of time*? (1 = "Not clear at all" to 5 = "Very clear" in 1 step increments)
- How much did you feel "in control" of where you were going in *A space of time*? (1 = "Not in control at all" to 5 = "Totally in control" in 1 step increments)

Enjoyment

Enjoyment: Level of enjoyment of the non-linear experience. The scale for enjoyment comes from a validated instrument to measure enjoyment in physical activities in adolescent girls (Motl et al., 2001). It has been adapted to suit the experiencing of *A space of time*.

Please read to the following assessments regarding your experience of *A space of time* and respond to it by choosing one of the responses on the scale from 1 to 5, where 1 = "Strongly disagree" and 5 = "Strongly agree."

While I experienced *A space of time*: (1 = "Strongly disagree" to 5 = "Strongly agree" in 1 step increments.)

I enjoyed it.	I felt bored.	I disliked it.	I found it pleasurable.
I got something out of it.	It was not at all interesting.	It felt as I would rather be doing something else.	

Table 4. Enjoy scale items.

Other research-related questions

Demographics

- How old were you on your last birthday (in years)? (18 to 99 in one year increments)
- How many years of college/university education have you completed? (0 to 10 in one year increments)
- What is your gender? (Male or Female)

Non-media schemata (spurious relationship)

- Did you identify with any of the characters? (Yes or No) If yes, contingency question: With which one of the characters you identified with? In 150 words or more, please describe why?
- Do you agree with the discourse of the movie about advertising, technology, and the economic system? (Strongly agree to Strongly disagree Likert-Scale)
- Have you ever been by yourself in an empty building as the one shown in *A space of time*? (Yes or No)

Attention Deficit Disorder (spurious relationship)

- Have you ever been diagnosed with Attention Deficit Disorder? (Yes or No)

Disorientation in everyday tasks (Spurious relationship)

According to Woodhead (1991), there is evidence "that individuals with higher spatial ability perform better on navigation tasks that those with comparable computer exposure and low spatial ability." (p. 138) If this would be the case, spatial ability might be a contributing factor or an alternative explanation of why subjects have a low interactive

95

behavior during the *A space of time* experience and why those same subjects do not use the web frequently.

- How easy it is for you to get lost in a city you don't know well? (1 = "Very easy" to 5 = "Very difficult" in 1 step increments)

Computer Anxiety (Spurious relationship)

Please read each item below and respond to it by choosing one of the responses on the scale from 1 to 5, where 1 = "strongly disagree" and 5 = "strongly agree." (1 = "Strongly disagree" to 5 = "Strongly agree" in 1 step increments)

- I look forward to using a computer.
- I do not think I would be able to learn a computer programming language.
- The challenge of learning about computers is exciting.
- Anyone can learn to use a computer if they are patient and motivated.
- Learning to operate computers is like learning any new skill –the more you practice, the better you become.
- I am afraid that if I begin to use computers I will become dependent upon them and lose some of my reasoning skills.
- I feel that I will be able to keep up with the advances happening in the computer field.
- I feel apprehensive about using computers.
- If given the opportunity, I would like to learn about and use computers.
- I have avoided computers because they are unfamiliar and somewhat intimidating to me.

96

SETTING

The experiment took place in a laboratory setting at the Multimedia Labs of the Communication Studies Department at California State University Sacramento. Subjects for the experiment were recruited with the help of 12 faculty members of the Communications Studies Department and the Art Department. Faculty members in new media and methodology related courses agreed to offer extra credit for participation in the experiment. More than 500 students were offered extra credit for participation in the experiment.

The experiment ran for 5 consecutive weekends. Each weekend day is divided in three segments with a maximum capacity of 25 subjects per segment. Each segment consisted of 1 hour and 30 minutes of browsing the non-linear experience and 15 minutes to respond to the questionnaire.

Subjects in the experiment were guaranteed anonymity and confidentiality. The experiment followed the Policy and Procedures for the Protection of Human Subjects at California State University, Sacramento.

Even though the tracking device is currently being implemented on any person who visits the non-linear experience on the World Wide Web, the laboratory setting provides a controlled environment where decision making process are isolated from external influences. The information that is received by regular Internet users may lack validity. While what is being measured is the impact of a person's media use schema, a non-controlled environment does not guarantee that other persons in the household are not influencing subjects or that other media is not being used while the browsing of the non-linear experience is taking place.

Contamination effects are considered to be small of negligible to some parts of the research but not for others. Under the scope of Schema Theory, browsing behavior and level of control should not be affected because it is assumed that the subjects' schemata determine both variables. Level of enjoyment may be affected by other subject commentaries and perception of the non-linear experience. Even though this contamination potential exists for one of the dependent variables, alternatives are not possible due to budgetary and resource limitations.

RESULTS

SAMPLE CHARACTERISTICS AND DEMOGRAPHIC INFORMATION

Out of the 477 subjects that participated in the experiment, 42 cases were classified as invalid for the following reasons (in order of importance):

Subjects accessed the questionnaire before they were instructed to do so. Because the data capturing process (both behavioral data and questionnaire responses) is integrated into the experience, subjects were able to access the questionnaire before completing the 90 minutes assigned to the experiencing of *A space of time*. Accessing the questionnaire at different moments was a concern because the subjects would be aware of the research questions present in the questionnaire before completing the experience. Furthermore, it would disrupt the homogeneity of the treatment invalidating the inferential power of the data gathered.

Program problems. In the first day of experimentation, the program for the experience had a broken link in one of the 180 QTVRs included in the virtual environment. Subjects that tried to access that link had a program failure warning on the screen before the experience would close. All of the subjects that had that experience on the first day of experimentation were excluded from the sample and changes were made to the program to correct the problem.

Other type of problems. One subject insisted in solving homework problems during the experience. One subject attended the experiment inebriated. One subject left the experiment after 30 minutes because he had other commitments.

Out of the 435 valid cases, 57.2 percent are female subjects and 42.8 are male subjects. The mean age is 25.4 years with a standard deviation of 7.6 years. Even though the distribution for age is skewed to the left, indicating a large proportion of typical students, it holds a fairly normal distribution to the right because the sample included a considerable number of older people. The range goes from 18 to 61 years of age. The

98

subjects in the sample have an average number of years in college of 3.8 with a standard deviation of 1.8 years and an overall normal distribution.

INTERNAL CONSISTENCY RELIABILITY

Three already validated scales were used in the project's questionnaire. The first, used as part of a scale to tap feelings of control vs. disorientation, comes from a validated disorientation scale by Otter & Johnson (2000), plus two extra questions based on the literature review covered in the second chapter. The second, the scale for enjoyment, is extracted from a validated instrument to measure enjoyment in physical activities in adolescent girls (Motl et al., 2001) and adapted to the experiencing of *A space of time*. The third one is a validated scale to measure Computer Anxiety, one of the variables that could introduce a spurious relationship into the data.

The results for the "control" or disorientation scale are presented in the following table:

	Scale Mean if Item Deleted	Scale Variance if Item Deleted	Corrected Item-Total Correlation	Squared Multiple Correlation	Alpha if Item Deleted
CONTROL1	13.1517	9.7603	.5943	.3591	.6945
CONTROL2	12.2943	10.3372	.5428	.3231	.7138
CONTROL3	12.5908	9.6018	.5830	.3794	.6978
CONTROL4	13.0391	11.0422	.4205	.1923	.7533
CONTROL5	12.8230	9.7267	.5115	.2631	.7259

Reliability Coefficients   5 items

Alpha =   .7609   Standardized item alpha =   .7611

Table 5. Cronbach's Alpha for the Control Scale

The three original control questions (CONTROL1, CONTROL2 and CONTROL3) give a Cronbach's Alpha of .7291, a smaller value than the one obtained when the scale includes the two items that were added from the literature review. If item CONTROL4 were to be removed ("How clear is the connection among the pieces that you saw in *A space of time*?") Cronbach's Alpha would increase to .7533; nevertheless, the original scale was kept because it is fairly good and it is consistent with the planning and execution of the research project. Therefore, the full set of items for the creation of a Control Scale was used for hypothesis testing.

In case of the scale used for enjoyment, the results are the following:

	Scale Mean if Item Deleted	Scale Variance if Item Deleted	Corrected Item-Total Correlation	Squared Multiple Correlation	Alpha if Item Deleted
ENJOY1	20.9310	35.2303	.7858	.6545	.9049
ENJOY2	21.0782	34.8556	.7547	.5953	.9077
ENJOY3	20.6966	34.2487	.7922	.6536	.9038
ENJOY4	21.2023	34.5995	.8084	.6786	.9024
ENJOY5	21.0690	36.1104	.6038	.4053	.9237
ENJOY6	20.3356	36.0945	.7619	.5856	.9077
ENJOY7	21.2667	32.8412	.7865	.6292	.9049

R E L I A B I L I T Y   A N A L Y S I S   -   S C A L E   (A L P H A)

Reliability Coefficients   7 items

Alpha =   .9201   Standardized item alpha =   .9220

Table 6. Cronbach's Alpha for the Enjoyment Scale

Cronbach's Alpha for the Enjoyment Scale is very good. If item ENJOY5 ("I got something out of it") is removed a slightly better Cronbach's Alpha would be achieved. Following the same decision rationale as in the Control Scale, the full Enjoyment Scale was taken into consideration because it is consistent with the literature review and the planning of the research project.

Finally, the Computer Anxiety Scale shows the following characteristics:

	Scale Mean if Item Deleted	Scale Variance if Item Deleted	Corrected Item-Total Correlation	Squared Multiple Correlation	Alpha if Item Deleted
ANXIETY1	17.0253	25.7805	-.4762	.3313	.7146
ANXIETY2	18.8460	16.9647	.3666	.1958	.5193
ANXIETY3	18.7080	16.5805	.4356	.4450	.4992
ANXIETY4	19.3586	18.8849	.2828	.2727	.5467
ANXIETY5	19.6897	19.6339	.3378	.2811	.5454
ANXIETY6	19.0529	17.9949	.2601	.1139	.5514
ANXIETY7	18.6851	17.3775	.3817	.2645	.5177
ANXIETY8	18.9701	16.9968	.3290	.2253	.5306
ANXIETY9	19.2276	17.6693	.4621	.3826	.5060
ANXITY10	19.4575	17.2580	.4478	.2818	.5033

Reliability Coefficients   10 items

Alpha =   .5774   Standardized item alpha =   .5953

Table 7. Initial Cronbach's Alpha for the Computer Anxiety Scale

The Computer Anxiety Scale, one of the variables that was used as a control variable due to its possible spurious relationship with feeling of control and level of enjoyment, presents a different scenario than the former two scales. By deleting item ANXIETY1 ("I look forward to using a computer") Cronbach's Alpha not only increases considerably but also changes from an unacceptable value of .5774 to a fairly good value of .7146. The new table minus the first item is the following:

	Scale Mean if Item Deleted	Scale Variance if Item Deleted	Corrected Item- Total Correlation	Squared Multiple Correlation	Alpha if Item Deleted
ANXIETY2	14.8690	20.4091	.3823	.1937	.6920
ANXIETY3	14.7310	19.3307	.5247	.3823	.6616
ANXIETY4	15.3816	22.5268	.2956	.2718	.7052
ANXIETY5	15.7126	23.4080	.3389	.2800	.7019
ANXIETY6	15.0759	21.6048	.2692	.1127	.7147
ANXIETY7	14.7080	20.5344	.4342	.2493	.6810
ANXIETY8	14.9931	20.5322	.3365	.2249	.7032
ANXIETY9	15.2506	20.7919	.5296	.3570	.6680
ANXITY10	15.4805	20.7295	.4624	.2803	.6767

Reliability Coefficients   9 items

Alpha =   .7146   Standardized item alpha =   .7248

Table 8. Final Cronbach's Alpha for the Computer Anxiety Scale

A very small increase in the internal correlation of these variables could be achieved by removing ANXIETY6; however, the increase is of a hundredth of a percent, making the exclusion of the item pointless.

As a result of the previous analysis, two out of the three scales will remain with all of their initial indicators. However, it is worth mentioning that the two unmodified scales with good alphas are the ones that were adapted to this specific research project (Feeling of control and Level of enjoyment.) The most tested scale, **computer anxiety,** and in theory the strongest of all, turned out to give the smallest alpha.

DESCRIPTIVE STATISTICS AND TESTING OF ASSUMPTIONS

Descriptive statistics will be divided into the three sections: Media use variables (independent variables); amount of interactive behavior, feeling of control and level of enjoyment (dependent variables); spurious relationship variables (control variables).

Descriptive Statistics for Media Use variables

	N	Minimum	Maximum	Mean	Std. Deviation
TV hours per week	435	0	40	8.49	7.672
Magazine hours per week	435	0	26	1.93	2.424
Newspaper hours per week	435	0	26	1.92	2.342
Reading Fiction Books per week	435	.0	20.0	1.47	2.5720
Reading Non-Fiction books per week	435	0	45	4.33	4.683
Radio hours per week	435	0	70	9.90	9.401
Internet hours per week	435	0	93	5.69	7.337
Video Games hours per week	435	0	25	1.00	2.820
Computer for Work hours per week	435	0	60	12.36	12.692
Computer for Fun hours per week	435	0	86	4.87	6.805
Movie theater hours per week	435	0	10	1.06	1.355
Number of Internet Months	435	0	120	54.51	26.399
Number of times experienced *A space of time*	435	0	10	.26	1.192
Number of hours experienced *A space of time*	435	0	25	.27	1.744
Valid N (listwise)	435				

Table 9. Descriptive Statistics for Media Use variables

The two most used media are television and radio. It is important to notice that not only the Internet is the third most used medium but also that the average longevity using the medium exceeds 4.5 years. The average number of hours using the computer for work and the average number of hours using the computer for fun are also worth a comment: in general the amount spent per week in a non-linear medium (Internet hours, computer for fun hours and computer for work hours) exceeds the amount of time spent in linear media.

The number of hours per week spent watching television exceeds the number of hours reading non-fiction books. This is consistent with previous research data that has been constantly used to indicate that Americans, throughout their education years, spend more time watching television than time in a classroom (Comstock, 1991) or that they spend more time watching television than reading their textbooks.

From the table we can determine that the normality assumption is at risk due to the high standard deviations and the small means. In many of the variables, the mean minus one standard deviation gives a negative number, showing that the distribution of the sample is skewed to the left. Initially, this situation could mean flaws in the program that extracts the information from the individual user databases. The only way to ensure that the data retrieved is correct is by applying the same transformations done by the program by hand. Ten users were selected at random from the sample and their data were computed manually. The results match the results obtained with the program, which indicates that there is an alternative explanation to the skewness in the majority of the distributions.

A plausible explanation comes from interpreting the meaning of the data according to the sample obtained. The vast majority of the subjects were students currently enrolled in college. The amount of time devoted to studying at the university level should take some time away from the subjects' media use. Therefore, it is possible to interpret the skew just as a descriptive characteristic of the sample obtained, making generalizations to a larger population (students and non-students) subject to external validity threats. The graphs are shown in Figure 30 are the media use histograms with normal curve and the graphs shown in Figure 31 are normal P-P plots.

The P-P plots show deviancy from normality in most of the variables with the exception of one variable: Internet Longevity or "How long ago (in months) did you start browsing the World Wide Web (NOT email)?" This fact strengthens the "lower media use than usual during college years" assumption and supports the assertion that the program made to extract the data is working properly. The Internet Longevity question escapes the rather usual "hours per week" operationalization, measuring instead the numbers of months using the Internet. The range for Internet Longevity goes from 0 to 120 months and has an average of 54.51 months; that is, it goes from 0 to 10 years and its average is 4.54 years.

This amount extends beyond the mean time of 3.8 years of college education. It would be expected to receive a fairly normal distribution when it comes to months using the Internet.

The final two variables have the biggest deviancy from normality. This is also expected because the variables are related to the number of times and the number of hours spent experiencing *A space of time* (even though the experience was tested on the Internet for several months before the experiment, no serious attempts to promote it or register it in search engines were made).

For the media use variables, a transformation is needed in order to sustain the normality assumption through the inferential analysis. The new variables consist of a (natural) logarithmic transformation preceded by the addition of a constant to all of the values. The addition of the constant has the effect of eliminating values equal to zero (which result in missing values when the natural logarithm is computed).

This transformation does not affect the result of the analysis. Following the properties of natural logarithms:

$$\ln(x+a) = \ln(x) + \ln(a) = \ln(x) + 0 \quad \text{(where a is a constant.)}$$

Equation 1. Additive property of natural logarithms.

The P-P plots for the transformed variables (Figure 32) show that the transformation had a positive effect on the distribution of the variables except for Internet Longevity which will be left on its original scale.

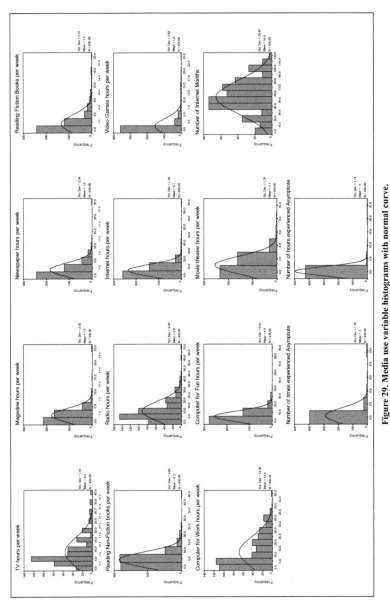

Figure 29. Media use variable histograms with normal curve.

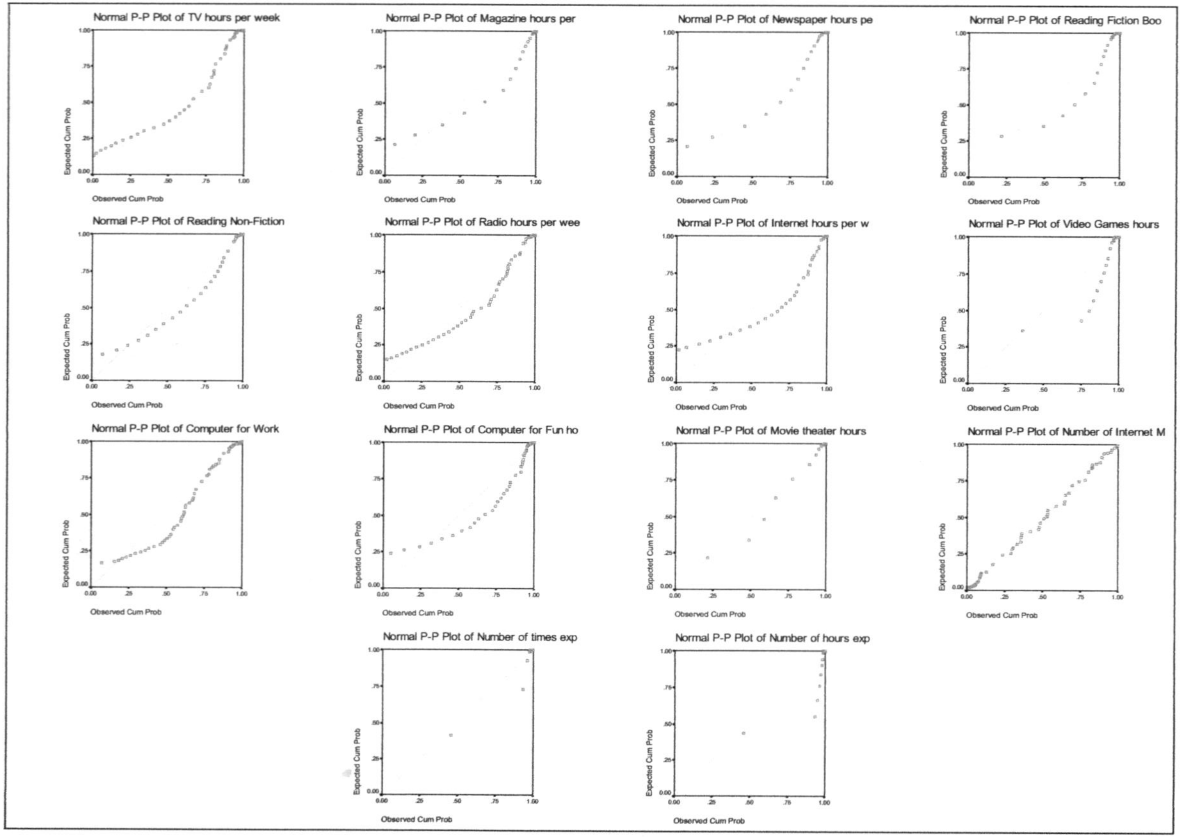

Figure 30. Normal P-P Plots for media use variables.

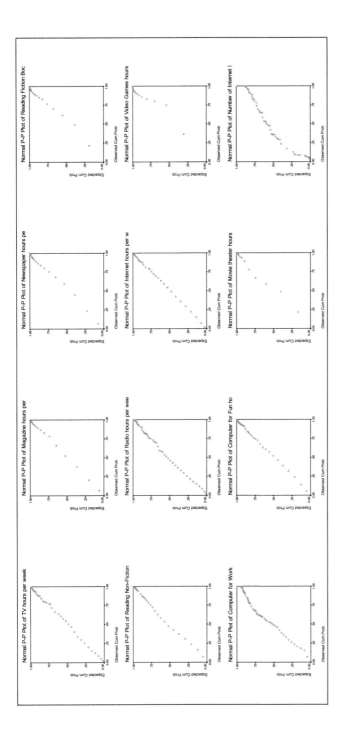

Figure 31. Normal P-P Plots for media use variables after transformation.

The two variables related to the experiencing of *A space of time* before the experiment will not be transformed but they will be recoded as a dichotomous variable: previously exposed and not exposed to the experience before the experiment. Both variables show a heavy abnormal skew to the left. The fact that these two variables are skewed to the left shows on one side that they fail to pass the normality assumption, but on the other side it helps understand that the treatment was largely unknown to the majority of the sample.

The second section is related to the dependent variables in the research design: 1) Interactive Behavior, 2) Feeling of Control, and 3) Enjoyment. Their descriptive statistics are the following:

Descriptive Statistics

	N	Minimum	Maximum	Mean	Std. Deviation
Amount of Interactive Behavior	435	3.00	483.00	51.5954	61.86537
Control Index	435	5.00	25.00	15.9747	3.85770
Enjoy Index	435	7.00	35.00	24.4299	6.84230
Valid N (listwise)	435				

Table 10. Descriptive Statistics for Amount of Interactive Behavior, Feeling of Control and Level of Enjoyment.

The normality assumption holds for both the Control Index and the Enjoy Index; however, as can be deducted by the size of the standard deviation in comparison to the size of the mean, it fails for Amount of Interactive Behavior. The following six graphs show the distribution of the dependent variables:

109

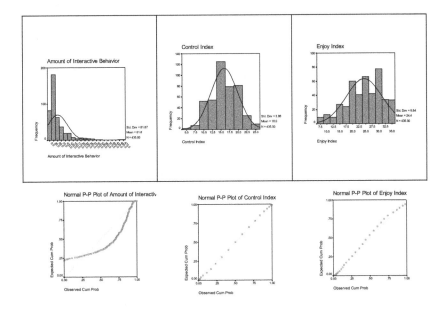

**Figure 32. Amount of Interactive Behavior, Control Index, and Enjoy Index histograms. Amount of
Interactive Behavior, Control Index, and Enjoy Index P-P plots.**

The Amount of Interactive Behavior curve is heavily skewed to the left and it has a
couple of outliers to the far right. The Amount of Interactive Behavior data needs a
(natural) logarithmic transformation to pass the normality assumption; the new variable
name holding the transformed values is named "Interactive Behavior (LN)." The new
histogram graph with normal curve and P-P plots show a considerable change in the
distribution of the variable.

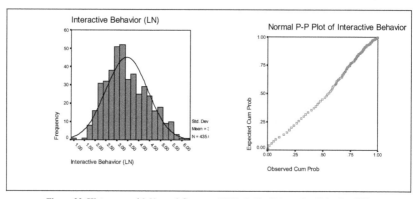

Figure 33. Histogram with Normal Curve and P-P plot for Interactive Behavior (LN)

Finally, the third and last section includes all the variables that could have a spurious relationship in the model and that might provide alternate explanations to the hypotheses being tested. Spurious relationship variables are nominal, ordinal and scale. The following table (Table 11) shows basic descriptive information about the nominal variables:

Variable (N=435)	Yes	No
IDCHAR (Identified with character)	31.5%	68.5%
AGREE (Agree with the experience's discourse)	77.2%	22.8%
BUILDING (Ever been in an empty building)	29.4%	70.6%
ADD (Attention Deficit Disorder)	3.7%	96.3%

Table 11. Descriptives for nominal controlling variables.

Both ordinal and scale controlling variables show a fairly normal distribution with the following basic descriptive information:

Descriptive Statistics

	N	Minimum	Maximum	Mean	Std. Deviation
Orientation in a city	435	1	5	2.75	1.192
Anxiety Index	435	9.00	38.00	17.0253	5.07745
Valid N (listwise)	435				

Table 12. Descriptive statistics for ordinal and scale controlling variables.

HYPOTHESES TESTING RESULTS

The first set of hypotheses are related to how media use schemata might affect the way the subjects browsed the interactive experience. Table 13 shows a correlation matrix between interactive behavior and self reported media use. Only the first column relates to the hypotheses. Because there is no previous research regarding media use schemata and its influence on how an interactive experience is browsed, a fairly flexible p-value of .10 has been used to accept or to reject hypotheses. This does not necessarily mean that the predicted direction of the correlation is the same as the stated hypothesis direction.

As it can be read from the correlation matrix (Table 13), seven out of the twelve tests have significant p-values. Newspaper hours per week (LN) and Interactive Behavior (LN) have a negative correlation of -.124 with a small p-value of .009. Hours reading fiction books (LN) and Interactive Behavior (LN) have a negative correlation of -.123 also with a small p-value (.01). Hours reading non-fiction books (LN) and Interactive Behavior (LN) have the strongest statistically significant negative correlation among the print media, it is -.158 with a very small p-value of .008. With one exception, all of print media with good statistical significance have also a negative correlation with Interactive Behavior; that is, the more the subjects read newspapers and books the less they interacted with the experience.

Correlations

		Interactive Behavior (LN)	TV hours per week (LN)	Magazine hours per week (LN)	Newspaper hours per week (LN)	Reading Fiction Books per week (LN)	Reading Non-Fiction books per week (LN)	Radio hours per week (LN)	Internet hours per week (LN)	Video Games hours per week (LN)	Computer for Work hours per week (LN)	Computer for Fun hours per week (LN)	Movie theater hours per week (LN)	Number of Internet Months
Interactive Behavior (LN)	Pearson Correlation	1	-.003	.011	-.124**	-.123*	-.158**	-.022	.126**	.192**	-.022	.140**	.017	.118*
	Sig. (2-tailed)		.946	.825	.009	.010	.001	.645	.008	.000	.645	.003	.722	.014
	N	435	435	435	435	435	435	435	435	435	435	435	435	435
TV hours per week (LN)	Pearson Correlation	-.003	1	.325**	.244**	.055	.037	.168**	.210**	.201**	-.038	.144**	.068	-.028
	Sig. (2-tailed)	.946		.000	.000	.252	.443	.000	.000	.000	.432	.003	.154	.555
	N	435	435	435	435	435	435	435	435	435	435	435	435	435
Magazine hours per week (LN)	Pearson Correlation	.011	.325**	1	.156**	.174**	.157**	.182**	.292**	.128**	.054	.196**	.147**	-.016
	Sig. (2-tailed)	.825	.000		.001	.000	.001	.000	.000	.008	.261	.000	.002	.739
	N	435	435	435	435	435	435	435	435	435	435	435	435	435
Newspaper hours per week (LN)	Pearson Correlation	-.124**	.244**	.156**	1	.156**	.196**	.149**	.191**	-.005	.033	.040	.074	.009
	Sig. (2-tailed)	.009	.000	.001		.001	.000	.002	.000	.909	.497	.404	.123	.846
	N	435	435	435	435	435	435	435	435	435	435	435	435	435
Reading Fiction Books per week (LN)	Pearson Correlation	-.123*	.055	.174**	.156**	1	.249**	-.001	.019	.000	.010	-.019	.068	.041
	Sig. (2-tailed)	.010	.252	.000	.001		.000	.978	.694	.998	.830	.698	.155	.391
	N	435	435	435	435	435	435	435	435	435	435	435	435	435
Reading Non-Fiction books per week (LN)	Pearson Correlation	-.158**	.037	.157**	.196**	.249**	1	.038	.078	-.055	.062	.007	-.011	.035
	Sig. (2-tailed)	.001	.443	.001	.000	.000		.434	.106	.254	.195	.881	.818	.472
	N	435	435	435	435	435	435	435	435	435	435	435	435	435
Radio hours per week (LN)	Pearson Correlation	-.022	.168**	.182**	.149**	-.001	.038	1	.153**	-.017	.157**	.062	.081	.108*
	Sig. (2-tailed)	.645	.000	.000	.002	.978	.434		.001	.728	.001	.196	.093	.024
	N	435	435	435	435	435	435	435	435	435	435	435	435	435
Internet hours per week (LN)	Pearson Correlation	.126**	.210**	.292**	.191**	.019	.078	.153**	1	.322**	.270**	.656**	.131**	.250**
	Sig. (2-tailed)	.008	.000	.000	.000	.694	.106	.001		.000	.000	.000	.006	.000
	N	435	435	435	435	435	435	435	435	435	435	435	435	435
Video Games hours per week (LN)	Pearson Correlation	.192**	.201**	.128**	-.005	.000	-.055	-.017	.322**	1	-.011	.382**	.086	.219**
	Sig. (2-tailed)	.000	.000	.008	.909	.998	.254	.728	.000		.818	.000	.077	.000
	N	435	435	435	435	435	435	435	435	435	435	435	435	435
Computer for Work hours per week (LN)	Pearson Correlation	-.022	-.038	.054	.033	.010	.062	.157**	.270**	-.011	1	.161**	-.056	.166**
	Sig. (2-tailed)	.645	.432	.261	.497	.830	.195	.001	.000	.818		.001	.247	.001
	N	435	435	435	435	435	435	435	435	435	435	435	435	435
Computer for Fun hours per week (LN)	Pearson Correlation	.140**	.144**	.196**	.040	-.019	.007	.062	.656**	.382**	.161**	1	.124*	.220**
	Sig. (2-tailed)	.003	.003	.000	.404	.698	.881	.196	.000	.000	.001		.010	.000
	N	435	435	435	435	435	435	435	435	435	435	435	435	435
Movie theater hours per week (LN)	Pearson Correlation	.017	.068	.147**	.074	.068	-.011	.081	.131**	.086	-.056	.124*	1	.000
	Sig. (2-tailed)	.722	.154	.002	.123	.155	.818	.093	.006	.077	.247	.010		.996
	N	435	435	435	435	435	435	435	435	435	435	435	435	435
Number of Internet Months	Pearson Correlation	.118*	-.028	-.016	.009	.041	.035	.108*	.250**	.219**	.166**	.220**	.000	1
	Sig. (2-tailed)	.014	.555	.739	.846	.391	.472	.024	.000	.000	.001	.000	.996	
	N	435	435	435	435	435	435	435	435	435	435	435	435	435

**. Correlation is significant at the 0.01 level (2-tailed).
*. Correlation is significant at the 0.05 level (2-tailed).

Table 13. Correlation Matrix between Media Use variables (independent variable) and Interactive Behavior (dependent variable).

The next four significant correlations between media use and Interactive Behavior (LN) are positive. Hours listening to the radio shows a correlation of .126 with an p-value of .008. Hours playing video games has a correlation of .192 with Interactive Behavior (LN) with a corresponding very low p-value (.000). Hours using the computer for fun also has a positive correlation of .140 and an low p-value (.003). Finally, the number of months using the Internet had also a positive correlation of .118 with a somewhat higher but still statistically significant p-value (.014). As it was expected, video games, using the computer for fun and Internet longevity had a positive relationship with the amount of interactive behavior while experiencing *A space of time*. This supports the idea that "related" schemata had an impact on the way the subjects interacted with the experience.

Also the correlation matrix shows positive correlations among common media use variables. Out of the 66 cross-media correlations that can be extracted from the matrix, 31 correlations have positive values and a maximum p-value of .003 . Some of the correlations understandably are very high; for example, the number of Internet hours per week (LN) and the number of computer hours for fun per week (LN) have a correlation of .656 with a very strong p-value (.000).

Table 14 shows the correlation matrix between Media Use and the feeling of control that the subjects perceived at the time of the experience. Three out of the twelve hypotheses related to media use and felling of control gave statistically significant correlations.

Correlations

		Control Index	TV hours per week (LN)	Magazine hours per week (LN)	Newspaper hours per week (LN)	Reading Fiction Books per week (LN)	Reading Non-Fiction books per week (LN)	Radio hours per week (LN)	Internet hours per week (LN)	Video Games hours per week (LN)	Computer for Work hours per week (LN)	Computer for Fun hours per week (LN)	Movie theater hours per week (LN)	Number of Internet Months
Control Index	Pearson Correlation	1	.067	.071	.061	.061	.021	.080	.077	.097*	-.006	.101*	.069	-.014
	Sig. (2-tailed)		.162	.142	.202	.202	.669	.094	.108	.043	.896	.035	.149	.765
	N	435	435	435	435	435	435	435	435	435	435	435	435	435
TV hours per week (LN)	Pearson Correlation	.067	1	.325**	.244**	.055	.037	.168**	.210**	.201**	-.038	.144**	.068	-.028
	Sig. (2-tailed)	.162		.000	.000	.252	.443	.000	.000	.000	.432	.003	.154	.555
	N	435	435	435	435	435	435	435	435	435	435	435	435	435
Magazine hours per week (LN)	Pearson Correlation	.071	.325**	1	.402**	.174**	.157**	.182**	.292**	.128**	.054	.196**	.147**	-.016
	Sig. (2-tailed)	.142	.000		.000	.000	.001	.000	.000	.008	.261	.000	.002	.739
	N	435	435	435	435	435	435	435	435	435	435	435	435	435
Newspaper hours per week (LN)	Pearson Correlation	.061	.244**	.402**	1	.156**	.186**	.149**	.191**	-.005	.033	.040	.074	.009
	Sig. (2-tailed)	.202	.000	.000		.001	.000	.002	.000	.909	.497	.404	.123	.846
	N	435	435	435	435	435	435	435	435	435	435	435	435	435
Reading Fiction Books per week (LN)	Pearson Correlation	.061	.055	.174**	.156**	1	.249**	-.001	.153**	-.017	.010	-.019	.068	.041
	Sig. (2-tailed)	.202	.252	.000	.001		.000	.978	.001	.728	.830	.698	.155	.391
	N	435	435	435	435	435	435	435	435	435	435	435	435	435
Reading Non-Fiction books per week (LN)	Pearson Correlation	.021	.037	.157**	.186**	.249**	1	.038	.078	-.055	.062	.007	-.011	.035
	Sig. (2-tailed)	.669	.443	.001	.000	.000		.434	.106	.254	.195	.881	.818	.472
	N	435	435	435	435	435	435	435	435	435	435	435	435	435
Radio hours per week (LN)	Pearson Correlation	.080	.168**	.182**	.149**	-.001	.038	1	.153**	-.017	.010	.062	.081	.108*
	Sig. (2-tailed)	.094	.000	.000	.002	.978	.434		.001	.728	.830	.196	.093	.024
	N	435	435	435	435	435	435	435	435	435	435	435	435	435
Internet hours per week (LN)	Pearson Correlation	.077	.210**	.292**	.191**	.153**	.078	.153**	1	.322**	.270**	.656**	.131**	.250**
	Sig. (2-tailed)	.108	.000	.000	.000	.001	.106	.001		.000	.000	.000	.006	.000
	N	435	435	435	435	435	435	435	435	435	435	435	435	435
Video Games hours per week (LN)	Pearson Correlation	.097*	.201**	.128**	-.005	-.017	-.055	-.017	.322**	1	.270**	.382**	.085	.219**
	Sig. (2-tailed)	.043	.000	.008	.909	.728	.254	.728	.000		.000	.000	.077	.000
	N	435	435	435	435	435	435	435	435	435	435	435	435	435
Computer for Work hours per week (LN)	Pearson Correlation	-.006	-.038	.054	.033	.010	.062	.010	.270**	.270**	1	.161**	-.056	.166**
	Sig. (2-tailed)	.896	.432	.261	.497	.830	.195	.830	.000	.000		.001	.247	.001
	N	435	435	435	435	435	435	435	435	435	435	435	435	435
Computer for Fun hours per week (LN)	Pearson Correlation	.101*	.144**	.196**	.040	-.019	.007	.062	.656**	.382**	.161**	1	.124**	.220**
	Sig. (2-tailed)	.035	.003	.000	.404	.698	.881	.196	.000	.000	.001		.010	.000
	N	435	435	435	435	435	435	435	435	435	435	435	435	435
Movie theater hours per week (LN)	Pearson Correlation	.069	.068	.147**	.074	.068	-.011	.081	.131**	.085	-.056	.124**	1	.000
	Sig. (2-tailed)	.149	.154	.002	.123	.155	.818	.093	.006	.077	.247	.010		.996
	N	435	435	435	435	435	435	435	435	435	435	435	435	435
Number of Internet Months	Pearson Correlation	-.014	-.028	-.016	.009	.041	.035	.108*	.250**	.219**	.166**	.220**	.000	1
	Sig. (2-tailed)	.765	.555	.739	.846	.391	.472	.024	.000	.000	.001	.000	.996	
	N	435	435	435	435	435	435	435	435	435	435	435	435	435

*. Correlation is significant at the 0.05 level (2-tailed).

**. Correlation is significant at the 0.01 level (2-tailed).

Table 14. Correlation Matrix between Media Use variables (independent variable) and the Control Index (dependent variable)

In contrast to media use and Interactive behavior, the direction of all the statistically significant correlations is positive. Hours per week listening to the radio is positively correlated (.080) with a fair p-value (.094). Hours per week playing video games and feeling of control have a correlation of .097, with a good p-value (.043). Finally, hours per week using the computer for fun and feeling of control have a correlation of .101 with an p-value of .035.

The three positive statistically significant tests of media use against feeling of control are also positive statistically significant tests of media use against Interactive Behavior. In both sets of hypotheses, radio use, video game use and using the computer for fun have a positive impact on the feeling of control and the amount of interactive behavior. These results also support the idea that media schemata have an impact on the way subjects experienced *A space of time.*

The final hypothesis meant to find support to the assertion that feeling of control is a significant determinant of the level of enjoyment while experiencing the non-linear story. The following table shows the results for the final hypothesis:

Correlations

		Control Index	Enjoy Index
Control Index	Pearson Correlation	1	.568**
	Sig. (2-tailed)	.	.000
	N	435	435
Enjoy Index	Pearson Correlation	.568**	1
	Sig. (2-tailed)	.000	.
	N	435	435

**. Correlation is significant at the 0.01 level (2-tailed).

Table 15. Correlation Matrix between Control Index (independent variable) and Enjoy Index (dependent variable).

The correlation between the control index and the enjoyment index is unusually strong (.568), and has a very low p-value. This finding raises important considerations in the production of an interactive experience, because it means a lot of emphasis has to be given to beta testing of a product to ensure that users feel in control as they use it.

In summary, the results from the hypothesis can be reduced to the following list:

Medium	Hypothesis	r	□
Newspapers	Hypothesis 3.1: The more hours of newspaper reading, the greater the amount of interactive behavior.	-.124	.009
Fiction Books	Hypothesis 4.1: The more hours of book reading (fiction), the greater the amount of interactive behavior.	-.123	.010
Non-Fiction Books	Hypothesis 10.1: The more hours of book reading, the greater the amount of interactive behavior.	-.158	.001
Radio	Hypothesis 5.1: The more hours of radio listening, the greater the amount of interactive behavior.	.126	.008
Radio	Hypothesis 5.2: The more hours of radio listening, the higher the sense of control.	.080	.094
Video games	Hypothesis 7.1: The more hours of videogame playing, the greater the amount of interactive behavior.	.192	.000
Video games	Hypothesis 7.2: The more hours of videogame playing, the higher the sense of control.	.097	.043
Computer for fun	Hypothesis 8.1: The more hours of computer playing, the greater the amount of interactive behavior.	.140	.003
Computer for fun	Hypothesis 8.2: The more hours of computer playing, the higher the sense of control.	.101	.035
Internet longevity	Hypothesis 12.1: The more Internet longevity, the greater the amount of interactive behavior.	.118	.014
N.A.	Hypothesis 14: The higher the sense of control, the higher the level of enjoyment.	.568	.000

TESTING FOR SPURIOUS RELATIONSHIPS

Causal relationship between two variables can be established if the variables are related to each other, the relationship cannot be explained by another variable (spurious relationship) and there is precedence in time of one variable over another. A statistically significant relationship has been supported by the data. Precedence in time was established in the literature review; basically, the way subjects behaved and felt during the experiment does not cause previous media use. The final condition for causality is finding a third variable (or as many they are) that would explain the relationship among the other variables. There must be some limit to the testing of spurious relationships because theoretically the potential number of possible causes in mass communications research and other social sciences typically remains undetermined.

In the literature review, the spurious relationships tested were those extracted from other research projects related to computer use or research made on human schemata. In particular, the spurious relationships tested are (the order does not indicate importance):

1) Do you agree with the discourse of the movie (an alternative to media schemata),

2) Identification with one of the characters (an alternative to media schemata),

3) Experienced an empty building before (alternative to media schemata),

4) Attention Deficit Disorder (the retrieving of schemata is affected by other psychological factors),

5) Disorientation on everyday tasks (problems retrieving spatial schemata, even if it is part of the experience or not), and

6) Computer Anxiety (schemata is retrieved inefficiently due to other psychological factors).

Demographic data are included also in the examination of spurious relationships as part of a wider exploratory analysis. The results of running partial correlations controlling for a set of variables can be found in Table 16. Vertically the table is divided in three sections. The first section contains the results for the correlations between media use and interactive behavior, feeling of control and level of enjoyment without any controls. The second vertical section contains the same variables as the previous one but in this case partial correlations controlling for all the possible spurious relationships apply. The results show an impact on the statistical significance and correlation strength of the variables. The correlation between interactive behavior and the number of hours spent reading newspapers increased in strength (from -.125 to -.1552) and its p-value decreased slightly. The correlation between interactive behavior and hours spent reading fiction books decreased and it became statistically irrelevant. In the case of interactive behavior and hours reading non-fiction books, the strength of the correlation decreased but remained statistically significant. In the case interactive behavior and radio, the correlation increased in strength and improved its p-value; nevertheless, the significance of the relationship between the latter and feeling of control disappeared. The relationships between number of hours playing video games and number of hours using the computer for fun and interactive behavior and feeling of control lost statistical significance.

Table of partial correlations (SPSS-style output). Each cell reports the correlation coefficient, the degrees of freedom in parentheses, and the significance level (P=).

	NO CONTROLS			AGE, COLLEGE, GENDER, IDCHAR, AGREE, BUILDING, ADD, ORNTCITY, ANXIETY				AGE, COLLEGE, ORNTCITY, ANXIETY	
	LNALLINT	CONTROL	ENJOY	LNALLINT	CONTROL	ENJOY	LNALLINT	CONTROL	ENJOY
CONTROL	-.019 (435) P= .689	1.0000 (435) P= .	.568 (435) P= .000	-.0611 (424) P= .208	1.0000 (0) P= .	.5597 (424) P= .000	-.0622 (429) P= .197	1.0000 (429) P= .	.5553 (429) P= .000
LNTV	-.003 (435) P= .946	.067 (435) P= .162	.059 (435) P= .216	-.0429 (424) P= .377	.0674 (424) P= .165	.0759 (424) P= .118	-.0051 (429) P= .916	.0770 (429) P= .110	.0678 (429) P= .160
LNMAG	.011 (435) P= .825	.071 (435) P= .142	.135 (435) P= .005	-.0057 (424) P= .906	.0479 (424) P= .324	.1232 (424) P= .011	.0222 (429) P= .647	.0639 (429) P= .186	.1256 (429) P= .009
LNNEWS	-.124 (435) P= .009	.061 (435) P= .202	.070 (435) P= .148	-.1552 (424) P= .001	.0457 (424) P= .347	.0455 (424) P= .349	-.1220 (429) P= .011	.0547 (429) P= .257	.3333 (429) P= .216
LNBOKFIC	-.123 (435) P= .010	.061 (435) P= .202	.075 (435) P= .119	-.0692 (424) P= .154	.0714 (424) P= .141	.0725 (424) P= .135	-.1186 (429) P= .014	.0705 (429) P= .144	.0791 (429) P= .101
LNBOKNF	-.158 (435) P= .001	.021 (435) P= .669	.124 (435) P= .010	-.0977 (424) P= .044	.0330 (424) P= .496	.1099 (424) P= .023	-.1345 (429) P= .005	.0364 (429) P= .451	.1311 (429) P= .006
LNRAD	.126 (435) P= .008	.080 (435) P= .094	.085 (435) P= .078	.1315 (424) P= .007	.0633 (424) P= .192	.0683 (424) P= .159	.1109 (429) P= .021	.0661 (429) P= .171	.0784 (429) P= .104
LNINTWK	-.052 (435) P= .279	-.077 (435) P= .108	-.088 (435) P= .067	-.0325 (424) P= .504	.0231 (424) P= .634	-.0668 (424) P= .169	.0181 (429) P= .708	.0276 (429) P= .568	.0511 (429) P= .289
LNVGAME	.192 (435) P= .000	.097 (435) P= .043	-.033 (435) P= .489	.0456 (424) P= .348	.0516 (424) P= .288	.0326 (424) P= .503	.1496 (429) P= .002	.0493 (429) P= .307	.0028 (429) P= .954
LNCOMPWK	-.022 (435) P= .645	-.006 (435) P= .896	.044 (435) P= .363	.0075 (424) P= .878	-.0452 (424) P= .352	.0219 (424) P= .652	-.0106 (429) P= .827	-.0383 (429) P= .427	.0088 (429) P= .856
LNCOMPFN	.140 (435) P= .003	.101 (435) P= .035	.085 (435) P= .076	.0177 (424) P= .716	.0536 (424) P= .270	.0871 (424) P= .073	.0831 (429) P= .085	.0527 (429) P= .275	.0596 (429) P= .217
LNMOVIES	.017 (435) P= .722	.069 (435) P= .149	.017 (435) P= .731	-.0313 (424) P= .519	.0344 (424) P= .479	.0128 (424) P= .792	-.0229 (429) P= .635	.0429 (429) P= .374	.0037 (429) P= .939
LNINTLON	.034 (435) P= .476	-.046 (435) P= .338	.066 (435) P= .167	-.0184 (424) P= .705	.0211 (424) P= .664	.0625 (424) P= .198	.0206 (429) P= .669	.0149 (429) P= .757	.0408 (429) P= .399

Table 16. Partial correlations for media use variables and interactive behavior, feeling of control, and level of enjoyment.

Nevertheless, some caution has to be taken when including variables like GENDER, IDCHAR, AGREE, BUILDING and ADD (gender, identified with a character, agree with the experience's discourse, been alone in an empty building and been diagnosed with Attention Deficit Disorder, respectively) because these variables are categorical and have been translated to dummy variables for the purpose of including them into the linear analysis of the joint variance and interaction among variables (where scale or at least ordinal measurements are required).

In the third column, all of the categorical variables have been left out of the partial correlation leaving only those variables with scale measurements. The results show that there was practically no change in strength or p-value in the majority of the previously significant correlations between media use and interactive behavior. However, it is important to notice that the same does not apply to the correlation between media use variables and feeling of control; all of the correlations lose their statistical significance.

In order to recover the effect of the possible relationships between categorical spurious variables and the dependent variables, an alternative form of correlation ratio test was performed. The name of the test is ETA and it is a coefficient of non-linear association between nominal and interval variables. The results of applying ETA tests to the categorical variables against the research project's dependent variables can be found on Table 17.

Independent Variable	Dependent Variable	E	E²
Gender	Interactive Behavior (LN)	.308	.094
Identified with character	Interactive Behavior (LN)	.133	.017
Agree with the experience's discourse	Interactive Behavior (LN)	.019	.000
Ever been in an empty building	Interactive Behavior (LN)	.058	.003
Attention Deficit Disorder	Interactive Behavior (LN)	.018	.000
Gender	Feeling of Control	.051	.003
Identified with character	Feeling of Control	.035	.001
Agree with the experience's discourse	Feeling of Control	.080	.006
Ever been in an empty building	Feeling of Control	.066	.004
Attention Deficit Disorder	Feeling of Control	.103	.010
Gender	Level of Enjoyment	.014	.000
Identified with character	Level of Enjoyment	.233	.054
Agree with the experience's discourse	Level of Enjoyment	.261	.068
Ever been in an empty building	Level of Enjoyment	.052	.002
Attention Deficit Disorder	Level of Enjoyment	.002	.000

Table 17. ETA correlation coefficients for nominal variables.

The ETA correlation coefficients' table shows a column for independent and dependent variables because ETA is asymmetrical; hence, ETA has different values when one of the variables is considered dependent and the other independent and vice versa. This asymmetry gives as a result two directional measurements, the one present in the table refers to the direction established in the hypotheses. ETA^2 is the percent of variation in the dependent variable that explains the independent variable and as it can be read from the table, none of the categorical variables (with a possible spurious relationship) has a meaningful impact on the dependent variables. Once again, level of enjoyment was only tested against feeling of control and its inclusion in this analysis has an exploratory purpose.

The same can be done with the scale variables (spurious) to get a sense of their relationship with the dependent variables. The results for interactive behavior can be found in Table 18.

Correlations

		Age	Number of years in college	Orientation in a city	Anxiety Index	Interactive Behavior (LN)
Age	Pearson Correlation	1	.345**	.075	-.162**	-.168**
	Sig. (2-tailed)		.000	.119	.001	.000
	N	435	435	435	435	435
Number of years in college	Pearson Correlation	.345**	1	-.023	-.043	-.143**
	Sig. (2-tailed)	.000		.637	.366	.003
	N	435	435	435	435	435
Orientation in a city	Pearson Correlation	.075	-.023	1	-.123*	.104*
	Sig. (2-tailed)	.119	.637		.010	.029
	N	435	435	435	435	435
Anxiety Index	Pearson Correlation	-.162**	-.043	-.123*	1	-.085
	Sig. (2-tailed)	.001	.366	.010		.078
	N	435	435	435	435	435
Interactive Behavior (LN)	Pearson Correlation	-.168**	-.143**	.104*	-.085	1
	Sig. (2-tailed)	.000	.003	.029	.078	
	N	435	435	435	435	435

**. Correlation is significant at the 0.01 level (2-tailed).
*. Correlation is significant at the 0.05 level (2-tailed).

Table 18. Person correlation coefficients possibly intervening variables and interactive behavior.

Age and the amount of interactive behavior are inversely related. Similarly, the number of years in college is negatively correlated with interactive behavior. This can be explained also by the positive correlation between age and the number of years in college. The data supports the assertion that younger subjects interacted more with the experience. Orientation in a city had a positive impact in the amount of interactive behavior, supporting the idea that some of the schemata used for spatial orientation inside and outside virtual environments have an impact on how subjects behaved during the experience. Contrary to this effect, computer anxiety (Anxiety Index) has a small negative impact on the amount of interaction. Orientation in a city is inversely correlated to the Anxiety Index; that is, the less oriented a person is the more anxious he or she will feel and vice versa (no causal relationship can be established in this case) . The negative correlation between Interactive Behavior (LN) and the number of years in college is quite interesting: it suggests that the younger the subject the more "playful" the subject will be in the virtual environment. This could indicate that the use of *A space of time* could vary from younger-less educated subjects to older-more educated subjects; it is possible that the former could be more interested in the functionality of the experience and the latter could be more interested in the content of the experience.

Correlations

		Age	Number of years in college	Orientation in a city	Anxiety Index	Control Index
Age	Pearson Correlation	1	.345**	.075	-.162**	-.057
	Sig. (2-tailed)	.	.000	.119	.001	.232
	N	435	435	435	435	435
Number of years in college	Pearson Correlation	.345**	1	-.023	-.043	.002
	Sig. (2-tailed)	.000	.	.637	.366	.970
	N	435	435	435	435	435
Orientation in a city	Pearson Correlation	.075	-.023	1	-.123*	.123*
	Sig. (2-tailed)	.119	.637	.	.010	.010
	N	435	435	435	435	435
Anxiety Index	Pearson Correlation	-.162**	-.043	-.123*	1	-.175**
	Sig. (2-tailed)	.001	.366	.010	.	.000
	N	435	435	435	435	435
Control Index	Pearson Correlation	-.057	.002	.123*	-.175**	1
	Sig. (2-tailed)	.232	.970	.010	.000	.
	N	435	435	435	435	435

**. Correlation is significant at the 0.01 level (2-tailed).

*. Correlation is significant at the 0.05 level (2-tailed).

Table 19. Person correlation coefficients possibly intervening variables control index.

Table 19 shows the same controlling variables against feeling of control while experiencing the non-linear story. Only two correlations present statistically significant p-values: Orientation in a city and computer anxiety. The former correlation (.123) supports the idea that orientation is a human characteristic that affects search-and-find tasks independently of their context (physical or virtual). The latter correlation has the same logical structure as that found in the literature: The more anxious the subjects were about using a computer, the less in control they felt during the experiencing of *A space of time*.

Correlations

		Age	Number of years in college	Orientation in a city	Anxiety Index	Enjoy Index
Age	Pearson Correlation	1	.345**	.075	-.162**	.007
	Sig. (2-tailed)		.000	.119	.001	.878
	N	435	435	435	435	435
Number of years in college	Pearson Correlation	.345**	1	-.023	-.043	.048
	Sig. (2-tailed)	.000		.637	.366	.318
	N	435	435	435	435	435
Orientation in a city	Pearson Correlation	.075	-.023	1	-.123*	.066
	Sig. (2-tailed)	.119	.637		.010	.166
	N	435	435	435	435	435
Anxiety Index	Pearson Correlation	-.162**	-.043	-.123*	1	-.146**
	Sig. (2-tailed)	.001	.366	.010		.002
	N	435	435	435	435	435
Enjoy Index	Pearson Correlation	.007	.048	.066	-.146**	1
	Sig. (2-tailed)	.878	.318	.166	.002	
	N	435	435	435	435	435

**. Correlation is significant at the 0.01 level (2-tailed).
*. Correlation is significant at the 0.05 level (2-tailed).

Table 20. Person correlation coefficients possibly intervening variables and enjoy index.

The third table (Table 20), as it was the case with nominal variables, has an exploratory purpose. The only statistically significant correlation is that between computer anxiety (Anxiety Index) and the level of enjoyment (Enjoy Index). As it was expected, the relationship between both variables is inverse: the more the subjects felt anxious about using a computer the less they enjoyed the experience.

Construction of linear multivariate models to improve inferential power

All of the information above coincides with the following models based on linear regressions. The first model includes all of the scale variables (media use and potential intervening variables) to make inferences about the amount of interactive behavior. The results are the following:

Model Summary[b]

Model	R	R Square	Adjusted R Square	Std. Error of the Estimate
1	.374[a]	.140	.107	.90604

a. Predictors: (Constant), Number of Internet Months (LN), Magazine hours per week (LN), Orientation in a city, Number of years in college, Movie theater hours per week (LN), Reading Non-Fiction books per week (LN), Radio hours per week (LN), Anxiety Index, Video Games hours per week (LN), Reading Fiction Books per week (LN), Computer for Work hours per week (LN), TV hours per week (LN), Newspaper hours per week (LN), Age, Computer for Fun hours per week (LN), Internet hours per week (LN)

b. Dependent Variable: Interactive Behavior (LN)

Table 21. Linear Regression R for Interactive Behavior (Dependent)

ANOVA[b]

Model		Sum of Squares	df	Mean Square	F	Sig.
1	Regression	55.794	16	3.487	4.248	.000[a]
	Residual	343.143	418	.821		
	Total	398.937	434			

a. Predictors: (Constant), Number of Internet Months (LN), Magazine hours per week (LN), Orientation in a city, Number of years in college, Movie theater hours per week (LN), Reading Non-Fiction books per week (LN), Radio hours per week (LN), Anxiety Index, Video Games hours per week (LN), Reading Fiction Books per week (LN), Computer for Work hours per week (LN), TV hours per week (LN), Newspaper hours per week (LN), Age, Computer for Fun hours per week (LN), Internet hours per week (LN)

b. Dependent Variable: Interactive Behavior (LN)

Table 22. Linear Regression ANOVA for Interactive Behavior (Dependent)

Using of all of the variables gives an R Square of .14 ; that is, the amount of variance in Interactive Behavior (LN) that is explained by the independent variables. As it is shown in the next table (Table 23), the explicative power of some of the variables included in the model is almost negligible:

Coefficients^a

Model		Unstandardized Coefficients		Standardized Coefficients	t	Sig.
		B	Std. Error	Beta		
1	(Constant)	3.985	.401		9.931	.000
	Age	-8.24E-03	.007	-.066	-1.240	.216
	Number of years in college	-5.68E-02	.025	-.110	-2.244	.025
	Orientation in a city	7.156E-02	.037	.089	1.911	.057
	Anxiety Index	-1.51E-02	.009	-.080	-1.592	.112
	TV hours per week (LN)	-5.43E-02	.064	-.043	-.848	.397
	Magazine hours per week (LN)	.121	.091	.072	1.334	.183
	Newspaper hours per week (LN)	-.192	.081	-.122	-2.364	.019
	Reading Fiction Books per week (LN)	-.113	.066	-.082	-1.714	.087
	Reading Non-Fiction books per week (LN)	-.123	.057	-.105	-2.156	.032
	Radio hours per week (LN)	.160	.053	.147	3.034	.003
	Internet hours per week (LN)	-7.33E-02	.079	-.061	-.928	.354
	Video Games hours per week (LN)	.206	.073	.144	2.798	.005
	Computer for Work hours per week (LN)	-2.41E-02	.040	-.030	-.600	.549
	Computer for Fun hours per week (LN)	8.552E-02	.072	.077	1.192	.234
	Movie theater hours per week (LN)	-5.14E-02	.079	-.030	-.648	.517
	Number of Internet Months (LN)	9.114E-03	.058	.008	.158	.874

a. Dependent Variable: Interactive Behavior (LN)

Table 23. Linear Regression t-values for Interactive Behavior (Dependent)

T values close to 0 are disregarded in order to find a model with **fewer** variables without sacrificing too much explicative power. The result of extracting some of the independent variables through the method of entering and removing variables can be found in the following table (Table 24):

Model Summary⁹

Model	R	R Square	Adjusted R Square	Std. Error of the Estimate	Change Statistics					Durbin-Watson
					R Square Change	F Change	df1	df2	Sig. F Change	
1	.192ª	.037	.035	.94205	.037	16.525	1	433	.000	
2	.242ᵇ	.059	.054	.93238	.022	10.035	1	432	.002	
3	.277ᶜ	.077	.070	.92435	.018	8.530	1	431	.004	
4	.306ᵈ	.094	.085	.91694	.017	8.001	1	430	.005	
5	.328ᵉ	.107	.097	.91102	.014	6.602	1	429	.011	
6	.342ᶠ	.117	.105	.90709	.010	4.729	1	428	.030	1.901

a. Predictors: (Constant), Video Games hours per week (LN)

b. Predictors: (Constant), Video Games hours per week (LN), Reading Non-Fiction books per week (LN)

c. Predictors: (Constant), Video Games hours per week (LN), Reading Non-Fiction books per week (LN), Radio hours per week (LN)

d. Predictors: (Constant), Video Games hours per week (LN), Reading Non-Fiction books per week (LN), Radio hours per week (LN), Number of years in college

e. Predictors: (Constant), Video Games hours per week (LN), Reading Non-Fiction books per week (LN), Radio hours per week (LN), Number of years in college, Newspaper hours per week (LN)

f. Predictors: (Constant), Video Games hours per week (LN), Reading Non-Fiction books per week (LN), Radio hours per week (LN), Number of years in college, Newspaper hours per week (LN), Orientation in a city

g. Dependent Variable: Interactive Behavior (LN)

Table 24. Stepwise linear regression for Interactive Behavior (Dependent)

The explanatory power (R square) of model "f" is .117; that is, a decrease of .023 over the R Square of the model including all of the variables. The number of variables decreases from 16 (plus a constant) to 6 (plus a constant). Therefore final model for the Amount of Interactive Behavior is as follows:

Model	Unstandardized Coefficients		Standardized Coefficients		
	B	Std. Error	Beta	t	Sig.
(Constant)	3.447	.187		18.441	.000
Video Games hours per week (LN)	.246	.065	.172	3.771	.000
Reading Non-Fiction books per week (LN)	-.154	.054	-.133	-2.862	.004
Radio hours per week (LN)	.165	.050	.151	3.280	.001
Number of years in college	-.065	.023	-.127	-2.793	.005
Newspaper hours per week (LN)	-.198	.074	-.126	-2.687	.007
Orientation in a city	-.08	.037	.099	2.175	.030

Table 25. Linear regression coefficients for Interactive Behavior (Dependent)

The same analysis can be applied to the independent variables and their impact on the subjects' feeling of control. Starting with the overall amount of explicative power if all the variables were to be included in the model:

Model Summary[b]

Model	R	R Square	Adjusted R Square	Std. Error of the Estimate
1	.265[a]	.070	.035	3.79047

a. Predictors: (Constant), Number of Internet Months (LN), Magazine hours per week (LN), Orientation in a city, Number of years in college, Movie theater hours per week (LN), Reading Non-Fiction books per week (LN), Radio hours per week (LN), Anxiety Index, Video Games hours per week (LN), Reading Fiction Books per week (LN), Computer for Work hours per week (LN), TV hours per week (LN), Newspaper hours per week (LN), Age, Computer for Fun hours per week (LN), Internet hours per week (LN)

b. Dependent Variable: Control Index

Table 26. Linear Regression R for Feeling of Control (Dependent)

ANOVA[b]

Model		Sum of Squares	df	Mean Square	F	Sig.
1	Regression	453.045	16	28.315	1.971	.014[a]
	Residual	6005.676	418	14.368		
	Total	6458.722	434			

a. Predictors: (Constant), Number of Internet Months (LN), Magazine hours per week (LN), Orientation in a city, Number of years in college, Movie theater hours per week (LN), Reading Non-Fiction books per week (LN), Radio hours per week (LN), Anxiety Index, Video Games hours per week (LN), Reading Fiction Books per week (LN), Computer for Work hours per week (LN), TV hours per week (LN), Newspaper hours per week (LN), Age, Computer for Fun hours per week (LN), Internet hours per week (LN)

b. Dependent Variable: Control Index

Table 27. Linear Regression ANOVA for Feeling of Control (Dependent)

The R Square for this model is small but statistically significant; indicating that the independent variables in the model help explain a small amount of the variance in feeling of control, and that the predictability of this small amount is quite high. The following table (Table 28) helps to determine which variables could be deleted in order to get a smaller model. Once again, the variables with small t-values are good candidates for removal:

Coefficients[a]

Model		Unstandardized Coefficients		Standardized Coefficients	t	Sig.
		B	Std. Error	Beta		
1	(Constant)	16.650	1.679		9.917	.000
	Age	-4.51E-02	.028	-.090	-1.623	.105
	Number of years in college	9.656E-02	.106	.047	.912	.362
	Orientation in a city	.329	.157	.102	2.102	.036
	Anxiety Index	-.133	.040	-.175	-3.356	.001
	TV hours per week (LN)	.226	.268	.044	.845	.398
	Magazine hours per week (LN)	6.034E-02	.379	.009	.159	.873
	Newspaper hours per week (LN)	.135	.340	.021	.398	.691
	Reading Fiction Books per week (LN)	.317	.276	.057	1.151	.250
	Reading Non-Fiction books per week (LN)	6.869E-02	.238	.015	.289	.773
	Radio hours per week (LN)	.269	.221	.061	1.220	.223
	Internet hours per week (LN)	-.203	.331	-.042	-.614	.540
	Video Games hours per week (LN)	.165	.307	.029	.536	.592
	Computer for Work hours per week (LN)	-.155	.168	-.048	-.924	.356
	Computer for Fun hours per week (LN)	.280	.300	.062	.934	.351
	Movie theater hours per week (LN)	.154	.332	.023	.464	.643
	Number of Internet Months (LN)	2.915E-02	.241	.006	.121	.904

a. Dependent Variable: Control Index

Table 28. Linear Regression t-values for Feeling of Control (Dependent)

The table shows how the majority of the variables will be deleted from the model, the small t values represent a smaller contribution to the acceptance or rejection of the model. The best models, through a process of entering and extracting variables from the model, are found in the next table (Table 29):

Model Summary^d

Model	R	R Square	Adjusted R Square	Std. Error of the Estimate	R Square Change	F Change	df1	df2	Sig. F Change	Durbin-Watson
1	.175^a	.031	.029	3.80230	.031	13.738	1	433	.000	
2	.203^b	.041	.037	3.78615	.010	4.704	1	432	.031	
3	.223^c	.050	.043	3.77344	.009	3.915	1	431	.048	2.004

a. Predictors: (Constant), Anxiety Index
b. Predictors: (Constant), Anxiety Index, Orientation in a city
c. Predictors: (Constant), Anxiety Index, Orientation in a city, Age
d. Dependent Variable: Control Index

Table 29. Stepwise linear regression for Feeling of Control (Dependent)

The best model is model "c"; which only maintained 3 variables (Anxiety Index, Orientation in a city and Age) out of the previous 16 variables. The decrease in the amount of variance explained by the 16 variable model and the 3 variable model is: .042 (from .265 to .223). The final coefficients for the model that explains how much the subjects felt in control is as follows:

Coefficients(a)

Model	Unstandardized Coefficients		Standardized Coefficients	t	Sig.
	B	Std. Error	Beta		
(Constant)	18.509	1.053		17.571	.000
Anxiety Index	-.135	.036	-.177	-3.704	.000
Orientation in a city	.350	.153	.108	2.284	.023
Age	-.047	.024	-.094	-1.979	.048

a Dependent Variable: Control Index

Table 30. Linear regression coefficients for Feeling of Control (Dependent)

Finally, after analyzing the impact of traditional media use on the amount of interactive behavior and feeling of control, the next step is to find a model that could explain in what way feeling in control is related to the enjoyment of the experience. Because there is only one proposed independent variable for this model the analysis is quite simple.

Model Summary[b]

Model	R	R Square	Adjusted R Square	Std. Error of the Estimate
1	.568[a]	.322	.321	5.63918

a. Predictors: (Constant), Control Index
b. Dependent Variable: Enjoy Index

ANOVA[b]

Model		Sum of Squares	df	Mean Square	F	Sig.
1	Regression	6549.049	1	6549.049	205.943	.000[a]
	Residual	13769.562	433	31.800		
	Total	20318.611	434			

a. Predictors: (Constant), Control Index
b. Dependent Variable: Enjoy Index

The amount of level of enjoyment variance that is explained by the variance in the subjects' feeling of control while experiencing *A space of time* is considerable. As it would be expected with a very strong relationship, the p-value for the Feeling of Control – Level of Enjoyment model is very small.

TIME SERIES ANALYSIS

Exploratory analysis of the data retrieved in *A space of time* has rendered meaningful and important results. The data used for hypothesis testing are cumulative in nature (it is the accumulation of the behavior of 435 valid cases). Nevertheless, each one of the subjects has an individual database describing their behavior throughout the experience in relationship to the type of content they are receiving, QTVR panoramas, QuickTime movies or interface elements of the experience. Because the tracking device registered each action and the amount of time spent for each one of those actions, it is possible to recreate the behavior graphically.

The following graphs (Figure 35 to Figure 40) depict the behavior of several subjects when interacting with the QTVR panoramas during the experience. The X-axis in the graph shows the number of QTVR experienced and the Y-axis shows the amount of time spent on each one of those panoramas. Even though the number of QTVR panoramas is different on each one of the graphs, they all were experienced in the amount of time allotted for the experiment (1.5 hours). A bigger number of QTVRs experienced (X) would also be reflected in the time spent on each one of them (Y); *ceteris paribus*, if the number of QTVRs increases in 90 minutes, necessarily the average amount of time spent on each one has to drop.

TimeQTVR

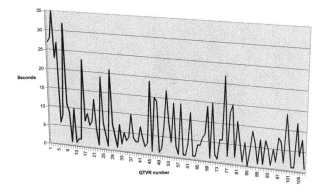

Figure 34. Time series for Subject 27

TimeQTVR

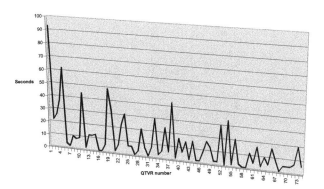

Figure 35. Time series for Subject 89

134

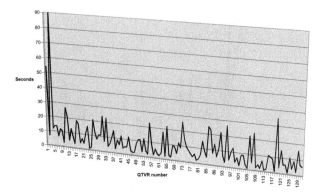

Figure 36. Time series for Subject 191

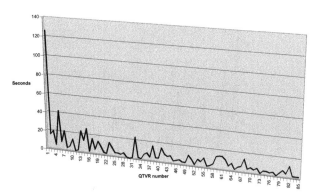

Figure 37. Time series for Subject 282

TimeQTVR

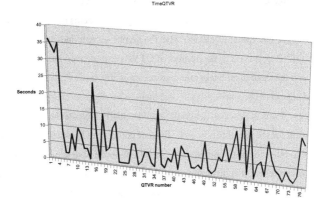

Figure 38. Time series for Subject 310

TimeQTVR

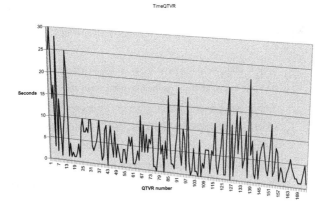

Figure 39. Time series for Subject 414

By simple visual inspection, the graphs seem to have a lower range of variation towards the end of the experience. This funneling effect seems to be present in the majority of the individual databases. Also the graphs seem to indicate that the time spent on each QTVR decreases as the number of QTVRs experienced increases. Schema Theory and the theoretical background presented in this book would suggest that subjects acquired cognitive structures that allowed them to be more efficient in their use of QTVR technology. If this is the case, the graphs could actually indicate the speed of schemata construction for the use of this specific form of content, and possibly show if previous exposure to other forms of content have any effect on the skill acquisition speed.

Nevertheless, it is difficult to make overall assessments about the whole sample from the 6 subjects selected. To form a better opinion for all valid cases not only the same visualization is needed for the entire sample, but also a mathematical approach is needed to reduce the subjectivity of the visual analysis. At this moment, a technical constrain of performing individual analysis of the tracking data arises: How would it be possible to obtain information summarizing the behavior of 435 cases?

The following process was undertaken to overcome the complexity of analyzing the QTVR time series for each one of the valid cases in the sample:

> Step 1: Make working hypothesis for the induction of general trends based on basic visual analysis as the one performed above.
> Step 2: Make a computer program to 1) work on the individual cases in order to graph individual behavior, and 2) obtain descriptive statistical information to avoid subjective interpretations.
> Step 3: Make another program to recover and integrate the results of all the individual analyses to make overall assessments about the sample.

The working hypothesis extracted from the initial visual analysis of the individual time series indicate the possibility of a downward slope in the use of the QTVRs, therefore:

Working hypothesis 1: The amount of time spent on each QTVR decreases as the number of QTVRs experienced increases.

If there is such behavior, it would be feasible to expect the same pattern in other forms of content; however, QTVRs and QuickTime movies differ in the fact that:

1) QTVRs needs some sort of interaction in order to provide more content (other views of the same room), while QuickTime movies run from beginning to end without the need of any interaction;

2) QTVRs are not time bound, the subjects had control on how much time they wanted to explore the content of the panorama before clicking on a hotspot, while QT movies are delimited to the amount of time predetermined by the author of the experience.

Despite these differences, the user also had the ability to rewind or fast-forward the QT movies, making it feasible that the amount of time spent on each one of them is less as the experience progresses. A second working hypothesis aims to find if there are differences in use depending on each type of media or if the same type of slope occurs in both of them:

Working hypothesis 2: The amount of time spent on each QT movie decreases as the number of QT movies increases.

Step 2 included the process of running a descriptive analysis, a linear regression and graphing of different measurements for each valid case in the sample. If this task was to be performed on each one of the subjects with SPSS, the process would have been lengthy and prompt for error (a not very practical task in the case of an inductive process that may yield no meaningful results). Also, once the analysis had been performed, a program would be needed to extract results from each output file and include them in a single database for subsequent analysis.

Another way of doing it is to use the "Production Facility" in SPSS. The following is an extract of the help menu of the "Production Facility" (SPSS 11): "Production mode is useful if you often run the same set of time-consuming analyses, such as weekly reports. The Production Facility uses command syntax files to tell the program what to do. A command syntax file is a simple text file containing command syntax." Instead of using the "programming" capabilities of SPSS to simplify the repetition of analyses in time, it can be used to simplify the repetition of statistical procedures in a large number of different databases like the ones obtained by tracking device of *A space of time*. The repetition is not based on longitudinal data entries but across a large number of cases originated in a single experiment.

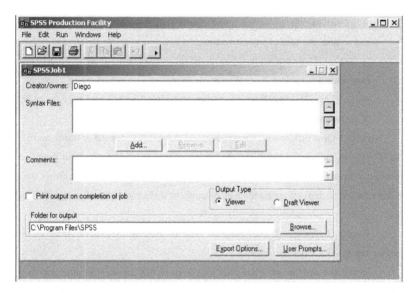

Figure 40. SPSS 11 Production Facility

The following is an example of the type of scripting needed to obtain descriptive information, linear regressions and different time series graphs for the first subject:

```
GET DATA /TYPE=XLS
    /FILE='H:\TimeSeriesQTVR\qtvrTS1.xls'
    /SHEET=name 'qtvrTS1'
    /CELLRANGE=full
    /READNAMES=on .
COMPUTE step = $casenum .
EXECUTE .
VARIABLE LEVEL panleft (SCALE) .
VARIABLE LEVEL panright (SCALE) .
VARIABLE LEVEL deltapan (SCALE) .
VARIABLE LEVEL zoomin (SCALE) .
VARIABLE LEVEL zoomout (SCALE) .
VARIABLE LEVEL deltazoo (SCALE) .
VARIABLE LEVEL timeqtvr (SCALE) .
VARIABLE LEVEL step (SCALE) .
```

```
IGRAPH /VIEWNAME='Scatterplot' /X1 = VAR(step) TYPE = SCALE /Y =
VAR(timeqtvr) TYPE = SCALE /COORDINATE = VERTICAL  /SPIKE X1
/SPIKE Y /FORMAT SPIKE COLOR=OFF STYLE=OFF /FITLINE METHOD =
REGRESSION LINEAR INTERVAL(95.0) = MEAN LINE = TOTAL SPIKE=ON
/X1LENGTH=5.0 /YLENGTH=4.0 /X2LENGTH=4.0 /CHARTLOOK='C:\Program
Files\SPSS\Looks\Classic.clo' /SCATTER COINCIDENT = NONE.
*Sequence Charts .
TSPLOT VARIABLES= panleft
  /ID= step
  /NOLOG
  /FORMAT BOTTOM REFERENCE
  /MARK deltapan.
TSPLOT VARIABLES= panright
  /ID= step
  /NOLOG
  /FORMAT BOTTOM REFERENCE
  /MARK deltapan.
*Sequence Charts .
TSPLOT VARIABLES= deltapan
  /ID= step
  /NOLOG
  /FORMAT BOTTOM NOREFERENCE.
*Sequence Charts .
TSPLOT VARIABLES= zoomin zoomout
  /ID= step
  /NOLOG
  /MARK deltazoo.
DESCRIPTIVES
  VARIABLES=panleft panright deltapan zoomin zoomout deltazoo
timeqtvr
  /STATISTICS=MEAN STDDEV MIN MAX .
REGRESSION
  /MISSING LISTWISE
  /STATISTICS COEFF OUTS R ANOVA
  /CRITERIA=PIN(.05) POUT(.10)
  /NOORIGIN
  /DEPENDENT timeqtvr
  /METHOD=ENTER step   .
EXE.
REGRESSION
  /MISSING LISTWISE
  /STATISTICS COEFF OUTS R ANOVA
  /CRITERIA=PIN(.05) POUT(.10)
  /NOORIGIN
  /DEPENDENT deltapan
  /METHOD=ENTER step   .
```

The bold letters are used in this case to emphasize the only part of the text that needs to change from one subject to the next to perform the entire analysis; besides these changes in line 2 and 3 of the script, the rest of the text indicates to SPSS routine procedures necessary to obtain the data. Macromedia Director was brought in again to generate the program that would run SPSS. By making a counter that would go from 1 to 435, only the necessary parts of the script would be changed and added to an overall text file.

The resulting syntax file for SPSS exceeded 500 pages and took several days to be completed on a PC running at 2.4 Ghz. The resulting .SPO file from SPSS had to be fragmented into several parts (5) in order to be manageable for the extraction of the information calculated by the statistical package.

So the technical maneuvers to make the data ready for analysis and interpretation did not end with the programming of the syntax file. Each one of the subjects gave as a result 11 images depicting the 2 linear regressions aforementioned (for QTVRs and QT) and 9 other measurements related to the use of both types of media (times the user panned to the left, times the user panned to the right, total amount panned to the left or to the right, times the user zoomed, fast-forward clicks, rewind clicks, amount fast-forwarded, amount rewound, pause-and-play), for a total of 56555 images. Disregarding the amount of processing power to open the SPSS output files, the visual analysis became difficult because between each QTVR regression graph laid 10 other images, and daunting task when 435 cases are taken into consideration.

Director had to be used again to display the results in a way in which not only all the linear regressions would be displayed consecutively but also all the other graphs contained in the SPSS output. The following is a depiction of the menu screen of the program made only for the visualization of the results given by SPSS:

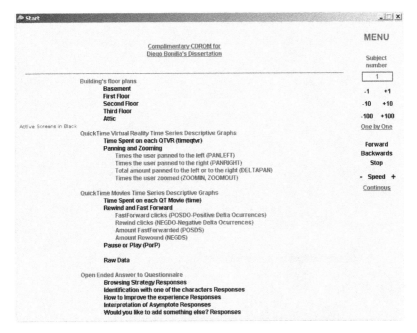

Figure 41. Program to display the visualization of behavior within the environment

On the right hand side of the screen, interface elements allow fast access to the SPSS output graphs for each individual subject (above "One by One") and the manipulation of animation controls that facilitate the consecutive visualization of the graphs related to each specific measurement (above "Continuous"). Consecutive visualization empowers the finding of trends by providing immediate comparison across subjects.

The following are independent screen of the visualization program for subject 1:

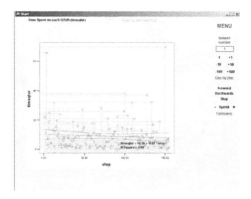

Figure 42. Time Spent on each QTVR

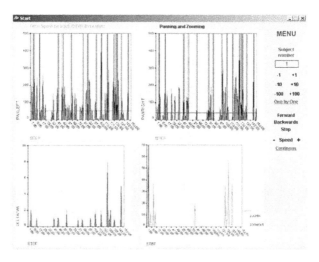

Figure 43. Times the user panned to the left (upper left), times the user panned to the right (upper right), total amount panned to the left or to the right (lower left), times the user zoomed (lower right)

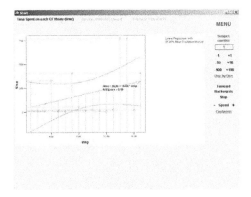

Figure 44. Time Spent on each QT

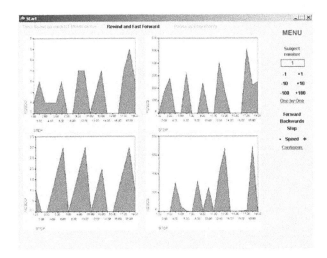

Figure 45. Fast-Forward clicks (upper left), rewind clicks (upper right), amount fast-forwarded
(lower left), amount rewound (lower right)

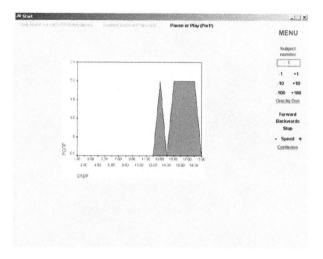

Figure 46. Pause-and-play clicks

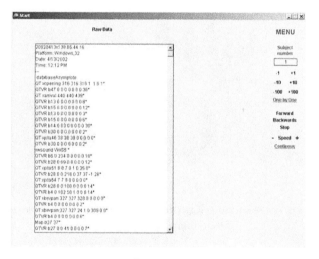

Figure 47. Raw Data.

Visual inspection supported the first working hypothesis and did not support the second working hypothesis. For QTVRs, even though few regression lines showed a positive slope, the majority showed a negative slope with different strengths. In the case of the QT movies, positive and negative slopes of different strengths were found, giving no evident patterns in their use.

A second stage involved a Director program that would extract numeric information from the SPSS output files to organize them in a database format so further summarizing and analyzing of the time series the data could be performed without subjective human interpretations. This process was possible due to the consistency in the SPSS output layout; by analyzing the output file and counting the number of words from specific "anchors" in the document (i.e., "Descriptive Statistics" or "Model Summary") to each of one of the estimates (i.e., mean, standard deviation, beta, t-value, significance, etc.)

The results did show common trends in the time series data. 406 subjects showed a negative slope and 29 subjects have a positive slope, supporting the idea that the common trend in the sample for the experiment is that subjects will spend less time on each QTVR as the number of QTVR experienced increases.

Out of the 435 valid cases, 282 of the regression lines showed a p-value smaller than .1 . The mean of the standardized slopes is -.2722; in other words the average decay in time with each extra QTVR is .2722 seconds. These 2 values might indicate that the fall in time spent on each QTVR is a result of an acquisition of cognitive structures that facilitate the use of this type of content.

When the slope measurement is included in the overall database, relationships between the slope strength and media use can also be found by running correlations. From this set of correlations one meaningful correlation appeared. The number of months using the Internet and the slope strength showed an Pearson's R equal to -.102 with a p-value of .033 . Following Schema Theory, this result supports the idea that the effects of using an interactive medium are small, but significant and cumulative; the same overall conclusion about the effects of television watching that Cultivation Theory supports.

So far, the analysis undertaken has operated under the assumption that the relationship between the amount of time spent on each QTVR and the number of QTVR

146

experienced is linear. The data collected about how the data fits to a line seems to indicate otherwise; the range of the fit of the regression lines go from 0 to .3 , a weak fit for conclusive inference.

Further analysis with the visualization program of subjects' behavior during the experience points to the following pattern:

- The first QTVRs experienced required significant more time that the average amount of time spent on the QTVR throughout the experience.
- A fast fall in the amount of time spent on the QTVRs.
- A stabilization period where the amount of time spent on each panorama remains almost stable.

This pattern would resemble a simple rational function like the one shown in Figure 49 with a range of 1 to the number of QTVRs experienced by each individual subject.

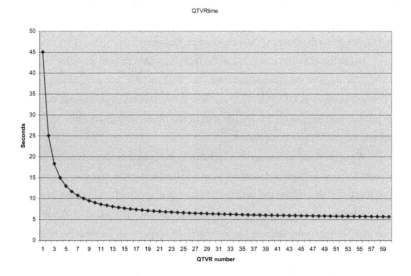

Figure 48. Tentative model: f(x) = 40/x + 5

So a third working hypothesis, derived from working hypothesis 1, point towards an equation in which the amount spent on each QTVR decreases with each QTVR experienced but in a curvilinear fashion.

Working hypothesis 3: The relationship between amount of time spent on each QTVR and QTVR number is not linear but curvilinear.

The function $f(x) = 1/x$ has a behavior similar to the one apparently present throughout the experiments sample; however, to adjust the function to values similar to the ones present in the database, some mathematical adjustments have to be made to the equation. The initial value of 40 represents the amount of time spent on the first unit and the initial value of 5 represents the amount of time spent during the stabilization period; both values were selected just exemplify their relevance in the function and have no specific value for the experiment's sample.

The speed of the fall in the amount of seconds spent on each QTVR with each QTVR experienced can be manipulated by multiplying x by a number; if the number is bigger than 0 and smaller than one, the speed of the fall will be slower; if the number is bigger than 1, the speed of the fall will be faster.

The general equation suggested has the following form:

$$f(X) = \frac{a}{bX} + c$$

Equation 2. Curvilinear equation to describe the amount of time spent on each QTVR

Once again, one way to find out if this curve fits better than a straight line for all the cases would be to generate a Syntax script for SPSS and let a computer perform the necessary number of calculations for each one of the cases. The script would contain instructions to apply the formula to each one of the QTVRs experienced for each subject, subtract the expected value from the observed value to obtain an error estimate and then calculate the average of the errors to obtain an overall measure of the fit. Starting this process would entail making the best possible guess about constants in the equation; the initial amount of time spent in the first unit (a), the speed of the fall in the amount of time spent on each QTVR (b) and the average amount of time spent on the last units (c)

Instead of guessing the first values for a, b, and c using the visualization tool, another program was applied to calculate the average time spent on each QTVR in all of the valid cases in the sample. This process would give us the average amount of time spent on the 1st QTVR for all the valid cases, the average amount of time spent on the 2nd QTVR for all the valid cases, the average amount of time spent on the 3rd QTVR for all the valid cases, and so on. This process can only be applied for a certain number of QTVRs because the total number of QTVRs experienced by each subject varied. The smaller number of QTVRs experienced by any of the subjects is 41; therefore the program designed to extract and calculate the average time across cases included only the first 39 panoramas.

The result yielded a curve, not a line, with a similar shape to the graph shown in Figure 49. The following table and graph show the result of this process:

QTVR number	Average time spent in seconds
1	53.3195
2	19.9678
3	25.023
4	15.1586
5	14.4138
6	13.7149
7	12.2644
8	12.3632
9	10.7885
10	10.1862
11	9.8575
12	9.4
13	9.9816
14	10.046
15	10.1149

16	9.1425
17	8.7126
18	9.3655
19	9.9241
20	9.5149
21	8.6966
22	8.6713
23	9.2989
24	9.2759
25	9.1402
26	8.1379
27	8.7839
28	8.5678
29	8.9195
30	8.8805
31	8.2874
32	8.931
33	8.4069
34	8.2874
35	8.1885
36	7.6552
37	7.6989
38	8.046
39	8.6299

Table 31. Average time spent on each QTVR across cases

150

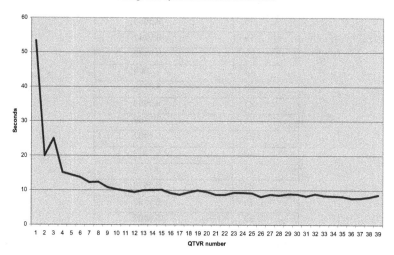

Average Time Spent on each QTVR across cases

Figure 49. Average Time Spent on each QTVR across cases

The table and the graph not only strongly support a curvilinear relationship but also provide a good guide for initial values for a and c; 58 and 8, respectively.

Finally, if the graph above shows average times for each QTVR experienced across the sample, it is reasonable to use these data to find an equation that could be used to describe the subjects' use of QTVRs during the experience. There are several programs in the market that can perform iterative processes for modeling. These programs help find the best possible estimates for an equation based on specific data. The program chosen for this project was CurveExpert[13] (see Figure 51).

---

[13] http://curveexpert.webhop.net/

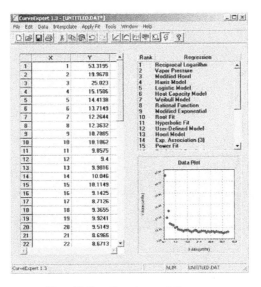

Figure 50. CurveExpert screenshot

The best estimates for the average time spent on each QTVR are the following: a = 49.45, b = 1.15 and, c = 6.75. In mathematical notation:

$$f(X) = \frac{49.45}{1.15X} + 6.75$$

Equation 3. Final model for the average amount of time on each QTVR.

The standard error for these estimates is 1.77 seconds with a very strong correlation coefficient (R) of .97, a vast improvement from the [0, .3] straight line range. The next figure (Figure 52) shows both the data and the curve in the same graph:

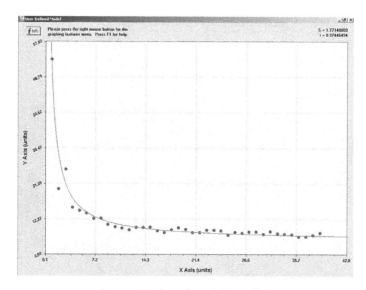

Figure 51. Final equation and data graphed

The following is a Residuals Plot (Figure 53):

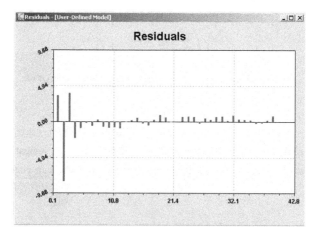

Figure 52. Residuals for the final equation

The previous two graphs give insights into the overall fitting of the equation to the sample data. Even though the fitting of the data to the equation is quite good, visual analysis of both graphs point towards even more complex analysis. It appears that not only there is a fall and then a period stabilization but also there is a cyclical behavior in the data. This cyclical behavior can be noticed by observing the wavering pattern of the data around the line depicting the curve. The formal term for this type of behavior is *positive correlation*, but will not be covered in this book. More complex time series analyses that include the evaluation of trends and seasonal variations is needed and encouraged.

In traditional time series analysis, the work performed on the data so far is related only to trends and it has been only applied to the averages of the time spent on each QTVR across the sample. An obvious next step would be to write a program that would apply this equation to each individual database trying to find how well it adapts to each subject's use of QTVRs, but that in itself is another book (and most probably in the field of mathematics or biostatistics).

154

USING THE TRACKING DATA TO IMPROVE THE EXPERIENCE

The databases can also provide a means to visualize navigation in the experience. The practical use of visualizing navigation is not only to understand if all the media has the same accessibility within the structure but also if the interface design weakens acquisition of content. By using the floor plans of the building, the navigation can be reconstructed as it happened giving an insight on the type of choices taken by the users. The following images are extracts of a program made to reconstruct the subject's navigation:

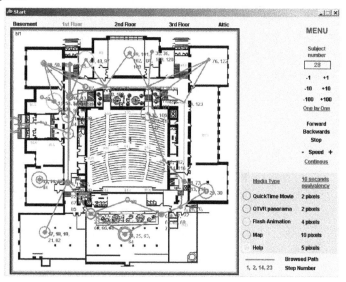

Figure 53. First floor navigation for Subject 28.

155

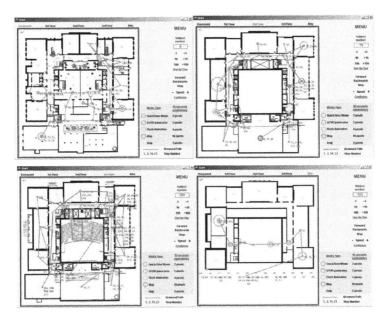

Figure 54. Basement, Second Floor, Third Floor and Attic navigation for several subjects.

Figure 54 is the floor plan for the first floor, the entrance point for the experience. The numbers beside the dots indicate the step number in the navigation of the virtual environment (same step number as those used in the time series analyses). The circles' radii represent the amount of time spent with different media. The lower right image in Figure 55 is the attic; in the lower part it has a series of numbers in columns. These numbers are related to different stair case's QTVRs; the longer the columns, the bigger the use of stair cases during the experience.

The graphical depiction of the users' behavior showed that some users returned more than once to the same set of rooms. "Looping" behavior, as explained earlier in the book, is one of the symptoms of disorientation. Emerging from a mistake in the programming of navigational paths in the floor plans, looping behavior appeared more frequently in the attic than in any other floor of the building. Originally the navigation pattern of every valid cases was supposed to be drawn in different maps to obtain graphical representations as the once shown in Figure 55. The program failed to switch the maps from one subject to the next, making the computer graph the behavior of all the subjects in one single map floor. Figure 56 shows the results of the process. The first row of maps show basement and floor 1, the second row shows floor 2 and 3, and the third row shows the attic.

The first floor shows high density on the left side. The accumulation occurs because this is the entry point to the building; all subjects, after the first two introductory scenes are left inside the building in the promenade, and from that initial position they started moving inside the virtual environment. This also explains why the first floor exhibits more activity than the basement, second floor or third floor. The attic shows probably the same amount of behavior than the first floor, but in a lower set of nodes; the first floor has 46 nodes while the attic has 15 nodes. The amount of behavior can be deduced from the long lines of numbers in the attic floor map, which indicate the subjects that reached the attic engaged in a constant looping behavior.

The visualization process unveiled the possibility of analyzing the impact of each room on the overall enjoyment of the experience. From the theoretical background in disorientation, looping behavior is one of the symptoms of "feeling lost". If "feeling lost" creates frustration then it is possible that subjects that experienced the attic enjoyed less the experience than those who didn't.

157

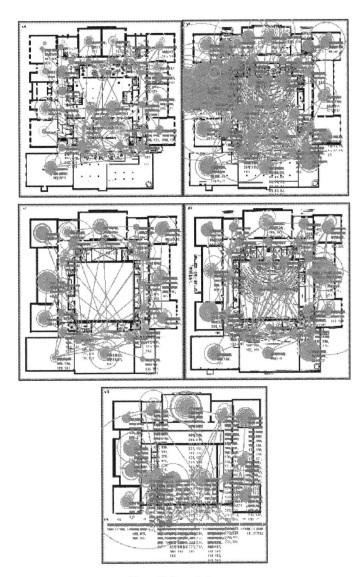

Figure 55. Serendipity maps.

The tracking registered each one of the nodes that were visited, making it possible to incorporate this information into the database by creating dummy variables representing each QTVR panorama, each QT movie and each Flash animation in the entire virtual environment. Every unit of content is coded as a 1 or 0 depending if the content was experienced or not. The resulting database contains rows representing each valid subject in the sample and columns representing units of content; for example, QTVR B4 in the first floor, QTVR E10 in the attic, QT "Doctor Scene" in the basement, etc. If the number of columns are added for one subject we would obtain the overall number of times the subject was exposed to a unit of content. If the number of rows are added for one single QTVR (for example, C3 in the 2nd floor) we would obtain the number of times that unit of content was experienced by the entire sample.

Once the dummy variables are in place, then it is possible to add at the end of the database the information related to the enjoyment of the experience (the enjoyment index) and look for relationships between the experiencing of specific units of content and how much the experienced was enjoyed. Figure 57 shows a reduced database with the dummy variables. The first row in the database shows the label for each one of the columns; showing 6 out of 37 basement QTVRs, 11 out of 46 first floor QTVRs, 5 out of 26 second floor QTVRs, none of the 32 third floor QTVRs,, 9 of the 15 attic QTVRs and the enjoy index value at the end.

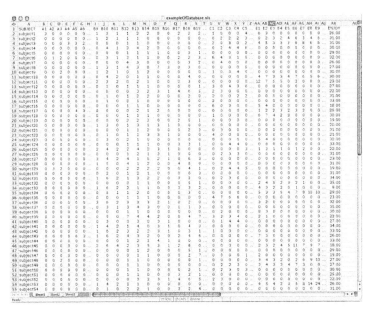

Figure 56. Example of Dummy Variables database

Correlations run on SPSS gave and indication of what units of content contributed negatively to the enjoyment of the story. The following image (Figure 58) shows the beginning of the output table given by SPSS:

		Enjoy Index	A1	A2	A3	A4	A5	A6	A7	A8	A9
Enjoy Index	Pearson Correlation	1	-.021	-.092	-.044	-.070	-.020	-.001	.028	.054	-.044
	Sig. (2-tailed)		.663	.054	.362	.143	.678	.989	.555	.262	.359
	N	435	435	435	435	435	435	435	435	435	435
A1	Pearson Correlation	-.021	1	.341**	.295**	.338**	.168**	.203**	.172**	.009	.134**
	Sig. (2-tailed)	.663		.000	.000	.000	.000	.000	.000	.858	.005
	N	435	435	435	435	435	435	435	435	435	435
A2	Pearson Correlation	-.092	.341**	1	.325**	.231**	.088	.065	.055	-.025	.021
	Sig. (2-tailed)	.054	.000		.000	.000	.066	.177	.256	.603	.656
	N	435	435	435	435	435	435	435	435	435	435
A3	Pearson Correlation	-.044	.295**	.325**	1	.323**	.135**	.133**	.230**	.028	.108*
	Sig. (2-tailed)	.362	.000	.000		.000	.005	.005	.000	.554	.025
	N	435	435	435	435	435	435	435	435	435	435
A4	Pearson Correlation	-.070	.338**	.231**	.323**	1	.315**	.189**	.217**	-.026	.129**
	Sig. (2-tailed)	.143	.000	.000	.000		.000	.000	.000	.582	.007
	N	435	435	435	435	435	435	435	435	435	435
A5	Pearson Correlation	-.020	.168**	.088	.135**	.315**	1	.853**	.482**	-.030	.214**
	Sig. (2-tailed)	.678	.000	.066	.005	.000		.000	.000	.531	.000
	N	435	435	435	435	435	435	435	435	435	435
A6	Pearson Correlation	-.001	.203**	.065	.133**	.189**	.853**	1	.437**	.009	.204**
	Sig. (2-tailed)	.989	.000	.177	.005	.000	.000		.000	.846	.008
	N	435	435	435	435	435	435	435	435	435	435
A7	Pearson Correlation	-.028	.172**	.055	.230**	.217**	.482**	.437**	1	.036	.410**
	Sig. (2-tailed)	.555	.000	.256	.000	.000	.000	.000		.451	.000
	N	435	435	435	435	435	435	435	435	435	435
A8	Pearson Correlation	.054	.009	-.025	.028	-.026	-.030	.009	.036	1	.151**
	Sig. (2-tailed)	.262	.856	.603	.554	.582	.531	.846	.451		.892
	N	435	435	435	435	435	435	435	435	435	435
A9	Pearson Correlation	-.044	.134**	.021	.108*	.129**	.214**	.204**	.410**	.151**	1
	Sig. (2-tailed)	.359	.005	.656	.025	.007	.000	.008	.000	.892	
	N	435	435	435	435	435	435	435	435	435	435
A10	Pearson Correlation	-.031	.249**	.220**	.245**	.223**	.289**	.271**	.349**	.184**	.504**
	Sig. (2-tailed)	.517	.000	.000	.000	.000	.000	.000	.000	.001	.000
	N	435	435	435	435	435	435	435	435	435	435

Figure 57. SPSS correlation between the Enjoyment Index and each unit of content

Reading column one for all of the rows (or reading row one for all the columns) gives the correlation coefficients between each QTVR panorama and enjoyment. The rest of the cells in the table give a correlation coefficient that indicates the relationship between individual QTVRs. This relationship reflects the structure of the environment and could be used to answer questions like: How probable it is to experience QTVR panorama A5 if I am located in A10? If the SPPS is read diagonally it is possible to see that the strongest correlations, with statistically significant p-values, occur the those

QTVRs that are adjacent to each other; for example, A5 and A6, A6 and A7. The relationship disappears in non-adjacent cells; for example A1 and C3. This data may be used for an evaluation of the virtual building as narrative device for the story by analyzing what units of content might be not be experienced. If two adjacent QTVR panoramas do not have a statistically significant correlation, it might be possible that the hot spots that connect both rooms are not intuitive enough causing users to omit them.

In terms of enjoyment, out of the 187 QTVRs, 27 QTVRs presented a statistically significant negative correlation with enjoyment and 1 QTVR presented statistically significant positive correlation.

QTVR	Correlation w/Enjoyment
a12	-0.13 *
a13	-0.11 *
a14	-0.14 **
a23	-0.09 *
a31	-0.11 *
a32	-0.11 *
b2	-0.15 **
b3	-0.10 *
b10	0.09 *
b13	-0.11 *
b21	0.10 *
b23	-0.10 *
b26	-0.10 *
b29	-0.10 *
b35	-0.16 **
c18	-0.10 *
c20	-0.14 **
c21	-0.10 *

d14	-0.11 *
d19	-0.14 **
e1	-0.11 *
e2	-0.11 *
e3	-0.15 **
e4	-0.14 **
e6	-0.12 *
e7	-0.10 *
e8	-0.11 *
e9	-0.11 *

Table 32. QTVR panoramas and Enjoyment Index (* p-value < .05, ** p-value < .01)

Upon revision of these QTVR panoramas, a common element was found: The QTVRs are dark and difficult to explore. This is specially true in the case of the rooms coded "e", the rooms of the attic. This QTVRs contain very little light because there are no windows in the attic of the building except for a couple of rooms. Navigation is difficult because the darker the panorama, the more difficult it is to finding the visual cues that indicate hot spots (normally doorways). The same is true for some rooms in the basement of the building; specifically the ones that show a negative correlation with enjoyment. This rooms are located in the old part of the building where the basement hallways get very dark.

The visualization tool could render more data upon analysis, an analysis not undertaken as part of this research project due to time limitations. Nonetheless, it is important to notice that the tracking device in the communications medium can affect positively the content of the medium. This approach would seem to indicate that the creation of multimedia interactive content can be a constant reiterative process and that this process applies not only to a product in development (CDROMs and DVDROMs) but also to a final product which is in constant state of refinement (mostly websites).

DISCUSSION

The tracking device provided evidence of practical use for both deductive and inductive research. Table 16 shows that with or without controls, the amount of interactive behavior within the experience was negatively correlated to two forms of print media: Newspapers and non-fiction books. To the contrary, Radio, video games and computer (for fun) show a statistically significant positive correlation with and without some control variables. Small correlations (between .1 and .3) might entail problems when the sample does not distribute normally or in the presence of outliers. Because most of the data, with the exception of "Internet months," were transformed with natural logarithm before obtaining Pearson's correlation coefficients, it can be assumed that the data presented fairly normal distributions (See Figure 32). Within the theoretical framework, readers probably are interacting less with the experience because they have a "reinforced" print schemata and using the computer for fun are interacting more because they have a "reinforced" multimedia non-linear schemata. The correlation between the sum of time spent reading and the sum of time spent playing with a computer showed no relationship (i.e., readers do not play video games and viceversa). The small correlations, even though meaningful, indicate that there are more factors than media use affecting the amount of interaction with the experience. No single schemata can be considered causal.

The user brings many elements into the experience of A space of time. The ones sought for in this project were integrated in the hypothesis (media use) and were considered when testing for spurious relationships (for example, computer anxiety). Even though the correlations were small, building a model for inference of user behavior based on previously known data is not out of hand. The research project as a whole showed that the integration and evaluation of a multivariate model to determine behavior is foreseeable in the short term. The mathematical processes needed for the finding relationships using the General Linear Model can be processed effortlessly by common computers and what is missing is our ability to use that computing power to our benefit. Other factors that could have an impact on the experiencing of interactive media, from IQ scores to the reading of books like "Make your own story" could be good candidates.

This approach to research in the social sciences seems appropriate. The computer power to analyze multiple causal factors is available, this change needs to be supported also by a change in methodology that assumes that cognition is irreducible to a simple cause-and-effect model. A multiple-cause-and-effect model seems not only appropriate to the understanding interactive communications but also to the comprehension of cognitive processes that would explain how the human brain works. Actually, from a cognitive psychology point of view, a tracking device in an communications medium seems an ideal instrument to understand how the brain functions in relationship with complex-heuristic systems of knowledge.

The correlation between feeling of control and enjoyment, with and without controls, is statistically significant (.000) and strong (.55 or better). This connection supports the idea that feeling in control leads to the freeing of cognitive resources that will improve the possibility of enjoyment. However, even though there are statistically significant correlations in any of the scenarios shown in Table 16, media use is not a good indicator of how much in control the subjects felt while experiencing *A space of time*. When no control variables are taken into consideration, media use seems to have a very small impact on feeling of control. When partial correlations are run, media use variables lose their relationship to the Control Index completely.

The tracking device was very useful for inductive research. The work regarding the visualization of the behavior and time series analysis rendered important results. On one hand, time series yielded an equation regarding the use of QTVRs in this specific experience that could be very meaningful both for the study of human memory and for interactive design. An alternative explanation for the reduction of time spent of each QTVR that evolved with the research project is that subjects in the sample knew that they had a time limit for the experiencing of *A space of time*. If subjects had felt time pressured they might have been encouraged by the experimental design to spend less time on each extra QTVR; but this is not the case. The average number of QTVRs experienced in the hour and a half devoted to the experiment is 118. The equation obtained through time series analysis is based on the first 39 QTVRs. This means that the equation is representing approximately the first one third of the number of QTVRs and that the reduction in the amount of time spent on each QTVR didn't happen because of time pressure imposed by the length of the experiment.

The equation derived from the entire sample shows there is a quick drop on the time spent on each QTVR for the first 4 panoramas, the drop decelerates in the next 10 panoramas and gets "stable" around the 20th. This pattern possibly is describing how memory acquired mental structures to facilitate the viewing of this type of content. The acquisition of skills related to the use of QTVR technology is very fast and there are considerable improvements on each additional panorama. So the first part is a reflection of an overall understanding on how the technology works; for example, 1) the image on the screen is not simply an image, 2) the image on the screen can be manipulated with the mouse, it is interactive, 3) the image on the screen has hot spots that can be clicked, 4) the image on the screen if moved to the left or moved to the right returns to its original point, it is a panorama. The second drop represents a process of fine-tuning those mental structures and still acquire other skills related to QTVR technology; for example, 1) the more I drag with the mouse the faster it rotates and the faster I can explore the contents contained in the panorama, 2) each panorama is part of an interlinked set of panoramas, 3) it is possible to zoom in and zoom out. The third part represents the use of QTVR technology once that their features have been discovered and the stability period shows the amount of time required to obtain meaning from each QTVR throughout the experience. This stability period is as important and meaningful as the drop because it shows that there is an average amount of time to extract meaning from the panorama.

The model found through the time series analyses is a good representation of how schemata is acquired and could expanded to other forms of interactive media. In the case of QTVRs in *A space of time*, the model has the following equation (Equation 3):

$$f(X) = \frac{49.45}{1.15X} + 6.75$$

But the general model to describe the acquisition of skills for other media or other activities is the following (Equation 2):

$$f(X) = \frac{a}{bX} + c$$

The numbers can change to reflect different technologies or different interfaces. It would seem that the model could work for all media that act as an interface between the user and the content; that is, it can be applied mostly to "interactive communications" or a system in which a person is extracting structured content from what he sees in a screen.

An alternative would be to expand the use of the model to other activities not related to computer use. It is possible to imagine the application of this equation, for example, to the acquisition of skills to play chess. Probably the factors in the equation would change to reflect the greater amount of skills needed to play the game and the greater amount of time needed to acquire those skills (probably reflecting days instead of seconds). It seems that "learning curves" might do a better job explaining the amount of acquired knowledge. Nevertheless, chess is an activity in itself. The difference with the model presented is that it describes the speed of skill acquisition for the use of a communications medium; which is not an activity in itself. Even though it is easy to imagine a person interested in a website, it is hard to imagine a person just interested in the act of browsing; while we can image expert chess players, we might disregard someone stating an expertise in browsing, just browsing. Interacting with a communications medium is part of a process to obtain content and even though the content might affect our browsing, browsing without content seems meaningless.

Testing the application of the model to other forms of interfaces, as a first step, might render insights on human memory and how fast we acquire the skills necessary to interact with different forms of content. The model probably is useful for projects using the same technology (interlinked QTVRs) and not only in *A space of time*. However, it is important to mention that the main navigation tool to obtain the content is the QTVR structure, so the building and it's layout is serving as interface between the story and the user. The understanding of the building's structure as the story's interface is what make the generalization to other interfaces possible.

The experiment undertaken for this project assumed that subjects haven't had experienced anything similar to *A space of time*. Testing different media use against behavioral data captured by the tracking device had the purpose of finding what schemata were activated upon exposure to a different (not yet experienced) form of storytelling. One way to find substantially if there is a process of building schemata would be by following a different experimental design, one that would include the experiencing of the story only once for one group of subjects and twice for another group of subjects. If schemata were constructed from previous browsing of *A space of time*, then it would be expected to find a different behavior with the tracking device.

The following is an experimental design aimed to finding behavioral changes depending on previous exposure to the experience:

| Group A | No treatment | Experience A Space of Time |
| Group B | Experience A Space of Time | Experience A Space of Time |

Table 33. Experimental design to test schemata building for *A space of time*

The first hypothesis would be that there would be significant differences between Group A and Group B. Specifically, and using the time series results as a guideline, the amount of time spent on the first units of content will be smaller in Group B than in Group A. A second plausible hypothesis would be that the stabilization period would have a smaller average amount of time (probably slightly less.)

A factor that is worth mentioning is that the sample was composed by Americans in the United States. The self-reported media use from the sample, as stated in the results chapter, shows that subjects spend more hours per week using a non-linear medium that using a linear medium, and the average number of months using the internet is 54.51. It may be possible that this previous experience with the medium had an impact on the way the behaved. A way to find out would be replicating the experiment in another setting where media use and computer use are not as common as in the United States, and where English is the local language; for example, Belice. If there is a process of schemata building for new forms of transmission of content, it would be expected to find a slower, more exploratory behavior than the one obtained in the U.S. A finding in this respect would support the idea of a technological gap between advanced countries and countries in development.

Contrary to other media, interactive media can be a measure of its own effectiveness as a communication device. The tracking device and the visualization helped improve the experience by finding the relationship among individual units of content and enjoyment of the experience. The analysis of the time series and how subjects interacted with the QTVR panoramas sheds new light on of a possible definition of interactivity, specially one that is directly linked with cognitive processes: Interactivity equals attention. While watching television, listening to the radio and even reading a book can happen while we are distracted, thinking about something else, a communication medium based on choices will stop its flux of content unless there is interaction. In its most basic form, interaction entails visually or aurally locating elements in a whole so the choice (a behavior) can take place; so, if there is interactivity, there most be, in the worst case, minimal attention to cues, and in the best case, engaged cognitive processing of the content. Defining interactivity as attention is worth a project by itself.

The tracking device also was useful in determining other factors that helped improve the experience. For example, when correlating exposure to individual panoramas and enjoyment, several of them have a negative relationship. This finding supports the idea that in the same way a mathematical model can be improved by adding or subtracting variables, a plot can be improved by adding or subtracting individual units of content.

One of the most beneficial aspects of the tracking device is the amount of data that can be collected and the possibilities of retrieving meaning from that information. Even though exploratory undertakings with databases is often discouraged in social sciences, this should not be a rule of thumb in the case of data retrieved with a tracking device. The methodology applied in this project showed that every digital medium has the ability of creating a behavioral database that can be used for analysis; in fact, we are at a historical moment in which the biggest amount ever of human behavioral data is being collected (even if it is not being analyzed).

Both scholars in communications and professionals can attain the promises of behavioral data provided by the medium if they include in their set of skills knowledge about how interactive communications work (that is, hands-on knowledge of interactive multimedia creation), mathematical approaches to data outside the General Linear Model (the analysis of time series) and programming to benefit from the computational power that currently exists in the market. If tracking data can give us insights on how humans process information, then it is possible not only to understand more about cognition but also to improve our means to design better, more efficient and more enjoyable interactive communications.

APPENDIX 1. SCRIPTS WITH TRACKING COMPONENT.

Script with tracking component 1.

This script is placed on every frame script that controls a QTVR

```
global oneTimer, nuevamarca
global initialPan, currentPan, PanIzq, PanDer, deltaPan, deltaPanindicator, BeginPan
global initialZoom, currentZoom, ZoomIn, ZoomOut, deltaZoom, deltaZoomindicator,
BeginZoom
global tiempoInicialQTVR
global BtnAx, BtnAy, BtnBx, BtnBy, BtnCx, BtnCy, BtnDx, BtnDy, BtnEx, BtnEy
global BtnFx, BtnFy, BtnGx, BtnGy, BtnHx, BtnHy, BtnIx, BtnIy, BtnJx, BtnJy
global BtnKx, BtnKy, BtnLx, BtnLy, BtnMx, BtnMy, BtnNx, BtnNy
global DistToActivate, ButtonInterval, DistButtonTitle, ButtonRotation
global PlayBackFrom, TiempoSonidosVW, separator, folderMovie
global orientation

on enterFrame
  if oneTimer = 0 then
    put the frameLabel into temp1
    if temp1 <> "b47" and temp1 <> "b13" then
      put char 1 of temp1 into temp2
      if temp2="a" or temp2="b" or temp2="c" or temp2="d" or temp2="e" or temp2="h" then
        QuePaneoNorth2
      else
        QuePaneo
      end if
    else
      QuePaneo
    end if
    PanIzq = 0
    PanDer = 0
    deltaPan = 0
    deltaPanindicator = "PanDer"
    BeginPan = "start"
    ZoomIn = 0
    ZoomOut = 0
    deltaZoom = 0
    deltaZoomindicator = "ZoomIn"
    BeginZoom = "start"
    put the timer into tiempoInicialQTVR
    TiempoSonidosVW = the timer + TiempoSonidosVW
  end if
end

on exitFrame
  if TiempoSonidosVW < the timer then
    put the frameLabel into temp15
    put char 1 of temp15 into letrita
    if letrita <> "h" AND temp15 <> "b47" then
      SonidosVW
    end if
  end if
  if the mouseV > 300 then
    locationButtons
    workButtons
  end if
  rastreoPan
  rastreoZoom
  go to the frame
end

on SonidosVW
  SonidoOTiempo = random(100)
  if SonidoOTiempo < 40 then
    if soundBusy(1) = false then
      randomvws = random (43)
      if PlayBackFrom = 0 then
```

```
      sound playFile 1,
folderMovie&"vw"&separator&"soundsvw"&separator&"vws"&randomvws&".aif"
    else
      vwsInternet = "VWS"&randomvws
--            set the pathName of member vwsInternet =
folderMovie&"vwsounds/"&vwsInternet&".swa"
--            member(vwsInternet).fileName =
folderMovie&"vwsounds/"&vwsInternet&".swa"
      member(vwsInternet).URL = folderMovie&"vwsounds/"&vwsInternet&".swa"
      put member(vwsInternet).URL
      play member vwsInternet
    end if
    put "Sonido de tour: vws"&randomvws
  end if
else
  TiempoEntreUnoYOtro = random(3)
  TiempoEntreUnoYOtro = TiempoEntreUnoYOtro * 600 -- Times ten seconds
  TiempoSonidosVW = (3 * 600) + TiempoEntreUnoYOtro -- Between 30 and 60 seconds
  put "Silencio en tour por "&(TiempoSonidosVW/60)&" segundos"
  TiempoSonidosVW = TiempoSonidosVW + the timer
end if
end

on QuePaneo
  put the number of lines of field "QTVRdata" into temp10
  repeat with n = 1 to temp10
    if word 1 of line n of field "QTVRdata" = nuevamarca then
      put word 2 of line n of field "QTVRdata" into paneotemp
      set paneo = paneotemp * 1
      set the pan of sprite 1 to paneo
      set the width of sprite 1 to 600
      set the height of sprite 1 to 350
      set oneTimer = 1
      exit repeat
    end if
  end repeat
  put the fieldOfView of sprite 1 into initialZoom
  set initialPan = paneo
end

on QuePaneoNorth2
  put the number of lines of field "QTVRdataNorth" into temp10
  repeat with n = 1 to temp10
    if word 1 of line n of field "QTVRdataNorth" = nuevamarca then
      put word 2 of line n of field "QTVRdataNorth" into paneotemp
      put the pan of sprite 1 into temp11
      set paneo = (paneotemp * 1) + orientation
      set the pan of sprite 1 to paneo
      set the width of sprite 1 to 600
      set the height of sprite 1 to 350
      set oneTimer = 1
--       put " Paneo: "&paneo&" North: "&paneotemp&" Orientation: "&orientation
      exit repeat
    end if
  end repeat
  put the fieldOfView of sprite 1 into initialZoom
  set initialPan = paneo
end

on rastreoPan
  put the pan of sprite 1 into currentPan
  increment = currentPan - initialPan
  if increment <> 0 then -- If true it means there was movement in the QTVR
    absoluteIncrement = abs(increment) -- Protection for big jumps that go from 360 to 0
or vicevarsa
    if absoluteIncrement > 200 then -- There was a big jump, the value of 200 is
arbitrary
--       put "BigJump"
      initialPan = currentPan -- Set values to detect next change
    else -- There was a normal jump
      if increment > 0 then -- It moved to the LEFT
        PanIzq = PanIzq + absoluteIncrement
--         put "PanIzq :"&PanIzq
        -- This part establishes if there was a change in direction in the panning of the
QTVR
        if deltaPanindicator = "PanDer" then
          deltaPan = deltaPan + 1
--           put "Changes in Pan direction :"&deltaPan
          put "PanIzq" into deltaPanindicator
        end if
        if BeginPan = "start" then
```

```
                  deltaPan = deltaPan - 1
                  set BeginPan = "ready"
               end if
            else  -- It moved to the RIGHT
               PanDer = PanDer + absoluteIncrement
--             put "PanDer :"&PanDer
               -- This part establishes if there was a change in direction in the panning of the
QTVR
               if deltaPanindicator = "PanIzq" then
                  deltaPan = deltaPan + 1
--                put "Changes in Pan direction :"&deltaPan
                  put "PanDer" into deltaPanindicator
               end if
            end if
            initialPan = currentPan -- Set values to detect next change
         end if
      end if
   end if
end

on rastreoZoom  -- Same rationale as above but without the big jump routine
   put the fieldOfView of sprite 1 into currentZoom
   incrementZoom = currentZoom - initialZoom
   absoluteIncrementZoom = abs(incrementZoom)
   if incrementZoom <> 0 then
      if incrementZoom > 0 then
         ZoomOut = ZoomOut + absoluteIncrementZoom
--       put "ZoomOut :"&ZoomOut
         if deltaZoomindicator = "ZoomIn" then
            deltaZoom = deltaZoom + 1
--          put "Changes in Zoom direction :"&deltaZoom
            put "ZoomOut" into deltaZoomindicator
         end if
         if BeginPan = "start" then
            deltaZoom = deltaZoom - 1
            set BeginZoom = "ready"
         end if
      else
         ZoomIn = ZoomIn + absoluteIncrementZoom
--       put "ZoomIn :"&ZoomIn
         if deltaZoomindicator = "ZoomOut" then
            deltaZoom = deltaZoom + 1
--          put "Changes in Zoom direction :"&deltaZoom
            put "ZoomIn" into deltaZoomindicator
         end if
      end if
      initialZoom = currentZoom
   end if
end

on locationButtons
   -- This part of the script was cut.
end

on workButtons
   -- This part of the script was cut.
end
```

Script with tracking component 2.

This sprite script is placed over the QTVR itself

```
global nuevamarca, marca, cualpiso, NumID, PlayBackFrom
global PanIzq, PanDer, deltaPan, ZoomIn, ZoomOut, deltaZoom, tiempoInicialQTVR,
downloadTime
global marcaNorth, TiempoSonidosVW

on beginSprite
   set the triggerCallback of sprite 1 = #MyHotSpotCallback
   set the hotSpotEnterCallback of sprite 1 = #MyHotSpotEnter
end

on MyHotSpotCallback me, hotSpotID
```

```
  TiempoSonidosVW = TiempoSonidosVW - the timer
  put "hotSpotID = "&hotSpotID
  set NumID = hotSpotID * 1
  put the frameLabel into marca
  put char 1 of marca into cualpiso
  if hotSpotID < 49 then
    put ""&cualpiso&hotSpotID&"" into nuevamarca
    QuePaneoToNorth1
  end if
  if hotSpotID > 49 and hotSpotID < 72 then
    put "s"&hotSpotID&"" into nuevamarca
  end if
  if hotSpotID > 74 and hotSpotID < 88 then
    put "h"&hotSpotID&"" into nuevamarca
    QuePaneoToNorth1
  end if
  if hotSpotID > 89 and hotSpotID < 91 then -- If 90 then exits to building
    SelectRandomPlaceInBuilding
  end if
  if hotSpotID > 94 and hotSpotID < 96 then  -- If 95 then exits to house
    SelectRandomPlaceInHouse
  end if
  if hotSpotID > 99 then
    put ""&cualpiso&hotSpotID&"" into nuevamarca
  end if
  --  put nuevamarca

  createBehaviorDatabase
end

on endSprite me
  set the triggerCallback of sprite 1 = 0
  set the hotSpotEnterCallback of sprite 1 = 0
end

on SelectRandomPlaceInBuilding
  put the number of lines of field "QTVRdata" into temp10
  temp10 = temp10 - 13 -- Exludes the QTVRs of Pandora's house
  temp11 = random(temp10)
  put word 1 of line temp11 of field "QTVRdata" into nuevamarca
end

on SelectRandomPlaceInHouse
  temp11 = random(13)
  temp12 = temp11 + 74  -- Includes only the QTVRs of Pandora's house
  put "h"&temp12 into nuevamarca
end

on createBehaviorDatabase
  global PlayBackFrom, IDcookie
  global IDcookie, frameL, PanIzq, PanDer, deltaPan, ZoomIn, ZoomOut, deltaZoom,
timeOnQT, downloadTime
  frameL = the frameLabel
  PanIzq = integer(PanIzq)
  PanDer = integer(PanDer)
  deltaPan = integer(deltaPan)
  ZoomIn = integer(ZoomIn)
  ZoomOut = integer(ZoomOut)
  deltaZoom = integer(deltaZoom)
  timeOnQT = integer((the timer - tiempoInicialQTVR)/60)
  if PlayBackFrom = 1 then
    downloadTime = integer(downloadTime/60)
  end if
  put "QTVR "&frameL&" "&downloadTime&" "&PanIzq&" "&PanDer&" "&deltaPan&" "&ZoomIn&"
"&ZoomOut&" "&deltaZoom&" "&timeOnQT&"*" into lineaBehavior
  put the number of lines of field "behavior" into cuentalineas
  cuentalineas = cuentalineas + 1
  put lineaBehavior into line cuentalineas of field "behavior"
  go to frame "limpiar"
end

on QuePaneoToNorth1
  put the number of lines of field "QTVRdataNorth" into temp10
  repeat with n = 1 to temp10
    if word 1 of line n of field "QTVRdataNorth" = marca then
      put word 2 of line n of field "QTVRdataNorth" into marcaNorth
      set marcaNorth = marcaNorth * 1
      exit repeat
    end if
  end repeat
  put the pan of sprite 1 into temp11
```

```
    global orientation
    orientation = (marcaNorth - temp11) * -1
--    put "North: "&marcaNorth&" Departure: "&temp11&" Orientation: "&orientation
end
```

Script with tracking component 3.

This frame script is triggered at the end of the video scenes or at the end of one of

8 mm films in which Pandora appears

```
global marca, oneTimer, nuevamarca, NumID
global IDcookie, webMovie, PlayTime, AmountSeen, BeginDownloadTime
global posDelta, negDelta, posDeltaTot, negDeltaTot, PauseOrPlay

on exitFrame me
  QTBehavior
  set oneTimer = 0
  --  if marca = "b47" then set marca = "b13"
  getNewNumID
  set nuevamarca = marca
  puppetSprite 5, false
  puppetSprite 6, false
  puppetSprite 75, false
  go to frame "limpiar"
end

on getNewNumID
  put marca into temp1
  delete char 1 of temp1
  NumID = temp1
end

on QTBehavior
  -- IDcookie, QT, NameOfMovieSeen, DurationOfMovieSeen, AmountOftheMovieSeen,
InHowMuchTime
  -- Num of FastForwards, Num of Rewinds, TotAmount FastForwarded, TotAmount Rewound, Num
of PausePlays
  PlayTime = integer(PlayTime/60)
  AmountSeen = integer(AmountSeen/60)
  InHowMuchTime = integer((the timer - BeginDownloadTime)/60)
  posDeltaTot = posDeltaTot/60
  negDeltaTot = negDeltaTot/60
  put "QT "&webMovie&" "&PlayTime&" "&AmountSeen&" "&InHowMuchTime&" "&posDelta&"
"&negDelta&" "&posDeltaTot&" "&negDeltaTot&" "&PauseOrPlay&"*" into lineaBehavior
  put the number of lines of field "behavior" into cuentalineas
  cuentalineas = cuentalineas + 1
  put lineaBehavior into line cuentalineas of field "behavior"
end
```

Script with tracking component 4

This frame script tracks behavior while a video is plaiying.

```
global PlayTime, BeginDownloadTime, AmountSeen
global trackQTtime, posDelta, negDelta, posDeltaTot, negDeltaTot, PauseOrPlay, POPtrack

on exitFrame me
  if the movieTime of sprite 3 < PlayTime then
    AmountSeen = the movieTime of sprite 3
    detectQTdelta
    go to the frame
  else
    puppetSprite 5, false
    set the member  of sprite 6 to "redirectbox"
    go to the frame + 1
  end if
  if the movieRate of sprite 3 = 0 then
    puppetSprite 5, true
    set the member of sprite 5 to "slow"
    set the locH of sprite 5 to 160
    set the locV of sprite 5 to 405
    set the member  of sprite 6 to "redirect"
  else
    puppetSprite 5, false
    set the member  of sprite 6 to "redirectbox"
  end if
end

on detectQTdelta
  PauseOrPlayHandler
  deltaQT =  the movieTime of sprite 3 - trackQTtime
  delta = abs(trackQTtime - the movieTime of sprite 3)
  if delta > 60 then
    if deltaQT > 0 then
      posDelta = posDelta + 1
      posDeltaTot = posDeltaTot + delta
      put "pos "&deltaQT&" # pos so far "&posDelta&" Total pos Change "&posDeltaTot
    else
      negDelta = negDelta + 1
      negDeltaTot = negDeltaTot + delta
      put "neg "&deltaQT&" # neg so far "&negDelta&" Total neg Change "&negDeltaTot
    end if
  end if
  trackQTtime = the movieTime of sprite 3
end

on PauseOrPlayHandler
  if the movieRate of sprite 3 = 0 then
    if POPtrack = 1 then
      POPtrack = 0
      PauseOrPlay = PauseOrPlay + 1
      put PauseOrPlay
    end if
  else
    if POPtrack = 0 then
      POPtrack = 1
      PauseOrPlay = PauseOrPlay + 1
      put PauseOrPlay
    end if
  end if
end
```

Script with tracking component 5

This frame script is triggered at the end of any Flash animation

```
global marca, oneTimer, nuevamarca, NumID
global IDcookie, webMovie, PlayTime, AmountSeen, BeginDownloadTime
global TiempoSonidosVW, QueFlash

on exitFrame me
  FlashBehavior
  set oneTimer = 0
  if marca = "bfacade" then set marca = "b13"
  getNewNumID
  set nuevamarca = marca
  TiempoSonidosVW = the timer + 600
-- put "flash"&QueFlash into temp1
-- unLoadMember member temp1
  go to frame "limpiar"
end

on getNewNumID
  put marca into temp1
  delete char 1 of temp1
  NumID = temp1
end

on FlashBehavior
  InHowMuchTime = integer((the timer - BeginDownloadTime)/60)
  put "Flash flash"&QueFlash&" "&PlayTime&" "&AmountSeen&" "&InHowMuchTime&"*" into
lineaBehavior
  put the number of lines of field "behavior" into cuentalineas
  cuentalineas = cuentalineas + 1
  put lineaBehavior into line cuentalineas of field "behavior"
end
```

178

Script with tracking component 6

Generic sprite script for all of the buttons on the main interface, the only part that
changes on each case is the part of the script that sends the head of the program to a
different frame label. Seven different buttons use this generic sprite script.

```
on mouseUp me
  global marca, oneTimer, BeginDownloadTime
  BeginDownloadTime = the timer
  put the frameLabel into marca
  oneTimer = 0
  createBehaviorDatabase
  puppetSound 2, "engage"
  go to frame "ComConInitial"
end

on mouseEnter
  puppetSound 2, "Sound2"
end

on mouseLeave
  put "" into field "bLegend"
end

on createBehaviorDatabase
  global nuevamarca, marca, cualpiso, NumID
  global PanIzq, PanDer, deltaPan, ZoomIn, ZoomOut, deltaZoom, tiempoInicialQTVR,
downloadTime
  global PlayBackFrom
  global IDcookie, frameL, timeOnQT
  frameL = the frameLabel
  PanIzq = integer(PanIzq)
  PanDer = integer(PanDer)
  deltaPan = integer(deltaPan)
  ZoomIn = integer(ZoomIn)
  ZoomOut = integer(ZoomOut)
  deltaZoom = integer(deltaZoom)
  timeOnQT = integer((the timer - tiempoInicialQTVR)/60)
  if PlayBackFrom = 1 then
    downloadTime = integer(downloadTime/60)
  end if
  put "QTVR "&frameL&" "&downloadTime&" "&PanIzq&" "&PanDer&" "&deltaPan&" "&ZoomIn&"
"&ZoomOut&" "&deltaZoom&" "&timeOnQT&"*" into lineaBehavior
  put the number of lines of field "behavior" into cuentalineas
  cuentalineas = cuentalineas + 1
  put lineaBehavior into line cuentalineas of field "behavior"
  go to frame "limpiar"
end
```

APPENDIX 2. DATABASE EXAMPLES.

Session 1.

```
20010925x24.196.239.139
Platform: Windows,32
Date: 9/25/01
Time: 5:11 AM
---
 databaseA space of time
QT xopening 316 316 319*
QTVR b47 5 4 358 1 0 0 0 23*
QT xarrival 440 440 445*
QTVR b13 3 228 420 2 0 0 0 21*
QT xarrival 440 440 455*
QTVR b13 0 0 0 0 0 0 0 2*
QTVR b12 3 49 478 8 0 0 0 31*
QTVR b39 2 254 0 0 0 0 0 12*
QTVR b14 3 10 288 2 0 0 0 19*
QTVR b31 2 0 236 0 0 0 0 8*
QT xpita53 26 26 29*
QTVR b31 0 0 0 0 0 0 0 2*
QT xpita56 50 50 53*
QTVR b31 0 0 96 0 0 0 0 3*
QT xpita48 8 8 11*
QTVR b31 0 253 392 4 0 0 0 17*
QTVR b17 2 13 406 3 0 0 0 18*
QT xmaze 443 443 446*
QTVR b17 0 174 3 1 0 0 0 6*
QT xmaze 443 443 453*
QTVR b17 0 292 48 5 0 0 0 556*
QTVR b31 0 13 441 4 0 0 0 12*
QTVR b18 3 311 44 3 0 0 0 24*
QT xreal 325 325 328*
QTVR b18 0 87 319 2 0 0 0 12*
QTVR b31 0 372 79 3 0 0 0 13*
QTVR b19 3 235 716 9 0 0 0 23*
QT xpita41 19 19 22*
QTVR b19 0 22 0 0 0 0 0 2*
QT xpita45 16 16 19*
QTVR b19 0 21 0 1 0 0 0 3*
QTVR b20 3 315 193 5 0 0 0 13*
Flash flash6 0 3423 179*
QTVR b20 1 0 16 0 0 0 0 2*
QTVR b22 2 261 269 12 0 0 0 24*
QTVR b33 2 176 275 0 0 0 0 16*
QTVR b23 3 586 5 1 0 0 0 7*
QTVR b33 0 33 283 2 0 0 0 14*
QTVR b22 0 108 0 0 0 0 0 4*
QTVR b33 0 132 260 2 0 0 0 10*
```

```
QTVR b22 0 129 3 1 0 0 0 8*
QT xpita44 7 7 10*
QTVR b22 0 0 44 0 0 0 0 3*
QTVR b19 0 0 26 0 0 0 0 3*
QTVR b31 0 0 65 0 0 0 0 4*
QTVR b14 0 1 152 1 0 0 0 5*
QTVR b39 0 0 0 0 0 0 0 1*
QT xperform1 404 404 407*
QTVR b39 0 10 595 4 0 0 0 22*
QTVR b38 2 3 334 1 0 0 0 11*
QTVR b28 2 0 333 0 0 0 0 10*
QTVR b6 2 1 476 5 0 0 0 15*
Flash flash2 0 2780 233*
QTVR b6 1 0 210 0 0 0 0 12*
QTVR b30 3 113 26 1 0 0 0 5*
QTVR c19 2 80 351 1 0 0 0 10*
QT xpita37 33 33 36*
QTVR c19 0 0 0 0 0 0 0 3*
QTVR c20 2 0 0 0 0 0 0 4*
QTVR c6 3 0 0 0 0 0 0 2*
QT xghost 694 694 698*
Map c6 14*
QTVR c6 0 79 0 0 0 0 0 5*
QTVR c21 2 0 10 0 0 0 0 3*
QT xpita22 18 18 21*
QTVR c21 0 20 145 2 0 0 0 7*
QTVR c6 0 251 6 1 0 0 0 10*
QTVR c19 0 19 150 0 0 0 0 11*
QTVR c18 1 32 301 2 0 0 0 15*
QT xpita40 10 10 13*
QTVR c18 0 0 0 0 0 0 0 2*
QTVR h77 3 22 542 3 0 0 0 26*
QTVR h80 3 90 423 3 0 0 0 3*
QTVR h75 4 61 621 1 0 0 0 18*
QTVR h80 0 0 0 0 0 0 0 2*
QTVR h81 2 50 263 3 0 0 0 9*
QTVR h83 2 272 14 3 0 0 0 10*
QTVR h84 3 350 143 5 0 0 0 19*
QTVR h83 0 0 0 0 0 0 0 3*
QTVR h86 2 309 158 2 0 0 0 13*
QTVR h83 0 233 0 0 0 0 0 11*
QTVR h85 3 226 24 2 33 33 1 18*
QTVR h83 0 0 0 0 0 0 0 1*
QTVR h81 0 98 0 0 0 0 0 4*
QTVR h82 2 233 7 5 0 0 0 10*
QTVR h81 0 753 166 7 0 0 0 23*
QTVR h80 0 47 312 0 0 0 0 6*
QTVR h79 4 359 100 1 0 0 0 11*
QTVR h76 3 625 81 11 0 0 0 19*
QTVR h79 0 143 9 3 0 0 0 6*
QTVR h77 0 464 0 0 0 0 0 8*
QTVR h79 0 19 172 1 0 0 0 6*
QTVR h80 0 80 0 0 0 0 0 3*
QTVR b28 0 401 259 1 0 0 0 16*
QTVR b4 2 705 0 0 0 0 0 14*
QT xbevpan 327 327 331*
QTVR b4 0 8 99 0 0 0 0 5*
```

```
QTVR b27 2 216 35 2 0 0 0 7*
QTVR b4 0 90 0 0 0 0 0 3*
QTVR b28 0 0 196 0 0 0 0 6*
QTVR b27 0 139 145 1 0 0 0 6*
QTVR b1 3 64 0 0 0 0 0 2*
QT xtvroga 258 258 262*
QTVR b1 0 53 196 6 22 0 0 19*
QTVR b25 3 390 22 3 0 0 0 12*
QTVR b34 2 243 19 3 0 0 0 9*
QTVR b35 2 64 0 0 0 0 0 4*
QTVR c17 2 220 0 0 0 0 0 6*
QTVR c26 2 3 157 2 0 0 0 4*
QTVR d17 2 54 411 3 0 0 0 11*
QTVR d1 3 0 117 0 0 0 0 7*
QT xtvpana 314 314 318*
QTVR d1 0 1 454 0 0 0 0 10*
QTVR d17 0 2 214 0 0 0 0 7*
QTVR d1 0 348 129 4 0 0 0 10*
QTVR d16 3 10 0 0 0 0 0 2*
QT xlove 782 782 785*
QTVR d16 0 4 385 0 0 0 0 14*
QTVR d25 2 264 23 1 0 0 0 7*
QTVR d26 2 18 21 0 0 0 0 3*
QTVR d2 2 380 0 0 0 0 0 7*
QT xgemad 345 345 349*
QTVR d2 0 4 177 0 0 0 0 4*
QTVR d26 0 120 267 2 0 0 0 12*
QTVR d17 0 42 0 0 0 0 0 2*
QTVR d18 2 131 16 1 0 0 0 4*
QTVR h86 0 39 204 0 0 0 0 8*
QTVR h83 0 0 252 0 0 0 0 5*
QTVR h81 1 116 227 0 0 0 0 8*
QTVR h80 0 0 11 0 0 0 0 3*
QTVR h77 0 11 303 0 0 0 0 5*
QTVR h79 0 6 142 0 0 0 0 9*
QTVR h80 0 19 0 0 0 0 0 2*
QTVR d31 3 356 104 6 0 0 0 18*
QTVR d30 3 20 91 3 0 0 0 6*
QTVR d29 3 2 363 0 0 0 0 10*
QTVR d18 0 255 0 0 0 0 0 7*
QTVR d17 0 180 0 0 0 0 0 4*
QTVR d18 0 91 85 1 0 0 0 5*
QTVR d29 0 0 50 0 0 0 0 3*
QTVR d19 2 394 10 3 0 0 0 8*
QTVR d5 4 204 12 2 0 0 0 8*
QT xtvjessa 407 407 410*
QTVR d5 0 117 376 6 0 0 0 14*
QTVR d6 2 88 335 0 0 0 0 8*
QTVR d21 1 255 27 1 0 0 0 6*
QTVR d6 0 151 116 1 0 0 0 6*
QTVR d7 3 51 116 4 0 0 0 7*
QT xlaundry 670 670 673*
QTVR d7 0 111 282 0 0 0 0 7*
QTVR d6 0 160 12 1 0 0 0 4*
QTVR d7 0 26 270 1 0 0 0 5*
QTVR d22 2 178 3 1 0 0 0 5*
QT xpita12 22 22 25*
```

```
QTVR d22 0 274 1 1 0 0 0 8*
QTVR d23 2 0 356 0 0 0 0 9*
QTVR d8 3 0 0 0 0 0 0 1*
QT xsurveil 325 325 328*
QTVR d8 0 0 0 0 0 0 0 4*
credits exit 42*
```

Session 2

```
20020309x66.87.103.51
Platform: Windows,32
Date: 3/9/2002
Time: 11:07 PM
---
 databaseA space of time
QT xopening 316 0 3*
QTVR b47 7 3 356 0 0 0 0 26*
you start 4*
you 1*
QTVR b47 0 0 0 0 0 0 0 1*
QT xarrival 440 0 0*
QTVR b13 2 5 359 0 0 0 0 13*
QTVR b12 8 0 282 0 0 0 0 19*
Server Change
QTVR b30 5 0 17 0 0 0 0 3*
QTVR b6 4 31 440 0 0 0 0 48*
Flash flash2 0 2780 239*
QTVR b6 0 0 97 0 0 0 0 2*
QTVR b28 3 0 228 0 0 0 0 5*
QTVR b5 4 0 344 0 0 0 0 21*
QT xmarien 456 456 459*
QTVR b5 0 0 173 0 0 0 0 5*
QTVR b28 0 0 209 0 0 0 0 5*
QTVR b4 3 364 9 1 19 19 1 27*
QT xbevpan 327 28 35*
Server Change
QT xbevpan 327 327 330*
QTVR b4 7 0 117 0 0 0 0 3*
QTVR b27 2 23 220 0 0 0 0 6*
QTVR b3 3 14 219 0 0 0 0 22*
QT xceil 6 4 4*
QTVR b3 0 81 249 4 0 0 0 14*
QTVR b27 0 84 0 0 0 0 0 4*
QTVR b1 3 0 294 0 0 0 0 12*
QT xtvroga 258 258 262*
QTVR b1 0 0 129 0 0 0 0 4*
QTVR b25 4 0 319 0 0 0 0 6*
Flash flash11 0 54 7*
QTVR b25 0 0 0 0 0 0 0 1*
QTVR b34 3 68 14 1 0 0 0 6*
QTVR b24 6 24 367 1 0 0 0 16*
QT xthree 430 430 433*
QTVR b24 0 28 167 0 0 0 0 5*
QTVR b34 0 0 210 0 0 0 0 5*
QTVR b33 4 0 9 0 0 0 0 3*
QTVR b23 4 0 138 0 0 0 0 7*
QTVR b33 0 118 0 0 0 0 0 4*
QTVR b22 8 87 87 0 0 0 0 8*
QTVR b21 3 0 400 0 0 0 0 18*
QT xtvjessa 407 407 410*
QTVR b21 0 0 99 0 0 0 0 5*
```

```
QTVR b19 7 22 0 0 0 0 0 3*
QTVR b31 3 109 0 0 0 0 0 3*
QTVR b18 4 20 315 0 0 0 0 13*
QT xreal 325 325 328*
QTVR b18 0 103 0 0 0 0 0 4*
QTVR b31 0 75 16 0 0 0 0 5*
QTVR b17 5 0 380 0 0 0 0 745*
QT xmaze 443 443 446*
QTVR b17 0 0 78 0 0 0 0 3*
QTVR b31 0 52 0 0 0 0 0 6*
QTVR b14 4 357 224 3 31 31 1 25*
QTVR b15 3 0 335 0 0 0 0 6*
QT xanima 160 160 163*
QTVR b15 0 128 0 0 0 0 0 5*
QTVR b13 0 0 0 0 0 0 0 1*
QTVR b14 0 0 68 0 0 0 0 3*
QTVR b39 3 27 0 0 0 0 0 6*
QT xperform1 404 404 407*
QTVR b39 0 21 0 0 0 0 0 5*
QT xperform2 310 310 313*
QTVR b39 0 0 103 0 0 0 0 3*
QTVR b14 0 0 101 0 0 0 0 11*
QTVR b29 2 102 26 1 0 0 0 23*
QTVR b7 2 145 0 0 0 0 0 7*
QTVR a25 2 0 131 0 0 0 0 4*
QTVR a23 4 0 0 0 0 0 0 1*
QTVR a22 4 0 9 0 0 0 0 3*
QTVR a21 2 46 112 0 0 0 0 7*
QTVR a14 2 0 121 0 0 0 0 *
QTVR a32 3 86 0 0 0 0 0 5*
QTVR a31 2 66 0 0 0 0 0 4*
QTVR a12 3 144 323 0 0 0 0 8*
QTVR a30 3 0 347 0 0 0 0 19*
QTVR d24 3 0 74 0 0 0 0 6*
QTVR d15 3 0 288 0 0 0 0 18*
QTVR d24 0 66 0 0 0 0 0 5*
QTVR c24 2 0 50 0 0 0 0 8*
QTVR c25 2 0 0 0 0 0 0 1*
QTVR c26 2 0 0 0 0 0 0 1*
QTVR c2 3 51 256 0 0 0 0 29*
QTVR c17 2 12 0 0 0 0 0 2*
Map a32 6*
QTVR a32 0 16 123 1 0 0 0 6*
QTVR a22 1 0 84 0 0 0 0 4*
QTVR a3 2 96 214 0 0 0 0 7*
QTVR a21 0 254 0 0 0 0 0 15*
QTVR a3 0 90 0 0 0 0 0 4*
Map a13 3*
QTVR a13 4 0 37 0 0 0 0 2*
QTVR a12 0 0 419 0 0 0 0 6*
QTVR a30 0 0 63 0 0 0 0 4*
QTVR a31 0 0 0 0 0 0 0 1*
Map a32 4*
QTVR a32 0 116 74 1 0 0 0 6*
QTVR a3 0 42 264 0 0 0 0 7*
QTVR a21 0 198 507 1 0 0 0 22*
Map a15 4*
```

185

```
QTVR a15 3 0 136 0 0 0 0 3*
QTVR a21 0 0 0 0 0 0 0 2*
Map a22 2*
QTVR a22 1 0 356 0 0 0 0 12*
QTVR a23 0 0 0 0 0 0 0 1*
QTVR a4 2 72 366 2 0 0 0 7*
QTVR a23 0 0 0 0 0 0 0 4*
credits exit 43*
```

APPENDIX 3. PROGRAMMING SCRIPTS FOR SPSS

```
GET DATA /TYPE=XLS
  /FILE='C:\TimeSeriesQTVR\qtvrTS1.xls'
  /SHEET=name 'qtvrTS1'
  /CELLRANGE=full
  /READNAMES=on .
COMPUTE step = $casenum .
EXECUTE .
VARIABLE LEVEL panleft (SCALE) .
VARIABLE LEVEL panright (SCALE) .
VARIABLE LEVEL deltapan (SCALE) .
VARIABLE LEVEL zoomin (SCALE) .
VARIABLE LEVEL zoomout (SCALE) .
VARIABLE LEVEL deltazoo (SCALE) .
VARIABLE LEVEL timeqtvr (SCALE) .
VARIABLE LEVEL step (SCALE) .
IGRAPH /VIEWNAME='Scatterplot' /X1 = VAR(step) TYPE = SCALE /Y = VAR(timeqtvr
) TYPE = SCALE /COORDINATE = VERTICAL  /SPIKE X1 /SPIKE Y /FORMAT SPIKE
  COLOR=OFF STYLE=OFF /FITLINE METHOD = REGRESSION LINEAR INTERVAL(95.0) =
  MEAN LINE = TOTAL SPIKE=ON /X1LENGTH=5.0 /YLENGTH=4.0 /X2LENGTH=4.0
  /CHARTLOOK='C:\Program Files\SPSS\Looks\Classic.clo' /SCATTER COINCIDENT =
  NONE.
*Sequence Charts .
TSPLOT VARIABLES= panleft
  /ID= step
  /NOLOG
  /FORMAT BOTTOM REFERENCE
  /MARK deltapan.
TSPLOT VARIABLES= panright
  /ID= step
  /NOLOG
  /FORMAT BOTTOM REFERENCE
  /MARK deltapan.
*Sequence Charts .
TSPLOT VARIABLES= deltapan
  /ID= step
  /NOLOG
  /FORMAT BOTTOM NOREFERENCE.
*Sequence Charts .
TSPLOT VARIABLES= zoomin zoomout
  /ID= step
  /NOLOG
  /MARK deltazoo.
DESCRIPTIVES
  VARIABLES=panleft panright deltapan zoomin zoomout deltazoo timeqtvr
  /STATISTICS=MEAN STDDEV MIN MAX .
REGRESSION
  /MISSING LISTWISE
  /STATISTICS COEFF OUTS R ANOVA
  /CRITERIA=PIN(.05) POUT(.10)
  /NOORIGIN
  /DEPENDENT timeqtvr
  /METHOD=ENTER step  .
```

```
EXE.
REGRESSION
 /MISSING LISTWISE
 /STATISTICS COEFF OUTS R ANOVA
 /CRITERIA=PIN(.05) POUT(.10)
 /NOORIGIN
 /DEPENDENT deltapan
 /METHOD=ENTER step  .

GET DATA /TYPE=XLS
 /FILE='C:\TimeSeriesQTVR\qtvrTS2.xls'
 /SHEET=name 'qtvrTS2'
 /CELLRANGE=full
 /READNAMES=on .
COMPUTE step = $casenum .
EXECUTE .
VARIABLE LEVEL panleft (SCALE) .
VARIABLE LEVEL panright (SCALE) .
VARIABLE LEVEL deltapan (SCALE) .
VARIABLE LEVEL zoomin (SCALE) .
VARIABLE LEVEL zoomout (SCALE) .
VARIABLE LEVEL deltazoo (SCALE) .
VARIABLE LEVEL timeqtvr (SCALE) .
VARIABLE LEVEL step (SCALE) .
IGRAPH /VIEWNAME='Scatterplot' /X1 = VAR(step) TYPE = SCALE /Y = VAR(timeqtvr
) TYPE = SCALE /COORDINATE = VERTICAL  /SPIKE X1 /SPIKE Y /FORMAT SPIKE
 COLOR=OFF STYLE=OFF /FITLINE METHOD = REGRESSION LINEAR INTERVAL(95.0) =
 MEAN LINE = TOTAL SPIKE=ON /X1LENGTH=5.0 /YLENGTH=4.0 /X2LENGTH=4.0
/CHARTLOOK='C:\Program Files\SPSS\Looks\Classic.clo' /SCATTER COINCIDENT =
 NONE.
*Sequence Charts .
TSPLOT VARIABLES= panleft
 /ID= step
 /NOLOG
 /FORMAT BOTTOM REFERENCE
 /MARK deltapan.
TSPLOT VARIABLES= panright
 /ID= step
 /NOLOG
 /FORMAT BOTTOM REFERENCE
 /MARK deltapan.
*Sequence Charts .
TSPLOT VARIABLES= deltapan
 /ID= step
 /NOLOG
 /FORMAT BOTTOM NOREFERENCE.
*Sequence Charts .
TSPLOT VARIABLES= zoomin zoomout
 /ID= step
 /NOLOG
 /MARK deltazoo.
DESCRIPTIVES
 VARIABLES=panleft panright deltapan zoomin zoomout deltazoo timeqtvr
 /STATISTICS=MEAN STDDEV MIN MAX .
REGRESSION
 /MISSING LISTWISE
```

```
/STATISTICS COEFF OUTS R ANOVA
/CRITERIA=PIN(.05) POUT(.10)
/NOORIGIN
/DEPENDENT timeqtvr
/METHOD=ENTER step  .
EXE.
REGRESSION
/MISSING LISTWISE
/STATISTICS COEFF OUTS R ANOVA
/CRITERIA=PIN(.05) POUT(.10)
/NOORIGIN
/DEPENDENT deltapan
/METHOD=ENTER step  .

GET DATA /TYPE=XLS
 /FILE='C:\TimeSeriesQTVR\qtvrTS3.xls'
 /SHEET=name 'qtvrTS3'
 /CELLRANGE=full
 /READNAMES=on .
COMPUTE step = $casenum .
EXECUTE .
VARIABLE LEVEL panleft (SCALE) .
VARIABLE LEVEL panright (SCALE) .
VARIABLE LEVEL deltapan (SCALE) .
VARIABLE LEVEL zoomin (SCALE) .
VARIABLE LEVEL zoomout (SCALE) .
VARIABLE LEVEL deltazoo (SCALE) .
VARIABLE LEVEL timeqtvr (SCALE) .
VARIABLE LEVEL step (SCALE) .
IGRAPH /VIEWNAME='Scatterplot' /X1 = VAR(step) TYPE = SCALE /Y = VAR(timeqtvr
 ) TYPE = SCALE /COORDINATE = VERTICAL  /SPIKE X1 /SPIKE Y /FORMAT SPIKE
 COLOR=OFF STYLE=OFF /FITLINE METHOD = REGRESSION LINEAR INTERVAL(95.0) =
 MEAN LINE = TOTAL SPIKE=ON /X1LENGTH=5.0 /YLENGTH=4.0 /X2LENGTH=4.0
 /CHARTLOOK='C:\Program Files\SPSS\Looks\Classic.clo' /SCATTER COINCIDENT =
 NONE.
*Sequence Charts .
TSPLOT VARIABLES= panleft
 /ID= step
 /NOLOG
 /FORMAT BOTTOM REFERENCE
 /MARK deltapan.
TSPLOT VARIABLES= panright
 /ID= step
 /NOLOG
 /FORMAT BOTTOM REFERENCE
 /MARK deltapan.
*Sequence Charts .
TSPLOT VARIABLES= deltapan
 /ID= step
 /NOLOG
 /FORMAT BOTTOM NOREFERENCE.
*Sequence Charts .
TSPLOT VARIABLES= zoomin zoomout
 /ID= step
 /NOLOG
 /MARK deltazoo.
```

```
DESCRIPTIVES
 VARIABLES=panleft panright deltapan zoomin zoomout deltazoo timeqtvr
 /STATISTICS=MEAN STDDEV MIN MAX .
REGRESSION
 /MISSING LISTWISE
 /STATISTICS COEFF OUTS R ANOVA
 /CRITERIA=PIN(.05) POUT(.10)
 /NOORIGIN
 /DEPENDENT timeqtvr
 /METHOD=ENTER step  .
EXE.
REGRESSION
 /MISSING LISTWISE
 /STATISTICS COEFF OUTS R ANOVA
 /CRITERIA=PIN(.05) POUT(.10)
 /NOORIGIN
 /DEPENDENT deltapan
 /METHOD=ENTER step  .
```

APPENDIX 4. MAPS WITH QTVR CODING AND

NAVIGATIONAL DESIGN.

Map 1 (Basement)

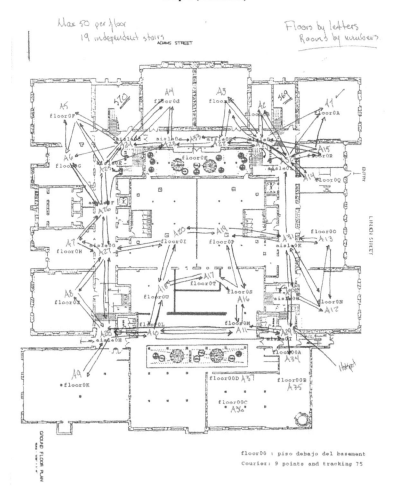

191

Map 2 (First floor)

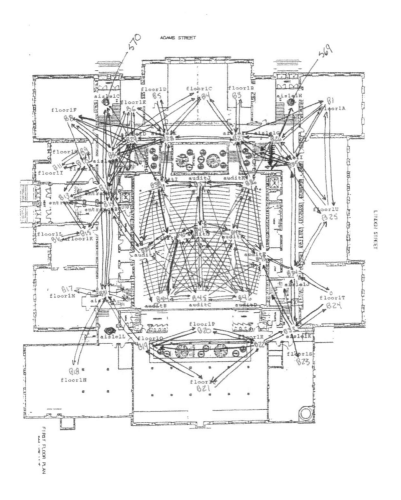

192

Map 3 (Second floor)

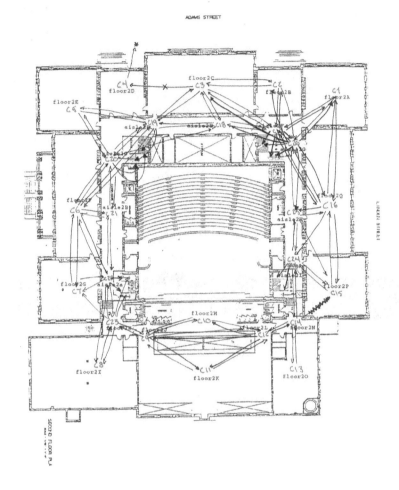

Map 4 (Third Floor)

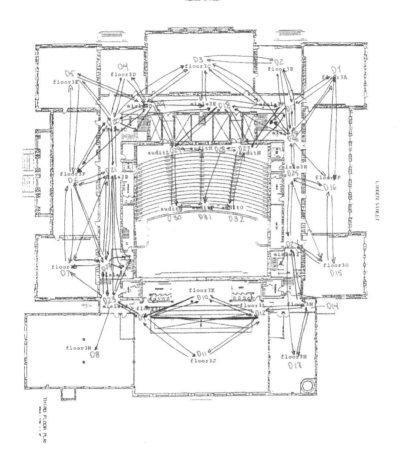

Map 5 (Attic)

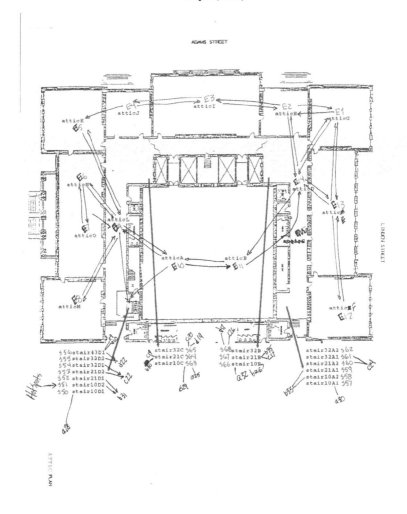

APPENDIX 5. A SPACE OF TIME, THE SCREENPLAY

A space of time

A non-linear film

by

Diego Bonilla

The first two scenes should be at the front of the rest of the experience. They can occur in any order. After that the rest of the scenes could happen at any moment. The last scene is the Death Scene, even though it can be chronologically misplaced. For the purposes of this copy, after the two scenes, the screenplay is presented in alphabetical order.

The container

Scene starts with random sequence extracted from the movie database.

1 Interior. Diner. Day.

>   David
>   (Making noises while he squeezes
>   cream cups over his coffee.)
> Old habits live long… At my age there's no reason why
> I should try to get rid of them.

>   Patty
> How old are you?

>   David
> I can't tell accurately anymore, I always end up
> rounding up… 60? 70?

>   Patty
> Oh! It can't be, you're younger than that…

>   David
> No, no, I've paid my dues… More or less 60.

>   Historian
> Oh, come on, you are still a very strong man….

> The tramp looks at him as if he has had this
> conversation many times in his life and is somewhat
> tired of it.

>   George
> Why don't you tell me how you got inside the
> building?

>   David
> How long is your attention span?

>   Historian
> I can focus, don't worry about me…

>   David
> I've been looking inside that building for quite some
> time. You really can't tell much about the upper
> floors from afar; well, maybe a little bit, if you go
> across the street. There is a big garage, you from
> there can take a good look from there into the
> northern side of the building… From there, those
> floors look empty… (Smiles.)

>   Doctor
>   (Inquisitive about the smile.)
> What?

                    David
                    (Paying no attention to the
                    question.)
But the lower floors, you can see what's in them from
the street, and believe me from outside they look
very interesting. There are chairs, there are
mattresses, small refrigerators, heaters, radios… You
name it (he looks very excited.) So I didn't get into
the building by coincidence, I waited patiently to
get myself inside. One day (voiceover) I was walking
along on one of the side streets and I saw the
janitor's nephew go outside the building, he was
taking something out -garbage maybe, I can't remember
what, he helps the janitor clean up the building in
exchange of money and favors.

                    Patty
Favors?

                    David
Yes, using the building for this and that… basically
the building is the nephew's playground. He invites
friends to the building to play hide and seek, run
remote control cars, do drugs… he's quite a
character. That day, he left one of the side doors
open and I found my way inside the building. I didn't
know the impact that the building was going to have
on me.

                    Historian
What happened?

                    David
That building is not just any building. That building
is a container of time…

                    Historian
It's a very old building, it will be one
hundred years old next winter… A lot of
people have many good memories of it,
especially when it was the district's main
school.

                    David
What I am trying to say is that the building is not
in everyone's memories, but the other way around:
everyone who has stepped inside the building has left
some part of them inside. The building is a
receptacle; it's a container of time…

                    Historian
I understand the metaphor…

                    David
There is no metaphor. You see, there is no metaphor.
The building contains time. All those walls, all

those rooms, all those corridors… There is something
in the air that holds or captures time… Almost as if
the building had a memory. I have come to believe
that… What I perceive in those rooms is just… is just
a combination of the time container with myself…

          Patty
You know how this sounds, right?

          David
Of course I know how it sounds! Imagine just living
it! It makes you question everything! But you just
raised a very important point: How much you are able
to take from that building depends entirely on how
comfortable you can get to be in an alternate
reality… So, I am sure that what I have seen is just
a combination of myself with the container.

          Patty
The building, you mean…

          David
The container… So I guess that we are going to have
some problems here. That's why I asked you about your
attention span, because if you are in a hurry, if you
have to get this done so you can get to the next
thing, or if you have appointments and time pressure
and you have to get somewhere… Probably it is better
that you don't sit through what I have to say…

          Doctor
Hi, it is Doctor Livingston, can you reschedule my
appointments to next week… I know, tell her that it
was an emergency… Well, I hope she does. Thank you.
(Hangs up.) I'll hear you.

          David
Good! I love to tell… Do you mind if I order some
donuts?

The detective makes a movement with his hand allowing
the tramp to order donuts.

          David
          (Calling the waitress. Raising his
          hand.)
Maggie, Maggie…

          Maggie
Hang on…

Straight cut to black.

The arrival

1. Exterior. Building's promenade. Day.

The scene starts with a panoramic view of the building. It is a shot of the façade taken from the buildings in the opposite side of the street. Jeremiah is walking down the street towards the building. Several friends are waiting for him. It's cold.

Claudia

There he is…

Zak

It's about time.

Kirk

Come on man, where have you been?

Jeremiah
(Imitating the voice.)

Come on man, where have you been? (He smiles coyly at Rene, grabs her and gives her a big smooch. Rene backs off.) Well, I try. (Jeremiah walks over to Bev and Julia and kicks Bev on the foot to rouse her.) Wakey, wakey Bev.

Bev

Oh you are such an annoyance at this hour of the day. Where is Phil with my coffee?

Jeremiah

Too much fun last night again?

Bev

Work, darling, work, some of us do that you know.

Julia

Could you just please open the door?

Jeremiah opens the door and they all enter the building.

2. Interior. Building. Day.

The scene cuts to a fast moving camera inside the building. It starts on the third floor, it moves from room to room in a very fast motion. At some point, the Tramp appears on camera, he is in a room in the third floor making measurements with a pendulum. He hears the sound of Jeremiah's group of friends and he picks up his tools and starts walking precipitously towards his room on the basement. The camera follows him until the second floor and then it departs to do a very fast motion throughout the second floor rooms, finally descending to the first floor.

200

                              Bev
                              (While the camera is moving through
                              the first floor rooms.)
          Oh my god, this building is impressive…

                              Claudia
          It gives me goose pumps…

                              Rene
                              (Walking away from the pack.)
          This place is too cold.

                              Jeremiah
                              (Introducing the building to
                              everyone.)
          The feeling of the building changes a lot with the
          temperature. When it is very cold it gets really
          creepy.

                              Rene
                              (To Jeremiah.)
          Are you going to turn the heat on?

                              Jeremiah
          It is already on; it is going to take a couple of
          hours.

                              Julia
          Listen to the echo. I love the echo of empty places.

                              Bev
                              (She sings to hear the echo of the
                              main entrance.)
          Sayonara baby, *au revoir monsieur*…

                              Panda
          It sounds like an aquarium.

                              Kirk
          This place is too weird. It reminds me of a Garcia
          Marquez story in which a group of kids break the
          light bulbs at their parents' house to fill up the
          rooms with fresh running light. Can you imagine?

                              Zak
          Great, keep up with the hard drugs.

                              Kirk
          It is a short story, Zak.

Jeremiah
(Through a megaphone.)
Hey, hey, over here… Rene, no, no, come over here.
Zak, Zak, get your ugly butt over here. Can I have
your attention for just a minute? Now, follow me.

Rene
Jeremiah, why do you have to use that thing? We can
all hear you.

Jeremiah
(Through the megaphone.)
You are I no position to ask me questions, my young
sweet concubine.

Rene
Oh please, who wound you up this morning?

More of the building at fast speed. The first lines of Jeremiah are
heard as a voiceover before the camera arrives to the auditorium.
Finally the camera synchs with the sound on a mid-shot of Jeremiah.

Jeremiah
(Through the megaphone.)
Welcome all to my playground. I know loved ones that
you are overwhelmed by the presence of this place,
but don't let yourselves be besieged by its surface,
if you go just a little bit deeper, you will see that
these walls have a memory… This used to be the
largest auditorium in the East coast; this is where
one of the best orchestras in the region played week
after week haunting concertos (pronounced in Italian)
and it is also the place where I, my friends, lost my
virginity.

Zak applauds and whistles.

Zak
Do we have to listen to this crap? I've got to use
the lou.

Jeremiah
(Through the megaphone.)
It was over there my loved ones where Caroline
Stanford took last glance at life before she plunged
into the sweet arms of death (Spinning fall from the
balcony to the floor of the auditorium). And it was
over there where my uncle asked my rest-in-peace-aunt
to marry him… And it was here, my loved ones…

Beverage
(Shouting.)
Get on with it. We want to have a look at the rest of
the building.

                              Jeremiah
            You are so impatient. Out of the kindness of my heart
            I have allowed Bev to work in the space, and after
            the rehearsal we are going to have some fun, but
            there are a few things you should know first, there
            are house rules: First, the building may seem empty,
            it's not. My uncle keeps a very detailed inventory of
            the building. Do not take, do not hide, and do not
            damage anything. Simply put, don't trash the place.
            Second, do not prop open the street doors. You are
            here by invitation, if you open those doors we will
            have uninvited guests. (A random sequence extracted
            from the tramp's scenes flashes quickly.) Finally,
            and this is the fun part, we will be locked in here
            overnight. If any of you leave without telling me,
            the police will come, and believe me you don't want
            that to happen.

A banging sound is heard from outside of the auditorium.

                              Claudia
                              (Slightly frightened.)
            Does anyone hear that banging?

                              Rene
            Someone's at the door.

                              Bev
            Oh! That better be Phil with my coffee. When are we
            going to load the equipment?

                              Jeremiah
            When we finish the grand tour. Now that you all have
            learned how to be naughty, and under what
            circumstances you will receive a spanking. Please
            follow me.

Straight cut to black.

203

Jeremiah and Phil's acid scene

Scene starts with random sequence extracted from the movie database.

1 Exterior. In front of the building. Day.

Jeremiah and Phil arrive to the building. Jeremiah pulls out a set of key from his pocket. He opens the main door. Phil follows him inside the building; he seems nervous, he is looking left and right to see if anyone is around.

2 Interior. Building's Lobby. Day.

>   Jeremiah
> Alright, if Ira is not around we are good to go. Let me see the ball.

>   Phil
>   (Pulling a box out of his
>   backpack.)
> Man, I spent the entire day looking through the store, I opened all the boxes and all I could find was purple and pink.

>   Jeremiah
> Phil this is going to be amazing. This is what we were looking for. You blow it up, I am going to check for Ira.

>   Phil
> Cool, man.

A random sequence is extracted from the movie's database.

3 Interior. Trotting around the building. Day

Jeremiah walks to each one of the staircases and yells for Ira. The camera follows. It takes Jeremiah some time to go around the entire structure (emphasis on the size of the building).

>   Jeremiah
> Ira!

A random sequence is extracted from the movie's database.

>   Jeremiah
> Ira! Yo, Ira, are you here? Yo, Ira, are you here? Ira? Ira? Yo, Ira? Ira…?

4 Interior. Building's Lobby. Day.

When Jeremiah returns, Phil has inflated most of the ball.

                    Jeremiah
          Yo, Phil, you're almost finished! This ball is
          amazing.

                    Phil
                    (Laying back in the couch.)
          Oh, man, I have a headache.

                    Jeremiah
                    (Ironically.)
          You should do this for a living. It suits you. So
          amazing. Lets drop!

                    Phil
          Are you totally sure your uncle is not coming?

                    Jeremiah
                    (Opening a plastic bag. From inside
                    the bag he takes out a two pieces
                    of paper.)
          When Ira is not around he is not around, besides
          probably he is with that chick he met a couple of
          weeks ago. It's cool.

                    Phil
                    (Grabbing the acid tablet.)
          Oh, man, this is so intense, man.

                    Jeremiah
          Screw reality.

Both drop the acid and they give each other mischievous looks.

                    Phil
                    (Both put the acid in their
                    mouths.)
          Oh, momma, here we go.

                    Jeremiah
                    (Surprised by the thought of it.)
          Oh, you know something?

                    Phil
                    (Nervously.)
          What, what's up?

                    Jeremiah
          I'm gonna get something.

A random sequence is extracted from the movie's database.

Jeremiah runs to one of the side doors and grabs a megaphone. In his
way back, Jeremiah hides behind a column and triggers a melody on the
megaphone.

                              Phil
                    What the hell is that?

                              Jeremiah
                              (Through the megaphone.)
                    Come out with you hands up… Women and babies first!
                    Stop or I will shoot.

                              Phil
                    Man, you scared the hell out of me. Jesus, I almost
                    had an out of body experience.

                              Jeremiah
                    Here, have it, you are going to die of a heart attack
                    at the age of forty… (Jeremiah grabs the ball.) Come
                    on, let's go!

A random sequence is extracted from the movie's database.

5 Interior. Staircase. Day.

Jeremiah starts leading the way to the third floor using the stairway
that it is closest to the main entrance. On the first landing he hears
the phone ringing, sits down on the stairway. Ira is on the other end.

                              Jeremiah
                              (Bluntly.)
                    Hi… No, no, I'll do that tomorrow, I'll do it
                    tomorrow. Ira: Are we going to have any visitors
                    tomorrow? No? So, I I'll do it tomorrow. OK? Yeah!
                    Yes, ok, fine. Bye. Cool. OK. Bye. (To Phil.) Yes! We
                    have the entire building just for ourselves.

                              Phil
                    Oh, that's good news, very good news. Do you think
                    your uncle's done stuff like this in the building?

                              Jeremiah
                    Oh, man, he used to come to this building a lot.

A random sequence is extracted from the movie's database.

6 Interior. Third floor, big room. Day.

                         Jeremiah
             I am sure he has done pretty memorable things in
             here.

                         Phil
             Your uncle kinda freaks me out. It is like one of
             those people who live in an alternate universe. You
             know what mean?

                         Jeremiah
             He's cool, yeah he is a little bit weird, but he's
             cool.

Jeremiah kicks the ball across the room. Phil leaves the megaphone on
the floor. They both start playing with the ball, kicking it at each
other. Music starts. Suddenly, Jeremiah sees a bright coming of the
wall, the acid has kicked in. The ball escapes to another room and Phil
follows it. They get separated. Jeremiah observes how the wall inflates
and deflates.

                         Jeremiah
                         (Conclusively.)
             You are alive… And you breathe.

A random sequence is extracted from the movie's database.

7 Interior. Hallways in the building. Day.

Phil starts feeling a headache. Everything looks distorted. Jeremiah
starts walking away from the room.

                         Jeremiah
             I just know stuff… I've never seen anything myself…

                         Pandora
                         (Voiceover with echo.)
             What makes you think that there is something to see
             here?

                         Jeremiah
             I know! you can feel it all over!

                         Pandora
                         (Voiceover with echo.)

             What if the building is simply empty?

                         Jeremiah
             Then it is just me, and that can't be. (Jeremiah runs
             up the stairs frenetically.)

A random sequence is extracted from the movie's database.

                    Pandora
                    (Voiceover with echo.)
          You are wrong. There is nothing here.

                    Jeremiah
          I know! I know there is. A hundred years do not go
          away without leaving a mark. (One of the walls in one
          of the staircases breathes again.)

                    Pandora
                    (Voiceover with echo.)

          It's only you, it's the acid.

                    Jeremiah
          See?

                    Pandora
                    (Playfully, voiceover with echo.)
          Jeremiah? You are peaking…

                    Jeremiah
          I am not! Oh, maybe I am.

A random sequence is extracted from the movie's database.

                    Pandora
          Are you sure you're not looking in the wrong place?

                    Jeremiah
          No, I'm not sure!

                    Pandora
          What would happen if you only see yourself?

                    Jeremiah
          No, no, that's impossible.

                    Pandora
          What if you find nothing?

                    Jeremiah
          I've seen something! Oh, man, oh man. I never seen
          anything. Oh, man. No. I have. It's not just me.

When Jeremiah reaches one of the corners of the building he stops
abruptly. Circus music starts playing. A bright light lights up
Jeremiah's face. He is surprised, he is scared. Inside the room, two
Pandas float above the floor, one of them is facing Jeremiah, and the
other one is not. The light gets brighter and brighter. Fade out to
white.

Bath

Scene starts with random sequence extracted from the movie database.

1. Interior. Upstairs bathroom in the house. Night.

Pandora walks into the bathroom. She carries a glass of wine. After she preps the bathtub the inner dialog starts.

>   Panda
>   (Voiceover.)
>   I have to let go.
>   "Who is not revolutionary at the age of 20 has no
>   heart, who is not conservative at the age of 40 has
>   no brain," I hate you for saying that… 24, 24 and I
>   am already tired. Where am I gonna get with this
>   rants? After that what? It is not the first time I
>   have to walk in the dark. I know how to trust myself
>   when I don't know where I am going. I have to let go.

Classical guitar starts. Panda undresses and steps into the bathtub.

>   Panda
>   (Voiceover.)
>   "Who is not revolutionary at the age of 20 has no
>   heart…" I won't be conservative at the age of 40, I
>   won't let go my revolutionary heart to be seized by
>   that which oppresses me. Is this a marathon instead
>   of a 100 yard dash, so be it. I am ready for the long
>   run. I'll break down every now and then and I will
>   keep on crying in the shower. I won't stop. I won't.
>   I will not be digested. I will not get attached to
>   the objects I have… It's fucking vane. "Who is not
>   revolutionary at the age of 20 has no heart, who is
>   not conservative at the age of 40" has a better shot
>   to live in peace.

A random sequence is extracted from the movie's database. Fade Out.

Claudia invites Pandora

1 Interior. House where Pandora is house-sitting. Day.

Scene starts with random sequence extracted from the movie database
followed by a series of images of Panda in her apartment. She is
uncomfortable, tired, depressed. The initial sequence stops with Panda
in front of the computer. She is sitting and she has her hand over her
face. She moves her hand to her forehead and looks at the monitor. Then
she starts typing.

>   Panda
>   (As she types her face changes. She
>   sheds a tear.)
>   I give up on you.

Pandora fades out and an animation fades in. In a black background,
small centered white words appear on the screen.

>   Panda
>   I give up on you.
>   The flow is so strong
>   That it is inhuman trying to resist it.
>   I give up on you,
>   Pal.
>   I will float to the end
>   With you
>   With the others
>   Alone.
>   Let's stream with all those
>   Blind
>   Silent
>   Accepting
>   Souls.
>   I give up on you,
>   And I know that you couldn't care less.
>   I taught myself to share your disdain
>   The hard way.
>   At least I am proud of putting up a fight,
>   I bled,
>   You were alienated from the very first moment.
>   Friend,
>   Neighbor,
>   Stranger,
>   Whatever,
>   I am ready to give up on you
>   And compete with you
>   For nonsense.
>   We won't do any better
>   Even if we try it.
>   It is you or me,
>   For no reason,
>   For the sake of it.
>   I finally give up on you.
>   I am done with this…

A close up of Pandora appears reflected on the screen. She looks absent
minded. She stands up, goes to the bathroom and opens the hot water in
the tub. A random sequence is extracted from the movie's database. The
telephone rings.

                              Pandora
                         (After reading the caller ID.)
          Hi.

2 Interior. Claudia's apartment. Day.

                              Claudia
                    Hi! I am glad you're home.

                              Panda
                    I wish I could be somewhere else.

                              Claudia
                    Perfect. Do you remember that guy Jeremiah that I
                    told you about? He hit on me and then he told me
                    thought hackers were heroic.

                              Panda
                    Yeah, I know the type.

                              Claudia
                    What do you mean you "know the type"?

                              Panda
                    He is resisting the system, and his only solution is
                    to be destructive… Basically, he is in pain, but he
                    doesn't know why.

                              Claudia
                    Panda, you don't even know this guy. That's a little
                    bit judgmental, don't you think?

                              Panda
                    Listen, Clo, the bath is running, lets talk about it
                    later.

                              Claudia
                    Look, I'm sorry. I didn't mean to snap at you. OK?
                    Anyhow, this guy is throwing a party…

                              Panda
                    Great, so can we talk about this later.

                              Claudia
                    Panda, just listen… The party is now.

                              Panda
          Now? Clo, its 11 am, what is this? A picnic? Any
          other day would be a good, you just picked the
          crappiest moment. I'm not in the mood.

A random sequence is extracted from the movie's database.

                             Claudia
          Do you remember the Real Estate Gems show that you
          told me about one night at the ungodly hour of 3 am.
          Well, the party is there. Jeremiah is the nephew of
          the janitor and the party is inside that building.

                              Panda
          Clo, that building?

                             Claudia
          Yes, that building.

                              Panda
          I thought that the building was somewhere in Chicago.

                             Claudia
          No, the building is in town. Now, are you coming?

                              Panda
          Can you pick me up?

                             Claudia
          I'll be there in an hour.

                              Panda
          Thanks, Clo…

                             Claudia
          Bye.

A random sequence is extracted from the movie's database. Fade out to
black.

Detectives in the Building

Scene starts with random sequence extracted from the movie database.

   1. Exterior. Back of the Building. Afternoon.

Patty Alden and George DeLarossa are detectives and they are
investigating Panda's death.

                    Patty
                    (*Knocking at the back door of the
                    building.*)
Did he say he was going to be here?

                    George
  Yup, he did.

                    Patty
                    (*Getting closer to the glass door.*)
It seems pretty empty in there.

                    George
Do you have his phone number? (On the cell
phone.) Hello? This is detective George DeLarossa,
we're standing outside your building, we don't see
much activity inside... Oh, you are? That would be
great. Yes, we'll wait here. (To Patty.) He's inside,
he's coming.

Jeremiah comes to the door.

                    Patty
You're Jeremiah…

                    Jeremiah
Yeah.

                    Patty
We are detectives George DeLarossa and Patty Alden. I
spoke to you on the phone yesterday. Is Mr. Gilman
around?

                    Jeremiah
No he's not, he threw-out his back and he's at home.
He did ask me to give you his number, in case there
is anything you would like to talk to him about.

                    George
That's fine. Can we come in?

                    Jeremiah
Sure…

A random sequence is extracted from the movie's database.

2. Interior. A large room in the 1ˢᵗ Floor. Afternoon.

George
I've always dreamt of a house like this. Can you
image having your bed in the middle of this room?
Right there, in the middle, nothing but a bed, with a
golden frame, and two side tables. Oh, come on.
Forget about your boxy apartment for a while. You can
put the bed there and then instead of television, you
can have a projector that will project all over that
wall. Sweet.

Patty
Then what, when you want to go to the bathroom you
have to wait for a charter bus?

George
You're no fun.

Patty
I'm not when you come up with your dumb ass ideas.

George
(Starting to walk.)
Ok, so what's the deal here?

Patty
(She opens her notebook and reads from it
while she walks.)
Jeremiah…

George
That's the guy that we just met…

Patty
(She nods while she is talking.)
Jeremiah, in combination with a few of his friends,
decides to put on a performance or something like
that, here in the building. The performance is
supposed to happen Sunday afternoon… so they rehearse
and set up equipment the day before.

George
But the performance never happens…

Patty
(Looking at him, somewhat perplexed
again.)
You're so insightful it gives me goose bumps. Once
inside the building, they tour around and then they
start rehearsing, in the middle of it some go here,
some go there; but Pandora stays in the auditorium
throughout the rehearsal.

                    George
Pandora? Pandora… Who is Pandora?

                    Patty
The deceased.

                    George
No, no, I mean… the other Pandora, the old Pandora…

                    Patty
I don't know. Am I supposed to know everything? After
rehearsal, they all start drinking and partying. This
girl Pandora didn't know these people, but she came
to the building because her friend Claudia invited
her. Jeremiah…

                    George
The guy we just met…

                    Patty
                    (*Once again she stares at him.*)
Jeremiah and one of his friends prepare a little
ghost telling party where he is planning to scare
everyone else with a set of props laid out inside the
building… That's when they hear a big bang in the
upper floor.

                    George
Pandora…

                    Patty
Yup.

                    George
I bet THAT scared the hell out of them.

                    Patty
Four of them have counseling appointments for next
week, one of them is under close supervision…

                    George
And that is?

                    Patty
Zacarias Meredith. I hate it when you come here as
the boss…

                    George
Hey, that's what happens when you go on vacation; you
have to catch me up with stuff.

                    Patty
At least try to change the tone of your questions,
you make it sound as if you were calling the shots.

> George
> Listen, that's the way I am... My job description
> doesn't say anything about the way I'm supposed to
> talk.

> Patty
> Whatever.

> George
> (*Changing the tone of his
> questions.*)
> Do you happen to know where she fell from?

> Patty
> The attic.

A random sequence is extracted from the movie's database.

3. Interior. Building's Attic. Night.

> George
> So. It's almost midnight...

> Patty
> About 10:30 at night.

> George
> Everybody is in a room downstairs scaring themselves
> out of this world and Pandora is up here by herself?

> Patty
> Yup. And if you think it's scary right now, keep in
> mind that for the little ghost trick, Jeremiah turned
> off all of the lights in the building.

> George
> Do you know what happened when they heard the girl
> fall?

> Patty
> They ran to this room below us and the janitor
> ordered everyone not to move and called the police...
> The guys arrived 6 minutes after the call and closed
> the area.

> George
> That's when they found the tramp in the room
> downstairs...

> Patty
> Yup. We can't detain him because we don't have enough
> evidence. Sure, you can charge him with trespassing
> and let him go with murder, so I've made a deal with
> the owner of the building to let the tramp stay for a

little longer inside the building and I'm taking him
out for coffee and donuts in a few days.

                    George
Yeah, that's smart, because it doesn't make sense…

A random sequence is extracted from the movie's database.

  3. Interior. Building's main entrance. Night.

                    George
Hello? We are about to leave! Hello?

                         Jeremiah
                         (Appearing from one of the corners
                         to the front door hallway.)
Over here.

                    Patty
Is it ok if we use the front door? We would like to
walk around the building.

                    Jeremiah
Sure, go ahead…

                    Patty
Do you mind if I ask you a question?

                    Jeremiah
Sure.

                    Patty
If you turn all the lights off in the building, would
you be able to know your way in the darkness.

                    Jeremiah
Yes you would, but it would pretty damn scary. I
wouldn't recommend it.

                    George
But it would be even scarier in the attic, right?

                    Jeremiah
Oh, yes. The attic, even with lights on, is scary…
Are you thinking that she was there with the lights
off? No, no, because the lights in the attic are
independent from the lights of the rest of the
building.

                    Patty
I see… Thank you very much. Here's my card. If you
think about anything that could help us out please
gives us a call (she hand a business card to
Jeremiah.)

                    Jeremiah

Sure I will.

A random sequence is extracted from the movie's database. Fade Out.

Doctor's lecture

Scene starts with random sequence extracted from the movie database.

    1.   Interior. Small amphitheater in a School of Medicine. Day.

> Students are waiting for the professor (Doctor) to arrive. Suddenly, the doors open, the doctor appears carrying several folders and a briefcase.

> Doctor
> (*At the desk.*)
> Good morning. Mental illnesses and creativity, is there any connection? Is it unprofessional of me to associate brilliance and madness? Today we are going to talk about a specific type of mental abnormality that is often associated with creativity: Temporal Lobe Epilepsy. The seizures that typify this form of epilepsy are not the type of seizures that we see on TV -the grand mal sort of seizures; these seizures occur here. Believe it or not, many decades ago, when medicine was still unclear about what was temporal lobe epilepsy and what was schizophrenia, the symptoms were attributed to (*reading from his notes and smiling evidently*) "violent discharges of gray matter" inside the brain.

A random sequence is extracted from the movie's database.

> Doctor
> And what were the symptoms of these violent discharges of gray matter? In other words, what are the symptoms of temporal lobe epilepsy? Well, one of the regular symptoms is what is commonly known as (*he writes it on the blackboard*) *déjà vu* -or "already seen" in French. It is quite probable that you all have experienced *déjà vu*; it is the sensation that you are living again what you have lived before. A "*déjà vu*" is caused by sudden electrical discharges in the area of the temporal lobe, discharges that trigger memories or a discharge that triggers a feeling of familiarity in us -even if we are not familiar with the situation at all. The illusion of *déjà vu*, but in a lot stronger fashion, is probably the most common symptom among temporal lobe epileptics. Related to the feeling of familiarity there is also what in French is known as (*he writes it on the blackboard*) "*jamais vu*" -or "never seen" in French. For example, I come home and everything seems the same as always; however, when I enter the bedroom I find a strange person in the bed. (*The class laughs.*) The pictures on the walls, the decoration, and the clothes that I threw on the floor the night before are still there and everything is known to me... But who is that person in bed that calmly drinks a cup of tea while reading an archeology digest?! Well, the person is my wife, and everything

219

indicates to me that she's my wife, but I don't
recognize her facial features.

A random sequence is extracted from the movie's database.

Doctor
Followed by "déjà vus" and "jamais vus," the list
continues with stronger types of hallucinations.
Temporal lobe epileptics often describe the smell of
burned plastic or the taste of a metal coin. It is
worthwhile mentioning that many of the smells
reported by temporal lobe epileptics are present in
folk stories about demonic apparitions… which brings
us to the auditory and visual hallucinations in
temporal lobe epileptics. Have you ever been walking
down the street and suddenly you hear that someone is
calling you? You turn around but no one is there.
These types of subtle auditory hallucinations are
being triggered by electrical discharges. Temporal
lobe epileptics suffer stronger auditory
hallucinations that can be as dramatic as voices
inside their heads. By the same token, the visual
hallucinations can reach extraordinary instances in
which walls melt and things change color.

A random sequence is extracted from the movie's database.

Doctor
More complex hallucinations are related to the event
of finding oneself in a different person; for
example, I see myself attending this lecture and
sitting over there. The visuals can become so
powerful that it is possible to ask a temporal lobe
epileptic to read from a blank page and he will.
Here, have the class' notes. Another symptom, now
that we are talking about the length of your notes,
is something called "hypergraphia". Temporal lobe
epileptics compulsively produce vast amounts of
written material, paintings, or other creative works.
Recently, I've been working with a homeless man, whom
I believe has temporal lobe epilepsy. I came across
him as part of my civic duty to collaborate with the
police force in understanding criminal behavior. This
person, who is a suspect in a murder case, believes
that the place where he finds shelter, an abandoned
building, contains or traps time in some way. His
visual hallucinations go from depictions of people
floating in the air in the middle of a room -every
room, to vast reproductions of past events that
occurred inside the building or that have happened to
the people who have stepped inside the building. The
building is one hundred years old, but his
hallucinations only relate to the last year or so.

A random sequence is extracted from the movie's database.

Doctor
This person has written most of his hallucinations in
journals, as a good temporal lobe epileptic he
suffers from hypergraphia; nevertheless, his
handwriting is illegible and he is the only person
who can read them. I have tried to convince him to
allow me to perform an electroencephalogram on him
without any success. I gave him a small dose of
Tegretol, a central nervous system suppressant, and
he ended up spending many hours a day in a catatonic
state. Furthermore, his hypergraphia decreased
totally, which became a factor in a subsequent
depression. What is important to notice from all of
this is that temporal lobe epilepsy is a condition
correlated with highly creative people, BUT the
creativity does not come as a skill to imagine things
or situations. Creativity comes as direct result of
what the individual actually sees, hears, and feels.
Creativity is just a reflection of the individual's
reality, a reality probably as valid as our own.

A random sequence is extracted from the movie's database. Fade Out.

Ghost Story

Scene starts with random sequence extracted from the movie database.

1. Interior. A room in the building. Night.

Jeremiah is guiding everyone into the room. As people get into the room they exclaim admiration for the candles on the floor. Everyone is a little bit drunk. Beverage is carrying a guitar and she is playing pieces of tunes. Panda looks pensive, she is staring at the candles. Claudia passes by and grabs her arm.

                    Claudia
        Are you ok?

                    Panda
        I am ok.

                    Claudia
        Are you sure?

                    Panda
        I am ok.

                    Claudia
        Are you angry with me?

Panda stares back indicating that she is not in the mood to establish a conversation.

                    Panda
        I have to go to the bathroom.

                    Claudia
        Can I go?

                    Panda
        No. Sit with Jeremiah and Rene, I'll be back.

                    Jeremiah
        Ok, everyone, remain in the circle I'll be back.

A random sequence is extracted from the movie's database.

Once they are all seated, Jeremiah leaves the room and runs downstairs to turn off the hallway lights of the entire building. Before returning he grabs a handheld battery lantern and walks back to the room in the second floor. When he enters the room, Beverage is singing a song.

                    Jeremiah
                    (Hushes everyone from singing.)
        Ok, boy and girls, let's get started. It is time for
        some good old-fashioned ghost stories…

                    Zak
        What is this ghost stories crap?

                    Jeremiah
They happened right here in this building.

                      Zak
And you still believe in tooth fairy…

                    Claudia
Actually, I still believe in the tooth fairy…

                     Rene
There is real story isn't it? Your uncle has some
newspaper clips of a guy that was ran over right here
in front of the building.

                    Claudia
Oh, no guys. You are giving me goose pumps…

                    Beverage
Let me tell you, I am more afraid of the living than
the dead.

                      Phil
What happened?

                    Jeremiah
Nobody knows for sure. My uncle didn't see that one;
but he got to know because of newspapers. Ira says
that you can hear heavy breathing at dawn, like if
someone was jogging inside the building at that time.

                    Claudia
Oh, no. I hate this. La-la-la-la-la-la. Bev, lets
sing…

A random sequence is extracted from the movie's database.

                      Zak
I cannot help to be but skeptical about this…
rubbish. Who wants to bet money that whatever you
guys talk about, we are going to leave empty handed.
Do you know for how long I've been trying to see a
ghost? When I was about 17, I went to a cemetery at
night and I pleaded, I begged, I invoked the forces
of evil, I cursed god in any possible manifestation…
What did I get?

                      Kirk
A cold.

                      Zak
Yup, a cold, no kidding, no bullshit. I got so sick
that I missed school for a week.

Julia
Something happened to me once.

Claudia
La-la-la-la-la-la-la-la-la…

Julia
It was at night, I was entering a highway and I was
looking through the mirror, suddenly I felt a strong
hit on my shoulder. I stopped the car, right there,
on the highway and I cried like a baby…

Zak
Oh, come on. I wanna believe as much as you do, but
that was not a ghost, that was your brain… I saw this
TV show once: They grabbed this guy, who experienced
a classic haunt 4 years ago, and they exposed him to
1 microTelsa, I'm not kidding, 1 microTelsa
transcerebral magnetic field.

Kirk
What is that? A micro-Tulsa?

Zak
I don't know either but that's what they call them.
After 10 minutes, just 10 minutes, the man reported
rushes of fear… And guess what? He ended up
experiencing an apparition. Da-da, that's it...

Julia
Oh, you're so… you say: "that's it," like if you were
giving an absolute truth in simple terms. Any
explanation of what caused the magnetic field during
the classic haunting? You see, what bothers me is
that just because you bumped into the scientific
research, presented by guys in white lab coats, in a
cheese TV show, everything is explained, everything
is perfect…

Zak
Not perfect, but close…

Julia
Zak, You don't even know what a microTelsa is…
Believing blindly in science doesn't make you any
better than someone who believes blindly in the Holy
Ghost.

A random sequence is extracted from the movie's database.

Jeremiah
Actually I have proof. A couple of years ago, I was
having really horrible nightmares. During that time I
had that big mess up with my folks and Ira let me
stay here, in the building. The nightmares continued

and I writing them down, I would just wake up and
scribble whatever I could before I would fall asleep
again After a while I got bored, so I bought a tape
recorder so now I could narrate them instead of
writing them. The nightmares continued. I was scared
to death. But then I noticed that the recorder had
something called Voice Activated System. So
essentially, you put the tape in and if there is a
noise it turns on, if it is silent it stays off. And
I think that the things I recorded are pretty damn
amazing. So you can apply your scientific verbiage
leave the recorder on and whenever there is a sound,
the machine picks it up, and then if there is silence
it turns itself off… Well, the things that I recorded
are just incredible. And I have it right here for
your rigorous examination.

A random sequence is extracted from the movie's database.

Jeremiah turns on the tape player and they start hearing noises of him
sleeping, snoring and moving around. Finally, normal sounds of the
building appear among Jeremiah's sleeping sounds. They all stare at
each other in total fear. Suddenly, a big hit on the upper floor, above
their heads, is heard. They all jump and scream. Finally, Jeremiah
picks up the lanterns and runs out of the room, everyone follows him
except for Rene, who remains sitting in shock. When they reach the
floor above, Jeremiah stops at the door. Claudia enters, screams, runs
towards Panda and kneels beside her.

                    Claudia
          Panda, baby, baby, talk to me, Panda? Call 911! Go,
          now, go! Oh, no, my baby. Please.

                    Janitor
                    (Entering the room.)
          Oh shit, oh shit. What's going in here!?

                    Jeremiah
          We were downstairs and we just heard the fall.

                    Janitor
                    (Reprimanding Jeremiah.)
          Oh, no, you must be shitting me! And what was she
          doing up there?

                    Jeremiah
          I don't know.

                    Janitor
          I am going to call the cops. Nobody leaves the
          building, understood? Oh, man. Shit. Shit!

225

The Janitor leaves the room. The face of Panda appears in a close up.
Then the scene jumps to the dinner. The tramp is emotional about what
he is narrating.

                              Tramp
                You see? There, that girl didn't die. I have two
                theories about it: one, the building (he makes a face
                simulating suction and makes a suction noise) the
                girl, or, or, the girl exploded and then the building
                as a whole held her, stopped her expansion… It is an
                extremely intense warp zone.

                              Detective
                Or maybe it is only inside your brain.

A random sequence is extracted from the movie's database. Fade Out.

226

In a maze

Scene starts with random sequence extracted from the movie database.

1. Exterior. Corn Maze. Day.

Claudia meets Pandora in a corn maze. Pandora is by herself. Claudia is
there with sister and her nephews.

                         Claudia
        Julian!? Clo!

Claudia spots Pandora and follows her hoping that any moment Pandora
will make a bad decision and arrive to a dead end.

                         Claudia
             Hi.

                         Panda
        Hello. (Beat.) Yeah?

                         Claudia
It's obvious I couldn't help noticing you, but I though that instead of
relying some corny hit line I would try a hit silence. (Pandora doesn't
know what to do.) Are you here by yourself?

                         Panda
        I came to be alone.

                         Claudia
        Alone here?

                         Panda
        I came to get lost.

                         Claudia
                         (Flirting.)
        You definitely chose the right place to do that?

                         Panda
        Are you alone?

                         Claudia
        I am here with my sister and my nephews. I can't find
        them… So, can I get lost with you?

                         Panda
        I don't know, I came to be alone.

                         Claudia
             I'm Claudia?

                         Panda
        Panda… Pandora.

                         Claudia
        You must get a lot of crap for having that name.

                    Panda
Yeah… I do.

                    Claudia
So what do you think may I tag along?

                    Panda
Alright.

A random sequence is extracted from the movie's
database.

                    Panda
Have you ever thought about telling a stranger
something very personal just because they are a
stranger?

                    Claudia
                    (Lying.)
Yeah, but I never done it.

                    Panda
My name is Pandora cause my mom didn't want me, but
she felt obligated to have me. You know there's some
people who don't know how to be parental? That's my
mom. She thinks I was some type punishment for
something that she did…

Straight cut to the moment in which Pandora's mom is telling the priest
that what she did she did so voluntarily. Return to Panda:

                    Panda
So I remained nameless for a while, and my mom
realized that coming to this world for something that
she did, and my staying her… (Stumbling) Under her
protection… her responsibility… was going to alter
her live in ways she didn't even expect, ways she
wouldn't want…

                    Claudia
                    (Offering an exit.)
And then she named you Pandora…

2. Interior. Claudia's apartment. Day.

She opens the street door and gets in. After dropping her things here
and there she grabs the phone.

                    Claudia
Dad? Hi dad, it's me? I have kinda strange question
to ask you: Do you know who Pandora is? Some type of
mystical figure. Oh.

A random sequence is extracted from the movie's database. Fade Out.

I ran out of Piggies

Theme 1

Scene starts with random sequence extracted from the movie database.

1. Exterior. Building's esplanade. Night.

> Isobel
> (Isobel looks pale and in
> discomfort.)
> Hello, Ira.

> Janitor
> Hello, kid. What are you doing here? You know we do
> the business around the back.

> Isobel
> I ran out of "piggies" (pills).

> Janitor
> I don't know…

> Isobel
> (Pulling out a bunch of bills.)
> I have money.

> Janitor
> Put that money in your pocket, kid. Hold the door
> (Janitor looks around). Get in.

A random sequence is extracted from the movie's database.

2. Interior. Building's Entrance. Night.

> Janitor
> I usually don't do this. I am doing you a favor here.
> Do you understand? I don't like kids to come any day
> at any time, you know? Are we clear on that? I have a
> life too. I don't know why I got to deal with this
> shit.

A random sequence is extracted from the movie's database.

> Isobel
> (Offering the money once again.)
> Please, I'll go right away.

> Janitor
> (Pulling a little plastic bag from
> a closet.)
> I only have this one here. I am going upstairs to get
> some more.

                                        Isobel
                        Wait! Can I have that one?

                                        Janitor
                        But it is a double "piggie"!

                                        Isobel
                        I'll have it!

                                        Janitor
                        I'll be back…

3. Interior. Janitor's office. Night.

                                        Janitor
                                        (After putting more pills in a film
                                        canister.)
                        Ernie, Ernie, pick up the phone… Shit.

4. Interioir. Building's basement. Night.

When the Janitor returns, he finds her lying on the floor. Her shirt is
slightly unbuttoned, just enough for her bra to show. The Janitor gets
closer.

                                        Janitor
                        Oh, my, my… A full size "piggie," and what do we have
                        here? Relax… (Isobel retreats, she is somewhat
                        sleeping but aware.) I didn't touch you. I didn't.
                        Why would I like to touch a "piggie"? So where is
                        that other "piggie"? Should we find the other
                        "piggie"?

Fade out. A random sequence is extracted from the movie's database.

5. Interior. Building's basement. Night.

Isobel is lying asleep on the floor of the basement with her skirt up
to the level of her crotch and her blouse is out of her skirt. When she
wakes up she realizes that her skirt is up and she starts to cover
herself frantically. She breathes heavily. She doesn't know if the
janitor has raped her.

Theme 2

1. Interior. Janitor's office. Day.

The janitor is in his office sitting in front of the desk. He is having
a conversation with Ernie -a prescription drug dealer.

                    Janitor
Why do you think that I know about this shit? Aspirin
is all I have ever taken…

                    Ernie
Do you have a pen?

                    Janitor
I do have a pen, what do you want?

                    Ernie
Write this down.

                    Janitor
Write what down?

                    Ernie
Grab a pen a write this down…

                    Janitor
Ok, what?

                    Ernie
Florazepam.

                    Janitor
Oh, no. Put a god damn list on the mail…

                    Ernie
                    (Spelling Florazepam.)
F-l-o-r-a-z-e-p-a-m... Alprasolam... A-l-p-r-a-s-o-l-
a-m... Diazepam... D-i-a-z-e-p-a-m... Bromazepan...

                    Janitor
Oh, you must be kidding me... How many are you going
to give me? Why can't you just put a list on the
mail…

                    Ernie
Ira, are you in or are you out?

                    Janitor
I am in, but this is like a damn spelling contest.

                    Ernie
Bromazepan… B-r-o-m-a-z-e-p-a-n... Those are downers.

                    Janitor
Does anybody smoke pot any more?

                    Ernie
Ritalin… R-i-t-a-l-i-n... Dexedrin... D-e-x-e-d-r-i-
n... Efedrin... E-f-e-d-r-i-n... Those are
amphetamines.

                    Janitor
And how much are these for?

                    Ernie
Around $40 a canister.

                    Janitor
Ok, what else?

                    Ernie
Effexor… Effexor… Celexa… Celexa… Paxil… Paxil…
Elavil… Elavil… Zoloft… Zoloft… Welbutrin… Welbutrin…
Prozac… Prozac…

                    Janitor
                    (Trying to make a joke.)
With this we could kill a cow…

                    Ernie
I'll give a $2000 batch to try you out. Is that ok?

                    Janitor
Ok.

A random sequence is extracted from the movie's database. Fade Out.

Jess and Rogan PostMortem

Scene starts with random sequence extracted from the movie database.

1. Interior. Room where Pandora died. Day.

Jess and Rogan are standing staring up at the hole in the skylight. They hug.

>   Rogan
>   I gotta go upstairs. I have to…

>   Jess
>   (Almost in shock, crying.)
>   No.

>   Rogan
>   Stay here, wait here…

A random sequence is extracted from the movie's database.

>   Rogan
>   Stay here.

Rogan turns around a walks away. Jess runs after him and grabs his arm. They walk together towards the Attic. They both climb to the upper part, where the skylight is. They separate. Rogan stares at the skylight. Jess cries at a distance.

A random sequence is extracted from the movie's database.

>   Jess
>   I wanna go home. Rogan: I want to go home.

A random sequence is extracted from the movie's database. Fade Out.

Love Discussion

1. Interior. House. Night.

Theme 1

Panda is reading a website in the lower part of the house. The
fireplace is lit. Jess and Trevor (her current date) enter the house
and the living room. Panda doesn't pay attention to them. They take off
their coats and they place them above the piano stool. Trevor
approaches the fireplace and Jess approaches Panda.

> Jess
>
> Hi, baby. What are you doing?

> Panda
> (Reading from the screen.)
> Listen to this crap: "The Russian economy is in a
> horrible situation, Russian male expectancy is only
> 56, the women from Russia are beautiful, intelligent,
> and loyal. (Panda scrolls down the web page and then
> reads another fragment.) The average monthly income
> in Russia is 200 dollars, they all live in small
> crowded apartments, and their living standards are
> far below what we have here in the US".

> Trevor
>
> What is that?

> Panda
> It's a damn website that advertises Russian females
> to American males, and I… (She is son angry that she
> stops talking and gives a small-internalized scream.)

> Trevor
>
> Yes, I have seen those. They are quite popular now.

> Panda
> The arguments just make me sick! You the wealthy
> American should go find yourself a Russian princess
> that lives in poverty. Listen to the way they present
> their sales pitch, in the question and answers
> section it says Here it is: "The Russian women are
> beautiful, but I am average looking, why would they
> want to meet me?" You know what the answer is?
> "Russian women like inner qualities," like what? Like
> your income, which is way higher than that of the
> Russians.

> Jess
> (Reading from the website.)
> Oh, no… "Looks don't matter to this beautiful
> creatures". So not having purchasing power makes you
> tasteless, huh?

Panda
(Scrolling.)
Read this, when questioned about the loyalty of those
beautiful creatures…

Jess
Why would you question it? Aren't they perfect when
acquired?

Panda
(Pointing somewhere in the screen.)
Here…

Jess
(Reading from the screen.)
"How loyal would they be? They are leaving their home
to a place thousands and thousands of miles away from
family and friends." Oh, that is just sick…

Trevor
(Sitting in the sofa in front of
the fireplace.)
Well, the thing is that these services are starting
to be quite popular…

Jess
Oh, it must strike you as extraordinary. I know it
does.

Trevor
I agree, it is extraordinary, but it seems like a
logical step…

Jess
Don't you think it's lame? Trevor, this is an ad for
humans, and what it is worse is that they use the
argument of love to sell… basically, they are saying
that the product will love you as part of the sales
pitch.

Panda
Listen to this, they even offer government visas for
the girl to come to the US fro 90 days to test her
out, if you are "incompatible" she goes back.

Trevor
Look, I don't mean offend you, but it has happened
throughout history… think about it as a modern form
of prostitution, people get lonely, people find ways
to be with someone not using love but cash as the
means to get it.

Jess
What?! Listen, go outside, stick your head in the
snow for half an hour and come back.

                              Trevor
              Babe, come on, it is such a cliché by this time to
              say that prostitution is one of the oldest
              professions…

Rogan steps into the living room and notices the discussion. He remains
under the threshold quite surprised by the fight attitude of Panda and
Jess. He is carrying a Gimmlet.

                              Jess
              You are really confused.

                              Trevor
              Hey, slow down, you are taking this too personally.

                              Jess
              Slow down? You just believe that trading sex is
              trading love, and I won't put any value judgment to
              the trading of sex, but trading love? It goes down to
              the inner bones of commercializing everything.

                              Rogan
              I don't what you are talking about, but if I can give
              my two cents on it, commercializing love is a big
              deal now.

                              Panda
              Rogan?

                              Rogan
              What do you think that those dating services on the
              web are all about? Ask people to separate themselves
              by variables… and the sad thing is that they do: sex,
              height, hair color, education, the goods (moving his
              hand in front of his chest as if he were delineating
              imaginary breasts), drinking, drugs, race… And then
              they select each other by choosing those variables,
              as if humans were nothing but a collection of pieces.

                              Trevor
              And what is the problem with that?

                              Rogan
              Well, it follows the idea that you can find love by
              reading the package.

                              Panda
              It is just an ugly extension of product-oriented
              marketing to people…

                              Trevor
              Ok, let me ask it again: And what is the problem of
              doing that?

                              Jess
              That people are not products, dumb ass…

                    Trevor
Careful…

                    Jess
Careful with what?

                    Rogan
There is a problem, it is innocuous. What happens
today in politics? You have these bozos reading the
surveys and pondering what is the most attractive
position to attract that biggest number of votes.
Depending on what corporate pressures they have, they
take this and drop that to keep the majority in their
pocket, right? Well, that's why we end up with
android-like candidates… and it doesn't matter how
many speeches they give, they always seem fake, not
human… something is very awkward about them. Do you
get my point?

Rogan sips from his drink a little bit, Panda smiles gently at him.

                    Panda
What the hell… We're talking about love here and you
are talking about android politicians?

                    Rogan
That's exactly what I am talking about. These
politicians change to fit the market and there's
nothing left of the human.

                    Jess
And prostitution might be the oldest profession, but
this a current trend, the system promotes ever
lonelier but successful entrepreneurs, these little
laborious units of production with huge dreams but
not a lot time to seek for the right person.

                    Panda
Feed the machine…

                    Trevor
                    (Standing up, agitated.)
Oh, my god, this is so sixties, this is so absolutely
sixties. Now the next thing is to smoke a joint, run
naked on the streets and have wild orgies…

                    Rogan
That's part of the problem, falling into extremes.
You don't have to become a pot smoker and have orgies
to stop being the ever-working ever-pushing employee.
There is a big gray zone in the middle.

                    Trevor
Ok, you want to pick up a fight? Want to talk about
love? There is no single proof that human feelings -
love, jealousy, loyalty, are nothing more than what

nature has forced us to do to prevail, not to perish
as a species. All of these feelings are hardwired
directly to our hypothalamus (points the back of his
neck). You are giving a sermon on the metaphysics of
love. That's your problem. You don't see that love is
nothing more than what we feel in order to keep the
species alive.

                    Jess
          Oh, you are such an idiot.

The theme stops to Panda and Rogan listening how Jess is fighting with
Trevor in the kitchen.

                    Panda
          I don't know if we did wrong or right by attacking
          him like that…

                    Rogan
          It's ok.

2. Interior. House. Late night.

Theme 2

Panda and Jess are sitting in Panda's bed. The conversation between the
two of them started not too long ago. They are talking about what
happened with Trevor. Jess is crying.

                    Panda
          Are you ok?

                    Jess
          I don't even want to talk about it, it's just another
          variation to the same story.

                    Panda
          I'm sorry, Jess.

                    Jess
          I'm not. You know what is terrible about it?

                    Panda
          What?

                    Jess
          That I am just about to quit relationships for good.
          I am so tired of the same old process. What I like,
          what I dislike, this and that that happened to me
          when I was a kid, I believe this, I believe that.
          Then starting, big hopes, perfection, my entire life

projected into the future, all the role playing, making the image fit…

                    Panda
I know.

                    Jess
The ass hole even talked to me about kids. Oh! He mentioned love as he had never felt it before and he mentioned marriage, and other stupid things. And then, you saw it, the exact same path again, with a little more or a little less pebbles than before: You end up with an ass hole that has learned the rhetoric to get himself laid. So what does it matter to have it deconstructed, you know? Who cares exactly what happened? Leave that to first lovers, teenagers, coffee shops, I don't know. I'm just so tired.

                    Panda
There is going to be someone out there, you know? Don't give up, it is foolish.

                    Jess
You don't give up. I don't have any strength left. Now when I start flirting again, I can't stop myself from feeling such apathy… not just towards the person in front of me but the entire situation. It's just senseless.

                    Panda
Come on. Things can be bad, but not helpless… That's why what we do makes sense.

                    Jess
I just look at this little cute guy making all his little cute faces at once and I just feel totally asexual, you know? It just kills me to go through all that rubbish again. And even more, at the beginning I thought that it was just a tough battle, you had to pay the price to get the right one, find the right one. There is no single good one… I'm sorry. I am going to stop.

3. Exterior. Outside Jess' house. Night.

Theme 3

Trevor steps out of his car, looks at a window of the house across the street, pulls out a cell phone and makes a call. Jess answers inside the house.

             Jess
Hello? Hello?

Jess looks out the window, sees Trevor outside and she closes the blinds.

          Trevor
        (Now screaming from the street.)
Jess! Jess!

          Jess
        (On the phone.)
He is stalking me, he is stalking me, he is out there right now. No, just like before! I am just sick of this bullshit, what am I supposed to do? I'll talk to you tomorrow ok? No, I'll talk to you tomorrow. Fine, fine, goodbye.

          Trevor
        (At the door of the house.)
Jess, I know you can hear me. Open the door. Open the god damn door. I know you can hear me. Open the door!

Jess storms towards a closet and pulls out a bat. Then she walks down the stairs and confronts Trevor.

240

Music for the Rants

Scene starts with random sequence extracted from the movie database.

1. Interior. House dinning room. Day.

Panda is in the dinning room. She has the velvet spread out over the table and she is taking photographs of little pieces of sculptures that she made. Jess is crossing the backyard towards the house, she is walking happily. She opens the kitchen door and the bells chime.

                            Panda
Rogan?

                            Jess
No, it's me… Hi!

                            Panda
Hi!

                            Jess
What's this for?

                            Panda
It is there so the cats don't get to this side of the house. One of the people that I am house-sitting for has an allergy to cats.

                            Jess
Are you too busy?

                            Panda
It's fine. I'm taking some photographs for the website, I think it is too plain… flavorless…

                            Jess
Wait, let me get some ice tea.

                            Panda
I'm competing against a lot of very flashy stuff on the web…

Jess goes to the kitchen. Fills her glass with ice tea, picks up her backpack and then walks around the house towards the dinning room. When Jess enters the dinning room Panda starts talking.

                            Panda
I've decided to give the rants an ad-like feel.

                            Jess
What?

A random sequence is extracted from the movie's database.

                    Panda
I think the problem with my rants is that they are
too textual. I'm targeting people who spend more time
watching ads than reading, so I've got to make them
look like ads even if they say something totally
different…

                    Jess
That would be a good contrast. Actually… this is a
nice introduction for what I wanted to talk to you
about… I took this without telling you, I hope you
don't mind.

                    Panda
It's ok, they're out in the public now anyway…

                    Jess
I did something else, I also thought that the rants
needed an extra push so… (She looks again inside the
backpack and pulls out a mini disk player.) There are
20 tracks, I like them all, but you don't have to use
them if you don't want to.

Panda takes the minidisk player, puts on the headphones and starts
listening. She hears the first rant put into music and she stares
angrily towards Jess.

                    Jess
I can explain…

Panda closes her eyes. She changes the track again a couple of times
and stands up abruptly a leaves the dinning room towards the kitchen
and then towards the backyard.

A random sequence is extracted from the movie's database.

                    Jess
                    (Looking through the windows
                    towards the yard.)
Rog, no, I've already done that… yes, no, well let me
put it this way, I still don't know if she loves me
or if she hates me.

Panda sits down on the swing. Slowly she changes from being concerned
to being entertained by the music. A random sequence is extracted from
the movie's database. Fade Out.

Panda and Rogan Asymptote

Scene starts with random sequence extracted from the movie database.

1. Interior. Laundry room at the house. Day.

              Rogan
So, what you've been up to?

              Panda
            (Doing laundry.)
Well, I went to the doctor yesterday and I told him
about my wrist problems and my changes in mood: How
one day I could be enthusiastic about my projects,
about my life, and some other day, or maybe the same,
drop in to this awful depression.

              Rogan
What did she tell you?

              Panda
What did he tell me?

              Rogan
He…

              Panda
Well, he said that the numbness in my fingers was
from spending too many hours at the computer; it
seems that I have joined the carpal tunnel club, so
he just gave some thing to wear on my hand while I
type. About the mood changes, he didn't give a shit
about my family propensity for hypoglycemia; he said
that I was bipolar and that he didn't treat mental
illnesses.

              Rogan
            (Helping Pandora.)
Wow. He said that? Just after 5 minutes? Way to go,
doctor…

              Panda
Yup.

              Rogan
You know, my grandmother has a theory for that.

              Panda
For what?

              Rogan
For those ups and downs you are having. One day, I
was about 16 at the time, she said to my face, really
straightforward: "Happiness doesn't exist".

                    Panda
Way to go grandma!

                    Rogan
Well, she put it this way. She said that life is
composed of a cycle of happiness and sadness that
always ends up being evened out. Very strong moments
of happiness will be paid with very strong moments of
sadness. So according to her, life is just a
manifestation of this process in which we are
overpaid with either happiness or sadness and at the
end we have to pay back. It's a big cycle.

A random sequence is extracted from the movie's database.

                    Rogan
Do you remember what I told you about my first
serious group of poems?

                    Panda
Remind me…

                    Rogan
The poems about mathematics?

                    Panda
Oh, yes, I remember. You brought that up at Jess' the
other day. You are such a dork.

                    Rogan
Well, the idea for making a series of poems about
math came from my grandma's concept of life. If
happiness and sadness fluctuate like that, then what
is life but a sine or a cosine function? Happiness,
sadness, happiness, sadness… And if you are bipolar,
or even bipolar but you have big mood swings, instead
of having a normal range you have these very big
highs contrasted with very big lows. So, it is a sine
or a cosine function with a multiplier larger than 1.
So happy, so sad, so happy, so sad… Those that cannot
deal with the roller coaster, what do they do? They
take antidepressants. An antidepressant just keeps
the multiplier somewhere between zero and one. The
result is a very neutral non-extremist life, very
close to the axis, very, to my taste, flavorless…

                    Panda
I really admire you.

                    Rogan
                (In a monologue, not really
                listening to Pandora.)
Well, if you analyze it a bit further, the cycles are
not identical. You can have a very strong moment of
sadness which will be paid with a very long but light
moment of happiness. So, basically what you have to

do is multiply intensity by time; how happy for how
long, how happy for how long…

A random sequence is extracted from the movie's database.

                         Panda
It doesn't work like that for me. It really doesn't.
I don't have any big theories. I just vomit to
provoke people, and the web is a medium custom-made
for all of my diatribes… Don't you think that we are
going at great speed? Everything is changing so fast.
Technology, relationships, capitalism, the
environment, it is like we are mounted in this car
that is moving at 200 miles an hour…

                         Rogan
Per hour…

                         Panda
And we all are blindfolded. A couple of years ago I
was extremely pissed at the idea of playing with
genes, and suddenly, out of nowhere, a sheep got
duplicated. Well, that scandal is gone. Today, just a
couple of years later, rich assholes are paying to
have their pets duplicated, artists are making glow
in the dark bunny rabbits, genetics are being
targeted to reconstruct tissue, and now I've even saw
a TV program where all the rhetoric floated around
the idea of improving human beings through genetics.
And now some group wants to get away with the cloning
of a human being.

A random sequence is extracted from the movie's database.

                         Rogan
What gets you so angry about that? Not that
I disagree, I just want to hear it.

                         Panda
My problem with genetics has nothing to do with the
issue of genetics itself. For god's sake, we don't
even know for sure the origin of life and we are
screwing around with genes in order to duplicate
living creatures… and we plan on improving ourselves
by tweaking the genetic code! So, I don't know if it
is right or wrong, but that is precisely my point. A
few years ago the debate began because someone
started experimenting with it, now, just a very brief
period of time afterwards, bang, changes have already
taken place. Don't you think that this issue should
be brought up in a large forum? Maybe the UN, a large
global forum that specially deals with this type of
issues. Cloning a human has become a competition for
a few to find a place in history. And genetics is
just one of the things, everything is moving as if we
were in a race against time… So, my main problem is

not the issue itself, but the speed at which we are
going.

> Rogan
> (Ironically.)
> So what is there to do about it?

> Panda
> What is there to do about it? Do you think that I am
> going to change something? Do you think my little
> animations on the web work at all?

> Rogan
> Why not?

> Panda
> How many times have you seen in the movies the theme
> of corporate life as an empty life, as a life without
> meaning, everyone living in a void from 9 to 5 on a
> daily basis? People go to the movies, watch that
> crap, consider it for half a second and then they go
> back, to do the exact same thing. They all are so
> alienated that for them it is only entertainment,
> nothing else, they agree with the discourse because
> they comply with their roles as moviegoers;
> everything is washed out by the time they wake up the
> morning after…

A random sequence is extracted from the movie's database.

> Rogan
> You know? I have a poem like that.

> Panda
> (Angry.)
> Oh, yeah! Like what?

> Rogan
> One of those poems about math. It simply says that
> the history of mankind resembles an exponential curve
> with an asymptote.

> Panda
> What is that?

> Rogan
> It is a curve like this… (Using magnets on the
> basement refrigerator.) Like this… There is a very
> long time of slow advance, you can think of it as all
> the time that it has taken us to go from tribal, to
> feudal, to the industrial revolution, etc. until the
> moment in which we are now, which it might be here or
> here or here, I don't know. The fascinating part of
> it is that the more you move to the right the faster
> you go. I won't go into many details…

                              Panda
          That would be nice.

                              Rogan
          I have to explain… The derivative of…

                              Panda
          No, stop, do you think that I know what are
          you talking about?

                              Rogan
          Listen, the derivative of this curve at this point is
          this… The derivative is the acceleration of the curve
          at that point. The more we move to the right, the
          more the acceleration increases, we go faster and
          faster and faster. But the most important thing about
          this curve, is that it never goes further than a
          specific X… At which we have this imaginary line,
          which is an asymptote. The curve accelerates and
          accelerates and it goes faster and faster up but it
          never touches this line, it never gets there…
          Technology is like that. A hundred years over here
          meant nothing in terms of technological advance, if
          you move here a hundred years mean a lot. And now
          that computers have evolved and we have artificial
          intelligence we are going to have the speed of this
          advance increasing enormously.

                              Panda
                              (Now, very interested in what Rogan
                              is saying.)
          What does it mean? What is that line?

                              Rogan
          I don't know. I would be rich if I knew. For a
          pessimist it could be dooms day, for an optimist it
          could be the moment in which we reach total
          understanding and an ultimate state of being. But
          this part, the part in which we are accelerating,
          that seems to be right on. I don't know if we are
          here, or here, or here… And the asymptote could exist
          in the year three thousand or before or after…

Panda Points to a place in the curve where the derivative has a high
slope.

                              Panda
          Here…

                              Rogan
          I don't know, but it seems that technological advance
          only pushes more technological advance.

                              Panda
          That's amazing, that's just incredible… It
          makes so much sense.

                        Rogan
Still, if it is true, I really don't think that you
or me can do anything about it. Even if we devote our
entire lives to that sole cause I don't think that we
can stop what is about to happen.

                        Rogan
                      (Voice-over.)
It keeps accelerating and accelerating and it never
gets there…

A random sequence is extracted from the movie's database. Fade to
black.

Panda and Prof. Tafford

Scene starts with random sequence extracted from the movie database.

1. Interior. Prof. Tafford's office. Day.

Theme 1

Panda appears sitting by herself in professor Tafford's office.

> Professor Tafford
> (Entering the room.)
> Sorry about that.

> Panda
> It's ok. What's up?

> Professor Tafford
> I'm just processing what Esther was telling me.

> Panda
> And what was that?

> Professor Tafford
> Well, I am asking for recommendations for my next job… She said that I should be careful who I ask.

> Panda
> Why?

> Professor Tafford
> Because some of the people I ask might be too truthful about me.

> Panda
> What is that supposed to mean?

> Professor Tafford
> Well, I have me conscience clear, so it doesn't matter that much… But when I asked what she meant with that… she said something that has me totally bewildered.

> Panda
> And you are going to tell me.

> Professor Tafford
> She said (imitating the colleague): "For example, some people might say that maybe you get too personal with your students," and that is just disturbing… Is there any problem with getting too personal with students?

                    Panda
Be careful, you are supposed to deposit your
knowledge by surgical methods.

                Professor Tafford
You are funny.

                    Panda
But wait, you shouldn't talk to the units of
production.

                Professor Tafford
You see, that is my point.

A random sequence is extracted from the movie's database.

                Professor Tafford
If I have something to show to my students it is that
you should question everything, everything. Knowledge
is a sand storm. You would be surprised about how
much of what we know in the social sciences is based
on things that we have only just agreed upon.

                    Panda
Well, at least someone tells the truth around here…

                Professor Tafford
Who discovered America?

                    Panda
What? Christopher Columbus.

                Professor Tafford
No. If you ask a Canadian, he would probably answer
that the Vikings were the ones who discovered
America, and if you ask some scholars in Mexico, they
might say that Asians were the first ones… The
Beiring stretch could have been crossed by primitive
people a long time ago, the racial and linguistic
similarities between Asians and indigenous Mexicans
is astonishing… So, does it matter that much? Yes, if
you are taught that a truth is absolute when it is
not.

A random sequence is extracted from the movie's database.

                Professor Tafford
                 (Out of nowhere.)
What's the origin of life?

                    Panda
I don't understand.

                Professor Tafford
Well, so many scientists agree that the origin of
life was this weird combination of proteins that

occurred at some point in the history of earth. You've seen the movie right? What… in fifth grade science class or on a PBS nature special? Super-cool animation about the origins of life, showing this lava-like pond with bubbles, everything in tones of ochre and reds and yellows… and the voiceover explaining: "suddenly, out of a chemical reaction… life". Just like that. Have you heard of any experiment in any part of the world by any scientist that has actually replicated this process? Has it ever been done? By anyone, anywhere… No! But it is already accepted as the truth by so many because it follows a quasi-deductive line of thought, which makes one believe it is scientific. And if it is scientific, for god's sake, it must be true!

A random sequence is extracted from the movie's database.

Professor Tafford
And those are the worst kind.

Panda
Who are the worst kind?

Professor Tafford
I call them religious scientists, the ones that dig into anything because there is some scientific undertone to whatever is being said, and that is so true of the social sciences. If you are a true scientist, if you are strict, if you do not allow any flaws in your rationale… very few things hold true. And while there are some of my colleagues here that would be anal for months about the mathematical details of a research project, nobody poses a question about the gap that the operationalization of variables creates.

Panda
I'm not sure what you mean by that.

Professor Tafford
The process that you have to go through if you want to translate real life into variables. How do you measure "apathy"? Think about it. Believe it or not, there are some researchers who would spend years on the details of the mathematical part of the research while disregarding totally, totally… the fact that they are not actually measuring apathy but what they have defined narrowly as "apathy," an infinitesimal portion of what they, in their limited capacity can only begin to understand. And then they base their generalizations on this scientific process and call it truth. You get my point…

A random sequence is extracted from the movie's database.

                    Professor Tafford
And then again, be careful to talk like this to
students… you might be "getting too personal". That
is a way of saying "we don't like your way of
thinking". You see, I am a threat to the status quo…

                    Panda
That's appalling. So they cannot hush you directly
because they would be censoring you, but there is a
lot of pressure for you not to speak out about your
ideas…

                    Professor Tafford
And only that, pressure if you are weak, pressure if
you need to keep your job at all costs, pressure if
you worry about being accepted as a means to accept
yourself. However, the better you are at what you do
the more space they will give you to dissent. So the
moral is: question everything, Panda, because
everything can be questioned. As in fashion,
scientists follow trends, but the trends last for
decades. So question everything and get ready to get
some ugly feedback. You will be threatening many who
have found a warm comfortable position at the expense
of others or at the expense of promoting a dull
existence, but at least you will have your conscience
clear.

2. Interior. Panda's house. Day.

Theme 2

Panda is working on a rant for the Internet. She is dancing around the
house third floor with her pajama shirt open; she is happy and
enthusiastic about the bitterness of her rant. Telephone rings.

                    Panda
                    (With her mouth with toothpaste.)
        Hello…

                    Jess
        Panda?

                    Panda
Hang on. (She spits.) Hi, sorry. I was brushing my
teeth.

                    Jess
        I am sorry.

                    Panda
It's ok, I am kicking ass big time.

                    Jess
        I am glad, baby.

252

                         Panda
          You should see what I am working on, oh my god, it's
          so offensive. Can I read it to you?

          A random sequence is extracted from the movie's
          database.

                         Panda
          Where are you? It will take me 30 seconds…

                         Jess
          Panda, baby, sit down. I have bad news.

                         Panda
          What?

                         Jess
          Panda, Tafford died this morning in a car accident?

                         Panda
          What?

                         Jess
          I am so sorry.

          A random sequence is extracted from the movie's database. Fade Out.

Panda meets Beverage

Scene starts with random sequence extracted from the movie database.

1. Interior. A room in the building. Day.

Panda and Bev bump into each other at some point. Bev excuses herself and starts walking away, and then Panda stops her.

                              Bev
            Have you seen Julia?

                              Panda
            No. Listen, Bev… That song that you sang, the second
            one… It is really good.

                              Bev
            Thank you. I make them for people like you… At least
            someone hears them.

                              Panda
            I am the author of the poem you used for the lyrics.

                              Bev
            I cannot believe it. Do you live here in town?

                              Panda
            Yes.

                              Bev
            I've tried to get in touch with you, but you never
            answered my emails.

                              Panda
            I'm sorry. I can't read them anymore. There are just
            too many, and sometimes I don't get very good
            responses.

                              Bev
            That cannot be true, your work is so ingenious, it's
            so overt, it's… I identify totally with it.

                              Panda
            I am glad to hear that. Well, you made them sound
            alive…

                              Bev
            I can't believe that we've been living in the same
            city.

                              Panda
            Feel free to use any of it anytime.

                         Bev
                (While hugging Panda.)
        You are offering me gold, darling.

                       Panda
It is hard to find someone that is not into the main
stream, and it just doesn't make a lot of sense to me
you know?

A random sequence is extracted from the movie's database.

                       Panda
Do you know how long I've been doing this? Two and a
half years. It started as a rant and now it has
become an obsession Now, I am pushing so hard, so
often, that I am starting to lose ground. Do you feel
something like that?

                       Bev
No, not really.

                       Panda
Oh, it is exhausting. I don't know if my work is
affecting me too much. Everything has started to move
very fast, I starting working and suddenly time just
flies by, it feels literally like time is speeding
up, the clocks speed up, the sunrises and sunsets
occur in a matter of seconds… But at least I believe
in what I am doing.

                       Bev
You shouldn't sacrifice yourself so much for the
cause that you lose your own life, going so far
radical that you come back around right again. It is
like you become that which you despise... Do you see
what I mean? Think about tolerance and what that can
accomplish. Why turn the whole world off? You can't
get anywhere that way; you just end up pissing people
off.

                       Panda
I think pissing people off doesn't bother me at all.
Quite the opposite, I believe we need to give
everyone a good shake and wake ourselves up from this
dream. We are just going way too fast.

                       Bev
                (Engaging in a somewhat drunken
                soliloquy.)
What's more, your own life begins to suffer, there is
no way you can live up to those expectations.

A random sequence is extracted from the movie's database.

                    Bev
You can never be entirely true to your own cause...
and you can kill yourself trying. Why create for
yourself a world you can never live up to? Don't get
me wrong I feel very strongly about certain issues
myself, and I guess you can see that in my work… our
work I should say. I still drive my car and pollute
the air, I still buy clothes at the local mall, I
still eat food and have no idea where it comes from.
I can chose to adjust my lifestyle to certain degree,
in hopes that it will have an effect, but chances are
I will die and never see the effect my words have
had.

                    Panda
I am not sacrificing myself for the cause, that's
just the way I am, I can't do anything but what I do…

                    Bev
                (Not listening.)
And it sucks! I'll be the first to admit it… But I
won't throw my hands up in the air and say, "Ah what
can you do?" I'm not going to starve myself, or live
in a tree for a month only to be killed by some
corporate logger.

                    Panda
I think I made myself misunderstood…

                    Bev
No, no, no. Think about what a long life could do.
Look at Pete Seeger... he's still singing and making
an impact. Kurt Cobain? Dead, dead, dead, and what
can we learn from him anymore? A voice of our
generation, completely gone.

A random sequence is extracted from the movie's database.

                    Bev
You see what I mean. It is the same idea as your love
poem: You say we don't know how too love for long,
well my contribution is that we don't know how to
fight for long. I not gonna go down into that room
with all those ass holes and the keg, and get knocked
out in the first round. I am gonna cause pressure
with time; pure, stable pressure.

                    Panda
Beverly, it feels like you are lecturing me.

                    Bev
I have grown wise and sexy, and I am going to
outsmart all this bastards. Come on, lets go get a
drink.

                    Panda
          Oh no, Beverly I …

                    Bev
          Beverly? Where did you get that name?

                    Panda
          Then what does Bev stand for?

                    Bev
                    (Strong French accent.)
          Beverage.

A random sequence is extracted from the movie's database. Fade out.

257

Community Access Channel

Scene starts with random sequence extracted from the movie database.

1. Interior. Panda's house. Day.

Panda is in the office room in the house. She has been working all day long.

> Panda
> (Whispering.)
> I am so burned out.

She looks at the computer to her right. The computer shows an on going rendering process. Then she looks behind her at the Macintosh. That computer also shows a rendering process. Finally, she looks at the computer next to the Macintosh. It is doing nothing. She stands up, heads to the TV room and turns on the TV. The real estate Gems Ad is on TV.

> Panda
> Let's see how you want me to understand the world today.

> Kathy Long (TV)
> This beautiful building is a four story construction with an overall "unusable" space of 168,000 gross square feet. A varied set of materials give a sense of belonging. Its uniqueness lies in a fluid transition from a stone and concrete solid foundation, brick and concrete perimeter walls, to steal and wood beams, to incredible floor decks, to ceramic tiles, terrazzo, marble and glass panels. The roof consists of shingles, tar, felt and gravel, in a wisely distributed flat and pitched styled construction.

A random sequence is extracted from the movie's database.

> Kathy Long (TV)
> Its construction started in the early 1900s and was finished a couple of years later. When walking around the hallways, one might find intriguing the interior windows that face the auditorium walls. The auditorium was constructed three decades later and became the largest auditorium in Eastern US until the mid century. Great plays, great voices and great musicians used this wonderful space as their inspiration. Every time that I visit this beautiful landmark I cannot help myself from going to the Attic…

She appears in the attic. In the room where there is only one circular window. While she talks, the upper part of a building with a light bulb clock appears through one of the circular windows of the attic. Even though the anchor speaks at regular speed, the clock at the top of the building is going extremely fast. Panda sits up widening her eyes in surprise.

                    Panda
          Oh, my god.

A closer shot of the circled window shows the clock speeding, minute after minute drift away as hundreds of a second.

                    Kathy Long
                    (In the background.)
          This building speaks through its walls. Its
          authoritative layout, turns, ceilings, beams, say to
          whomever lays eyes on it, that it is here to stay
          (the shot changes to the building's facade), it is
          here to show that Beaux Arts are an inherent part of
          our society and we are able to reflect that in our
          constructions. Time, strength, and beauty are values
          that a recognized by everyone and are proudly
          presented here… In Real Estate Gems.

                    Panda
                    (To herself.)
          I can't believe this… (She grabs the phone and dials
          Claudia.) Come on, Claudia, pick up the phone… (She
          hears an answering machine.) Damn! (She waits for the
          greeting to stop.) Claudia, answer me. Claudia… I
          just saw something on television, it was this show
          about historical Real Estate properties and when the
          program is about to finish… When the program is about
          to finish, the anchor appears in front of a window
          somewhere in the building, through the window you can
          see the clock of another building, you are not going
          to believe this, the clock… The clock was speeding
          and the anchor was talking normally… (She hears a
          beep indicating that the machine has stopped
          recording.)

Right after she hangs up the telephone starts ringing.

                    Claudia
                    (Sleepy tone.)
          Did you just called me?

                    Panda
          Yeah, sorry to woke you up.

                    Claudia
          What's wrong? Are you ok?

                    Panda

          Yes… I just saw this thing on television. There was
          this real estate show. I don't know, and this woman,
          and there is this window… and in the window this

clock and time is speeding up, it was going through
the minutes as if they were seconds… And the woman is
talking normally.

                    Claudia
What movie is this?

                    Panda
I'm sorry I woke you up.

                    Claudia
Are you sure? What's wrong, hon?

                    Panda
Nothing, really. I'll tell you tomorrow, go back to
sleep.

                    Claudia
Ok, good night sweety.

                    Panda
Bye.

Panda hangs up the phone. She closes her eyes. A random sequence is
extracted from the movie's database. Fade Out.

PANDA WRITING

Scene starts with random sequence extracted from the movie database.

1. Interior. Panda's house. Day.

Panda is typing one of her rants. The perspective is that of a webcam placed on the monitor.

                              Panda
                    It's all over the place.
                    Of all the monsters I could have found,
                    I chose to fight the biggest one.
                    A society…
                    A society that…
                    Evolves, a society that evolves through…
                    Greed and…
                    A society that evolves through greed
                    at the expense of its own psychological well-being…

A random sequence is extracted from the movie's database.

                              Panda
                    A society that evolves through greed
                    at the expense of its own psychological well-being.
                    The concept of a material world
                    has been so embraced
                    that it is already embedded in pop culture.
                    A playful concept of a mediocre life.

A random sequence is extracted from the movie's database.

                              Panda
                    Is there something more difficult than trying to show
                    everyone that reality doesn't have to be the wait it
                    is…

A random sequence is extracted from the movie's database. Fade Out.

261

Panda's childhood drawings

Scene starts with random sequence extracted from the movie database.

1. Interior. Third floor living room. Day.

Panda, Jess and Rogan are watching an old Panda video.

                    Jess
          Panda…

                    Panda
          I know, I'm just like that. I keep everything, I keep
          every single little thing.

                    Jess
          I know.

                    Panda
          You know what else? About once a year I go through my
          memory box and I look through everything… see where
          I've been, what I've done.

                    Rogan
          Your memory box?

                    Jess
          You haven't seen it Rogan.

                    Rogan
          No, what?

                    Jess
          You mean, you haven't seen this?

Jess stands up and goes to the closet, she returns with a large
suitcase.

                    Panda
          Oh no…

                    Rogan
          Why would I be snooping in the closets?

                    Jess
          Panda's memory box? Da-da…

A random sequence is extracted from the movie's database.

                    Rogan
          I don't understand, what… why do you keep this?

                    Panda
          Well, in a world without a god there isn't much more
          than your past, right?

                         Rogan
                         (Browsing a sketch book.)
          I can clearly see here the traces of an obsessive
          compulsive…

                         Panda
          What? (The laugh together.) If I show you something
          would you promise not to freak out?

                         Jess
          Yeah…

                         Rogan
          What?

                         Panda
          Just promise.

                         Jess
          You know whatever you do Panda we are going to love
          you even more.

Panda starts browsing among the many contents in the suitcase, finally
se pulls out a couple of white plastic bags. From the plastic bags she
pulls out two big stacks of white paper.

                         Rogan
          What are these?

                         Panda
          My earliest creative endeavors.

                         Jess
          You made all of this? They are all about families…

                         Panda
                         (Pointing at the other bag.)
          And clocks…

                         Jess
          Oh my god! Panda?

A random sequence is extracted from the movie's database.

                         Rogan
          When did you make these?

                         Panda
          In elementary school, between ages of 5 and 10, I
          think.

                         Rogan
          Was it part of the homework or what?

                         Panda
          No, I always drew families. I swear I was the perfect
          case for a child psychologist.

                    Jess
And the clocks…? Is that related to your feelings
about time?

                    Panda
I don't know. It would seem back then that time moved
so slowly. It is only recently that I feel that time
is speeding up.

A random sequence is extracted from the movie's database. Fade Out.

Patricia's confession

Scene starts with random sequence extracted from the movie database.

1. Interior. Church. Day.

The interior of a gloomy church with big stained-glass: The door opens and Panda's mother (Patricia) comes in. Slowly, she walks down the center corridor. She notices a priest placing pamphlets in the back of the long wood seats and she walks towards him. A baptism is taking place in one of the church wings, a baby cries.

                    Patricia
          Father, father…

                    Priest
          Good morning, sweetie.

                    Patricia
          Father, I would like to confess.

                    Priest
          I am very busy, love. Come back at 4, father Tom will
          be in the confessionary from 4 to 6.

Patricia stares at him. Her face denotes angst. The priest looks at her and extends his right arm towards her.

                    Priest
          Are you all right, child? Come sit with me.

A random sequence is extracted from the movie's database.

                    Patricia
          I have sinned. I have sinned and I need guidance.

                    Priest
          Open your heart to me, love.

                    Patricia
          I am pregnant, father.

                    Priest
          My child, that's not a sin, that's a blessing…

                    Patricia
          I feel trapped. I feel trapped by the one who is
          living inside of me. If this child comes to the
          world, father, it will be a bastard. I am 27, father,
          and I didn't have any intentions to procreate. I am
          not a good person for procreation. My role in this
          life is not that of a parent, taking care of small
          creature… I…

> Priest

You are being too hard on yourself. In deed, you have not followed the appropriate paths but should seek forgiveness and rise up to be a person of the lord.

> Patricia

I cannot have this child. Father, I feel guilt.

A random sequence is extracted from the movie's database.

> Patricia

This creature, this part of me will come to the world the wrong way. Father, this child was conceived out of the most extreme atrocities; I am being punished for what I did in the worst possible way… Father, is abortion justified in a case like mine?

> Priest

Did someone rape you?

> Patricia

No.

> Priest

What you did, you did so voluntarily?

> Patricia

Yes…

> Priest

No, my child, you have no option. You should learn to see that the way the lord is working on you is not vengeful, quite the contrary, you have been offered the opportunity to redeem yourself through the life of your child… Give your child a good Christian life.

> Patricia

How can I bring my own flesh to this world at this moment? Don't you see? The world is falling apart so fast.

A random sequence is extracted from the movie's database.

> Patricia

How can I bring someone to this world when there is so much evil around us? How do you think my baby will be able to manage?

> Priest

You will be there for it.

> Patricia

I don't want this baby. It wasn't conceived with love but violence, and I don't want that child to suffer, and I don't want dedicate my life to anyone while I don't know what to do with myself?

A random sequence is extracted from the movie's database. Fade Out.

Pandora's Death

Scene starts with random sequence extracted from the movie database.

1 Interior. Building's second floor. Night.

Panda leaves the room where the ghost stories are being told; she is in her way to find the room with the speeding clock that she saw on television. Jeremiah through the megaphone.

>   Jeremiah
>   Ok everyone, remain in the circle. I'll be back.

Jeremiah walks to the first floor and turns off the building lights. The Janitor, who is in a room in the third floor sees Pandora walking towards the attic and he starts following her. Panda finally reaches the door to the catwalk in the attic.

>   Panda
>   (Whispering to herself.)
>   Oh, god, I've been here before.

A random sequence is extracted from the movie's database.

When panda starts walking across the catwalk, the janitor closes the door of the attic very slowly and locks it.

A random sequence is extracted from the movie's database.

Panda advances until she reaches the room with the window where the clock can be seen. She stands in front of the window and looks up. The clock is not showing the time. She frowns.

A random sequence is extracted from the movie's database.

Suddenly, Panda hears a wood crack. The janitor is standing below the threshold. Panda screams at the sight of the janitor, but she recovers promptly.

>   Janitor
>   Oh, oh, I am sorry. I didn't want to scare you…

>   Panda
>   Who are you?

>   Janitor
>   (He hesitates considerably, up to
>   the point that it is evident that
>   he is about to lie.)
>   I own the building. I… I was noticing you in the
>   building… You are one of Jeremiah's friends. I came
>   up here cause… I kinda like you… and I thought that
>   we could talk for a while.

                    Panda
Sure we can talk, why don't we go downstairs? Get a
drink or something.

                    Janitor
No, no, we can't. Sorry we can't.

                    Panda
Sure we can, its downstairs, that's where everyone
else is…

                    Janitor
We can't, I locked the door.

A random sequence is extracted from the movie's database.

                    Panda
What do you want from me?

                    Janitor
Listen, I'm not gonna hurt you. I'd never hurt you...

                    Panda
                    (Interrupting him and almost
                    shouting.)
So why did you lock the door?

                    Janitor
I just find you very attractive… I… I want to…
Listen, I'm not into aggressive sex or anything like
that, as a matter of fact I'm a great lover… And I
believe that two people should have some rapport
between each other and… Let me prove it to you, it's
guaranteed…

                    Panda
You are the janitor, aren't you? Please, let me get
by. I am going to start screaming.

                    Janitor
I think it is time that we consent.

                    Panda
Consent?!

                    Janitor
                    (Stepping towards her.)
Listen, I… You are so beautiful, you are definitely
exquisite and I know…

                    Panda
Step back, oh, please, step back…

Panda screams for help. She tries to move fast pass the janitor and the janitor is able to grab her blouse. Panda pulls so hard that the he falls and looses her. Panda runs across the attic. She reaches the catwalk and she runs full speed across it. She runs down the stairs and tries to open the door without any success. She runs up the stairs. Panda realizes that she won't be able to hold the door for long and she runs into the attic room of the building's façade. The janitor enters the room and Panda runs to the platform.

> Janitor
> (Screaming angrily.)
> You hurt me, you hurt my arm!

The janitor gets closer and suddenly Panda slips and falls through the skylight to the lower floor. A big bang is heard. The janitor looks down and sees the body of Panda lying on the floor. The janitor runs down.

> Janitor
> Oh, shit. Oh, shit. Oh, shit!

After the big bang in the room below where Panda crashed (the ghost story room), everyone runs up to find out what happened –Jeremiah leads the pack. When they reach the scene, Jeremiah stops at the door. Claudia enters, screams, runs towards Panda and kneels beside her.

> Claudia
> Panda, baby, baby, talk to me, Panda? Call 911! Go, now, go! Oh, no, my baby. Please.

> Janitor
> (Entering the room.)
> Oh shit, oh shit. What's going in here!?

> Jeremiah
> We were downstairs and we just heard the fall.

> Janitor
> (Reprimanding Jeremiah.)
> Oh, no, you must be shitting me! And what was she doing up there?

> Jeremiah
> I don't know.

> Janitor
> I am going to call the cops. Nobody leaves the building, understood? Oh, man. Shit. Shit!

The Janitor leaves the room. The face of Panda appears in a close up. Then the scene jumps to the dinner. The tramp is emotional about what he is narrating.

                    Tramp
You see? There, that girl didn't die. I have two
theories about it: one, the building (he makes a face
simulating suction and makes a suction noise) the
girl, or, or, the girl exploded and then the building
as a whole held her, stopped her expansion… It is an
extremely intense warp zone.

                  Detective
Or maybe it is only inside your brain.

A random sequence is extracted from the movie's database. Fade Out.

Performance Rehearsal I

Scene starts with random sequence extracted from the movie database.

Sequence One.

1. Interior. Building's auditorium. Day.

Bev is working with Julia and Rene on a performance sequence.

> Bev
> Do you see what I'm going for here? I want you to hit
> the position tight and hard and then give it a beat
> and then the words.

> Rene
> Where did you want us to start out?

> Bev
> I'm thinking maybe, at the back of the house. Rene
> why don't you take house left and Julia, you house
> right and strut, really strut. Maybe we can even have
> you stop and pose in the aisle for the first set of
> phrases.

> Julia
> What's happening with the lights at this point?

> Bev
> You should be in a spotlight at this point but that
> all depends on our equipment. Once again my artistic
> vision is being joked by technology. Why I was given
> these visions? Why?

> Julia
> Because you can't resist.

> Bev
> How are we doing with the projector?

> Jeremiah
> Screw the projector!

A random sequence is extracted from the movie's database.

> Bev
> Could you guys try it out from when you enter the
> auditorium? Hit your first pose at the pillar, I like
> that, on the first phrase. OK, here we go.

> Julia and Rene strut from the back of the house, stop
> half-way strike a pose.

Julia
"Buy now, its guaranteed."

Rene
"Don't wait. Limited offer."

They hit the next pose in front of the staircases.

Rene
"Your friends will love it."

Julia
"Don't go without it."

They cross to center stage and hit the next position.

Rene
"Buy what you want."

Julia
"Don't miss this unique opportunity, get it now."

Rene
"Why wait? You are worth it."

Julia
"Anything more would be too much."

Rene
"Do it for yourself, do it for your loved one."

Bev
"So you think you know who you are?"

Julia, Rene & Bev
"Who are you?"

Bev
"What makes you so sure you haven't been made?"

Julia & Rene
"Made."

Bev
"Into a…"

Bev and Julia & Rene
"Ravenous, consuming, machine…"

Bev
"With little else to show for your effort than a lot
of things you don't need."

Julia & Rene
"What do you need?"

                    Bev
"So what is it you do need?"

                    Julia & Rene
"What do I need?"

                    Bev
"You don't know what you need, do you? Well, then,
isn't it bothering you?"

                    Julia
So, Bev, what are we supposed to be doing while you
are singing?

                    Bev
Actually, I should be in spot and the light should
dim, so you should be able to clear left and right.
Are we doing ok with that projector, Jeremiah? You
got it going?

                    Jeremiah
I got the projector going, Zak is going to run it for
you.

                    Bev
Ok, great.

A random sequence is extracted from the movie's database.

                    Bev
You guys can take a break but don't leave yet. Don't
go to far just in case I need you, right?

                    Julia & Rene
All right.

                    Bev
Ready Zak?

                    Zak
Ready.

Jeremiah walks towards one of the side aisles and meets with Rene.

                                        Bev (song.)
Isn't it bothering you?
Wherever you go,
no matter what you do,
isn't it bothering you?
Rapid suburban commercializing you.
Isn't it bothering you?

Everywhere you look things seem the same:

Strip malls & concrete walls the industrial food
chain,
There's no escape from the global take-over.
We are at war....
And you are the machine.

Isn't it bothering you?
Wherever you go,
no matter what you do,
isn't it bothering you?

It's not enough to simply live out your life.
You must have things to justify.
And when it's done what will your contribution be.
A pile of rubbish in an ever-increasing garbage heap.

                    Panda
It's spooky how close this is to what I do. Do you
know this Bev?

                  Claudia
No, I know she is a friend of Jeremiah's. I never
seen her sing before.

                    Panda
I would love to find out who she is.

                  Claudia
I bet you would.

                    Bev (song.)
Isn't it bothering you?
Wherever you go,
no matter what you do,
isn't it bothering you?

No room for the price you paid,
whatever happened to those plans you made?
We will jettison your remnants of life here on earth,
into outer space...
You are no more.

Isn't it bothering you?
Wherever you go,
no matter what you do,
isn't it bothering you?

Rapid suburban commercializing you.
Isn't it bothering you?

A random sequence is extracted from the movie's database. Fade Out.

275

Performance Rehearsal II

Scene starts with random sequence extracted from the movie database.

Sequence Two. Continuation of Scene one.

1. Interior. Building's auditorium. Day.

> Bev
>
> Jeremiah? Jeremiah? Where did that boy go? I can't
> see a thing, I'm blind as a mole. Zak, can we take it
> to the next number. It should be loaded and ready to
> go.

> Zak
>
> Oh, the bye-baby-monsieur thing?

> Bev
>
> Yes that's it.

> Zak
>
> You're good to go.

A random sequence is extracted from the movie's database.

> Bev
>
> This last song was inspired by the poetry of an up
> and coming artist in cyberspace. Bla, bla, bla. I
> have absconded some of the words for the lyrics…
> Anonymous collaboration… let's just say of it is an
> original collaboration with a nameless entity. Ok… "I
> want to talk about…" Where are they? I need those
> guys? Julia! Rene! Can someone go find them for me?

> Julia
> (Julia walks down from the back of
> the auditorium)
> I'm here, but I don't know where Rene took off to.

> Bev
>
> Great. Indulge me and just say the words, don't worry
> about the movement, just so I can get the rhythm
> down.

> Julia
>
> Ok? Thanks. "I want to talk about…"

> Julia
>
> "Love."

> Bev
>
> "Please. What do you know about love. First it's
> 'Hello'"

                                        Julia
            "Hello."

                                        Bev
            And then it's… "Sayonara baby." That would
            work.

A random sequence is extracted from the movie's database.

                                        Bev (song.)

            Sayonara Baby.
            Ourevoir monsieur.
            Hasta la vista, my darling.
            It's good-bye my dear.

                        I hear in your voice,
                        As you whisper goodbye,
                        A cold and vacant tone,
                        And start to wonder if you knew it at
                        all,
                        This thing you call love…
            But you know this has happened many time before,
            The world you knew has come to shades of gray,
                        Then you fill the pull the rush and then,
                        You get on the ride again…

                        And then it is:
            Sayonara Baby.
            Ourevoir monsieur.
            Hasta la vista my darling
            It's good-bye my dear.

                        Love for you is that accumulation
            Of simple characteristics
                        That subtle and bearable tone
            Of your fleeting existence
            And at least for a little while
            Until you need the thrill
            Of falling in love again
            This will do quite well.

                        And then you'll say...
            Sayonara Baby.
            Ourevoir monsieur.
            Hasta la vista my darling
            It's good-bye my dear.

            Then until what you looked for before
                        Bores you day by day
            Then you will be ready to change
            And change and change again
            And you will find the arguments
            To justify your abandonment
            Your lack of luck
            Your sorry fate
            Trust me, you don't love.

                    Panda
              (Knowing the lyrics of the song.)
        You have a propensity to breed.

A random sequence is extracted from the movie's database. Fade Out.

Poetry is Dead

Scene starts with random sequence extracted from the movie database.

1. Interior. Panda's house. Night.

Rogan, Claudia and Panda are having a conversation in the living room.
Claudia is lying on the futon with her head on Panda's lap and Rogan is
sitting in front of the computer. They are calmed, relaxed.

                    Rogan
          You know? It really doesn't matter how well you do
          it? It doesn't work that way. That's the problem:
          Stereotyping is the public's worst sickness. What is
          the typical poem that beginners write? Oh roses, oh
          love, my heart, my loneliness…

                    Claudia
          So, how should it be?

                    Rogan
          Poetry is not something that someone can tell you how
          to do. If Panda gives me a poem and it doesn't sound
          to me like her, she's faking it. She is writing the
          poetry that has been shown in the media. If Panda
          gives me a poem and it sounds like something she
          would say to me any day, then it would be different.
          I don't believe in those people who have 9 to 5 jobs
          and then come home to be poets. Much less do I
          believe in those who break up with their loved ones
          and get so depressed that then they write a poem.

                    Panda
          Yeah, that's pathetic. (To Claudia.) Want some tea?

Panda leaves the room.

                    Claudia
          Your poems don't sound like you, to me.

                    Rogan
          That's because you don't know me too well.

A random sequence is extracted from the movie's database.

                    Claudia
                    (Remaining quiet until Pandora
                    returns.)
          You see, it doesn't make sense, you criticize
          stereotyping but you are trying to give us the
          guidelines to be a perfect poet.

                    Rogan
          I am not telling you how things should be, I am
          telling you how things should not be. Because of this
          awful, nauseous, anachronistic, way of understanding

poetry, nobody gives a shit about it anymore. How
many hours a day does someone spend on the damn
computer? Ask Panda. (To Panda.) How many? 6? 7? And
even though we spend so much time on the computer,
dealing with software bugs, Internet relationships,
etc., etc., etc. How many poems have you heard about
the computer? How many poems have you read about that
"faceless creature that comes to my life in binary
form, who is going to tell me that the systole and
diastole of my heart could be in synch with those
electric impulses that come from afar"? (Panda and
Claudia laugh.) Exactly, exactly, you laugh?

                    Claudia
We laugh because it is ridiculous.

                    Rogan
                    (Angry.)
You laugh because I touched a cord. Because, someone
who is having an email love correspondence with
someone else in… Sydney, doesn't think about what
their emotions are really attached to… However, after
8 hours in front of the computer, they come back home
and they write a pitiful poem about longing and
nature, blooms and peaches… Just because they are so
damn trained to think about poetry in this way no
wonder no one sells a damn poetry book anymore.

                    Claudia
I am sorry; I didn't mean to upset you.

                    Rogan
To be a poet is to be authentic, but if you
accomplish being authentic, there is no way out…
That's how it comes, that's how it manifests. Things
really make no sense when you question their roots,
their basics.

                    Claudia
                    (She returns to the living room
                    with a glass of water in her hand.)
You see? This is the real reason why people don't
like poets. Your passion makes you stubborn.

                    Rogan
If I don't agree with you that doesn't make me
stubborn.

                    Claudia
Poets do not understand that after an 8 hour day at
work you arrive home burned, the last thing you want
to mess around with is real life. Your expectations
are based on the assumption that people have
vacations all year long and have the time to
speculate theories about life.

              Rogan
Claudia, you are giving me the cause as a premise
that we should all abide by because that's the way
things are. That's exactly why we need poets.
Working your ass off everyday so you return home
unable to give one single thought about what life is
all about, is precisely the reason why we need true
poets.

              Claudia
You know? I am not going to try to bring you down
from your cloud.

              Rogan
Cool.

              Claudia
              (Leaning towards Panda to whisper.)
Can I stay here tonight? I have a feeling he is not
going to give me a ride home.

              Panda
Sure.

Claudia runs up the stairs and when she arrives to Panda's bedroom she
jumps to the bed. Once on the bed, she starts undressing herself really
fast.

              Panda
This is why I like you…

              Rogan
It annoys me that, with her, I just can't get any
idea across. She is a damn wall.

              Panda
I don't think you understand her.

              Rogan
What is there to understand?

              Panda
You fool, she started an argument with you so she
could stay here tonight… You should write about her,
it is really fascinating how she works.

A random sequence is extracted from the movie's database. Fade Out.

281

Speedy Calm (Fish)

Scene starts with random sequence extracted from the movie database.

1. Interior. Panda's bedroom. Night.

Panda is sleeping in her bed. She has her mouth open wide and her face
denotes tranquility. The scene changes from the extreme close up to a
fish floating slowly in its tank. All of what can be heard is a very
slight hum, the hum of an aquarium.

                    Panda
                    (Voiceover.)
            I would prefer to dream about something else. I would
prefer a paranoiac dream in which a monster is
chasing me and I have to hide many times because it
will always find me. I would prefer one of those
dreams in which I have to go to school undressed or
one of those dreams in which I get lost. My worst
dreams are made of nothing but tranquility. A plain,
overwhelming tranquility. I would prefer to dream
about something else. If I could isolate this
quietude, this serenity…

A random sequence is extracted from the movie's database.

                    Panda
                    (Voiceover.)
            I guess that I could have been an absolute glutton
with moments of silence when I was little… But my
brain doesn't work like that anymore… I am being
forced into a different wavelength.

2. Exterior. Panda's old house. Day.

Panda appears a little girl. She is playing with Rogan.

                    Rogan
            This is very cool! You stand here, you wait 30
seconds, and then you let it loose. It will go up
automatically.

                    Panda
            I don't think it is going to work but ok, I'll try it
over here. (She starts pushing a column with her
arm.) It hurts. How about now?

                    Rogan
Yeah.

                    Panda
Ok. (She separates from the column.) I doubt it will
work. Wow. It did work!

                    Rogan
I know.

3. Interior. Panda's bedroom. Night.

                          Panda
                       (Voiceover.)
          Your mind does what your arm does. You see, your
          thoughts stream in this sea of peacefulness, where
          nothing really happens. Up… Down… Turn… Stare… Float
          limitlessly… It drives me mad; I believe that after
          one of these dreams I will wake up totally mad. It
          will happen during my sleep. It will happen during my
          sleep.

A random sequence of images, extracted from all the scenes shown here,
flashes at great speed for 10 seconds. A random sequence is extracted
from the movie's database. Fade Out.

Sometimes I hear a modem dialing

Scene starts with random sequence extracted from the movie database.

   1.Interior. Panda's house. Day.

Panda opens a closet in the dinning room and extracts a bottle of wine.
Suddenly she hears a modem dialing. She checks the computers around
here to see if any of them is on, but all of them are off.

                       Panda
                 (In a soft tone.)
I am sorry. Things are serious. Do you know the
reason why I am so paranoid? I understand the
potential the web has for surveillance, and I
recognize that legislation regarding commercial and
criminal issues is just not reacting at the same
speed as the technology. And the combination of those
two things makes me paranoid. Think about it. They
say current legislation is good enough to deal with
criminal activity on the web. What about those things
that are not considered criminal?

                       Rogan
Like what?

                       Panda
All this bullshit about tracking you in order to
provide you with better service, all this acquisition
of "statistical" data… So, what? If it is statistical
then it is ok? Of course it is statistical; they
don't gather it and store it just to reduce their
anxieties about running out of information.

                       Rogan
Now you are being the dork.

                       Panda
No, listen (Confessing.) I think that I hear the
sound of a modem dialing. I recognize the potential
in every communications medium as a surveillance
device. Think about it backwards; instead of thinking
of a convergence of previous media towards the
Internet -now video on the web, now your radio on the
web, your news on the web, etc., etc., think that
every preexistent medium has now a digital capability
to track you, to know what you listen to, what you
watch, what interests you. Scary isn't it. I don't
like feeling observed.

                       Rogan
I don't believe it; you actually hear a modem
dialing? You are loosing it.

                              Panda
          Oh, something new?

                              Rogan
          Ok. So, what is the big deal about knowing if you
          turn on the television at 8 pm? If you read
          technology news?

A random sequence is extracted from the movie's database.

                              Rogan
          What's the big deal?

                              Panda
          I can't believe that you, Rogan, can ask such a dumb
          ass question…

                              Rogan
          Excuse my ignorance…

                              Panda
          From a beautiful prince you just dropped to the
          category of a frog. What's the big deal? Do you think
          that the local mechanic is going to be tracking the
          corporation executives to know when their cars break?
          Yes? Do you think that corner bakery is going to know
          who orders bread on-line? Or do you think that the
          big corporations are going to track regular people?
          The problem is that this new toy doesn't work the
          same way for everyone. The ones with money and power
          track, the rest of us are being tracked. Besides, I
          don't have to give any big rationale to it. I have a
          right not to be subject to any data gathering? I have
          the right to be left alone!

                              Rogan
                              (Trying to calm her.)
          Panda, nobody is observing you right now…

                              Panda
          No, but I know where it is heading…

Suddenly the sound of a modem dialing is heard on the background. Panda
screams and jumps out of her chair.

                              Panda
          I am just going to go mad.

                              Rogan
          No, you are going hysterical. I heard it too… It's
          your neighbor's… Come on. (Panda draws her near a
          window.) It's your neighbor's, you hear it?

Panda looks very troubled. Rogan approaches Panda and opens his arms as an invitation for a hug. Panda accepts it and lays her ear against Rogan's chest. Then Panda's telephone rings, she closes her eyes. A random sequence is extracted from the movie's database. Fade Out.

Teenage angst

Scene starts with random sequence extracted from the movie database.

1. Exterior. Building's side. Afternoon.

A group of young teenagers stands outside the building. The sun is just beginning to set. They are looking down at a broken basement window that is covered over with cardboard.

                    Matt
          We can get in there; I know we can fit through this
          window.

                    Alison
          I don't know Matt, we might be able to get in, but
          the drop is pretty steep once you get through the
          window.

                    Matt
          I'm gonna try. It's fine, no problem. It's an easy
          jump.

The others follow one by one.

                    Sue
          I don't know if this is such a good idea guys.

                    Thurston
          I'll be fine; nobody's here and we are only going in
          for a second to have a look around. We'll be out
          before it's dark. Come on, it'll be OK. (Thurston
          lands with a large thump.) Oh, man, I think I broke
          my hand. (Fascinated by the echo.) Echo… Echo! Listen
          to me!

                    Alison
          Thurston, be quiet you'll get us caught.

They leave the room and head for the stairs. The janitor hears the noise and he is going to check what it is.

A random sequence is extracted from the movie's database.

                    Sue
          Wow, neat. There is an auditorium in here.

                    Matt
          Cool. Let's see if we can find it.

Quick shot of the janitor walking up the stairs with the bat in his hand.

                    Alison
          Shhh… Wait I thought I heard something. Did you guys
          hear that?

                    Matt
        It's an old building, probably shifts around a lot.
        Let's see if we can find the auditorium.

                    Sue
        You guys, I think we should go, it's starting to get
        dark.

                    Thurston
        Yeah, let's get out of here, I'm starting to get
        creeped out.

                    Sue
        Me too.

                    Alison
        Let's go back the way we came so we don't get lost.

She points in the direction where they came from. Suddenly, the figure
of the janitor appears turning around the corner at the end of the
hallway and walking briskly towards them. They see the janitor before
he sees them. All at once they scream. They begin to run away from the
janitor and he sees them clearly at this point. He begins to run and
holds the bat above his head. Jeremiah, who is cleaning one of the
upper floors, hears the chase.

                    Ira
        Ahhhh. I'm gonna kill you. Run little shits, run. Get
        out of my building!

The teenagers separate and Matt end up by himself. Ira follows Matt and
the other three escape through the main back door.

                    Ira
        You! I'll kill you!

Finally, Ira catches him, drops him to the ground and raises the bat
above his head.

                    Jeremiah
                    (Arriving to the same room.)
        Stop! What are you doing? Stop! He's just a kid.

A random sequence is extracted from the movie's database. Fade Out.

Jeremiah's threesome

Scene starts with random sequence extracted from the movie database.

1. Interior. Building's auditorium. Day.

Beverage has started rehearsing. In the middle of the song, Jeremiah turns to René and points to Claudia at the other side of the auditorium. Claudia is watching the rehearsal with Panda sitting next to her.

>   Jeremiah
> Let's go play.

>   Rene
> Right now?

>   Jeremiah
> Yes, now. I've seen this before.

>   Rene
> Just stand up and leave?

>   Jeremiah
> Why not? Bev is cool, she won't mind. Let's go.

Rene and Jeremiah stand up hunched over and start walking towards the left door of the auditorium. When Jeremiah crosses to the door, Rene looks back to catch Claudia's attention. Then she walks out the auditorium and goes to the building's gym where Jeremiah is bench pressing a small amount of weight.

>   Rene
> Guess what I did?

>   Jeremiah
> What?

>   Rene
> I stood up at the door until I got Claudia's
> attention…

>   Jeremiah
> And?

>   Rene
> She smiled at me. I think she might join us after
> rehearsal. She has to get away from Panda first.

>   Jeremiah
> Panda?

>   Rene
> Claudia's friend.

289

                           Jeremiah
          And she is coming with us?

                                 Rene
          She said "yes".

                           Jeremiah
          Does she know?

                                 Rene
          I guess… I think so…

                           Jeremiah
          How far should we go?

                                 Rene
          I don't know, let's play it by ear.

Jeremiah moves forward and kisses Rene. Tempestuously he tries to get
his hand inside her blouse, but she moves back. She looks entertained
by it.

                                 Rene
          Ease down boy. What are we going to tell her?

                           Jeremiah
          I don't know. Why not be somewhat evident about it?

                                 Rene
          What? Say: Hey, Claudia would you like to have sex
          with us?

                           Jeremiah
          Ok.

                                 Rene
          No! Are you nuts? You're just thinking with the
          little one.

A random sequence is extracted from the movie's database.

                           Jeremiah
          What about "hey, Claudia, how would you like to come
          on a nice tour around the building"?

                                 Rene
          What if she says "no"?

                           Jeremiah
          We have enough time to pick someone else.

                                 Rene
          Ok.

A random sequence is extracted from the movie's database.

Jeremiah, Rene and Claudia appear in one of the rooms of the second floor.

>   Claudia
>   So, if these walls could speak, what would they tell
>   me about the two of you?

>   Jeremiah
>   Oh, plenty but none of the stuff that you are
>   thinking about?

>   Claudia
>   And what am I thinking about?

>   Jeremiah
>   Oh, that part I won't tell you.

>   Rene
>   I can tell you what I am thinking.

>   Claudia
>   (Annoyed.)
>   What are you thinking?.

>   Rene
>   I think we should do something silly. Do something
>   different, get crazy, lose style!

>   Claudia
>   Like what?

>   Jeremiah
>   (Jeremiah runs towards the
>   hallway.)
>   I know, wait here, I have an idea.

>   Claudia
>   (To Rene.)
>   I know well what you guys are up to.

>   Rene
>   Are you ok with it?

>   Claudia
>   Don't get me wrong; I'm up for just about anything
>   involving you, but I'm not interested in him.

>   Rene
>   Would you consider it?

Jeremiah returns with a glass bottle in his hand. The conversation between the two of them stops abruptly.

>   Claudia
>   What's that for?

                    Jeremiah
    Well… You guys remember how to play spin the bottle?
    (Rene laughs.) No wait a sec., I don't mean spin the
    bottle like you did in the basement when your kids…
    let's up the ante. Whomever the bottle goes to, has
    to remove a piece of clothing.

                    Claudia
    There are people around.

                    Jeremiah
    So what? The party is downstairs, there not gonna
    come her. And if they do, maybe they would like to
    join the fun.

                    Claudia
    Let's make it a little bit more interesting: Whomever
    looses has to take off their clothes and gets to
    choose the next room where we'll spin in again.

                    Jeremiah
    Oh, we have a little exhibitionist here.

                    Rene
    I get to go first.

A random sequence is extracted from the movie's database.

                    Rene
    Here we go. (She looses.) No way, man, you've got to
    be kidding. (She gets the first round…and takes off
    her shoes)

They play the game. First shot of Rene holding her shoes in her hand as
she runs down the hallway chasing after Jeremiah and Claudia. It
escalates. They run from room to room, different shots, and different
clothes missing… The mood is jovial and playful. Suddenly there is a
scream. Claudia, while holding her clothes in her arms runs straight
into Pandora.

                    Jeremiah
    I forgot something back there guys… I better go look
    for it.

Pandora looks surprised. Claudia isn't able to move and stay standing
there. A random sequence is extracted from the movie's database. Fade
Out.

292

Time value of money

1. Interior. Panda's house. Day.

Jess walks into the house and runs up, she is excited about talking to Panda.

> Jess
> Panda? Panda?

> Panda
> Over here, in the cockpit…

> Jess
> I wanted to talk to you so badly, I ran half the way here. What are you doing reading a book? I thought that you were going to work on another rant.

> Panda
> I am. I have them all rendering…

> Jess
> I bet you do… I think I have another solution, once again it can be criticized as making the market inefficient but you know…

> Jess and Panda
> Making the market inefficient is a moral decision and bla-di-bla-bla-bla…

> Jess
> What is the reason why we have the wild pitches in advertising? Do you remember? That thing that was saying the other day about making people believe that with the click of the button you can send perfectly edited video anywhere in the world.

> Panda
> The argument is that people know that they are ads and that they are supposed to be persuasive, so people should not believe entirely those claims…

> Jess
> But they do…

> Panda
> Well, that is why people believe the Internet connects the "entire" world, when a lot of the underdeveloped countries have a very small telephone penetration rate.

> Jess
> Yes! Okay, so besides giving you a wild pitch like that, they normally state that if you don't have it…

Panda
You are going to be left behind.

Jess
Exactly! And then they throw other things like… give
it to your kids or they are going to be left behind
too, so they attack your parent responsibility, they
won't have access to…

Jess and Panda
Jess says: All the knowledge contained in the
information superhighway... Panda says: All the
knowledge there is…

Jess
This is so mean, this is so mean it is scary…

Panda
Jess? Nothing that we haven't talked about before.

Jess
Something just became really evident.

Panda
What?

Jess
Well, in finance class I raised today the point of
who profits most from lending money, that is… that
percentage rate that is charged to those who borrow
money is the reason why some people lend money,
right? Well, I wanted to know who is benefiting from
this. And as it is common now, I got a harsh answer
(faking the voice of the professor): "Certainly not
those who are asking for the money, isn't it?" This
is pure evil, baby…

Panda
What is?

Jess
Those damn commercials about computers and the
Internet, what is the typical line before the end of
the commercial? They lend you money to acquire the
computer, right? Pay it back in 24 months with this
"easy" interest rate… First the ad creates a false
perception of the computer and what it does, you can
make home videos of your children that look as a
professional TV production that later on you can send
to your parents…

Panda
You have access to all the knowledge there is…

Jess
If you don't acquire it you are going to lag behind,
and by the way let us lend you money so we can

squeeze out of you… first, a purchasing decision
based on false information… second, an extra
percentage above the price that you wouldn't have had
to pay if you had been patient…

                    Panda
First, they create the anxiety and then they profit
also on the people's inability to wait… Yes, yes it
is mean. So, what is the solution?

                    Jess
Besides regulating even more the advertising
industry, you regulate those who lend money and
profit from the time value of money…

                    Panda
Like what?

                    Jess
Well, you cannot tax it because you just shift the
entire market… maybe putting a quota, a maximum
profit that can be made out of lending money…

                    Panda
And that would make the market inefficient…

                    Jess
Obviously, but I have to know in what way… I have to
know in what way… I love you, you kick ass.

                    Panda
Where are you going?

                    Jess
I am going to talk to my economic professors.

                    Panda
They are going to hate you for it…

                    Jess
Of course they will, screw them, that's why I pay
them.

A random sequence is extracted from the movie's database.

Tramp about the Magnetic fields inside the building

Scene starts with random sequence extracted from the movie database.

1 Interior. Diner. Day.

>   David
> I believe there is a strange connection between the
> house that Pandora was asked to housesit for and the
> container.

>   Historian
> What kind of connection?

>   David
> I really can't tell accurately, because the
> instruments I have are somewhat… precarious.

>   Historian
> Instruments? What do you mean instruments? To measure
> what?

>   David
> Electromagnetic fields inside the container…

>   Historian
> I've been meaning to ask you this and this is the
> right time for it: what was your profession?

>   David
> I thought that you were interested in the building.

>   Historian
> Yes, yes I am, but I also find you to be a
> fascinating person.

>   David
> But I am not interested in talking about my past. If
> you want me to continue talking about the container,
> I will do so, but if not, we can stop.

>   Historian
> No, no, please continue… You were talking about the
> electromagnetic fields inside the building.

>   David
> When you are new to the building you don't notice the
> subtleties in the air… but when you know it by heart,
> you start realizing that the building contains
> electromagnetic waves inside… Those fields are
> circumscribed to a set of focal points.

>   Historian
> I don't think I have ever felt an… electromagnetic
> field.

                    David
It feels very weird, your body hair suddenly rises
and all of it points in a single direction. Also when
you breathe you can feel how the air not only reaches
your lungs but also your stomach. (The first scene of
the tramp making measurements appears on screen.
Voiceover.) It wasn't difficult to figure it out.
First, you set the weight from a string and you let
it rest. At moments of high activity, the weight will
start pulling right away towards the focal points,
which are located somewhere in the centre of the
container. Once you have the process nailed down, it
is easy to move from one room to the next. However,
it wasn't easy to figure out the location of the
focal points, so I started mapping out the building
and the direction of the pull from the weight.

                    Historian
                    (Voiceover.)
How much time would it take you to figure the pull in
each room?

                    David
                    (Voiceover.)
It would depend on the electromagnetic activity of
that day. Maybe between 10 to 30 minutes.

                    Historian
                    (Voiceover.)
I bet it was difficult to make the time with the
janitor around…

                    David
                    (Voiceover.)
Ira is never around, he is bad business for the
building. Besides, he only appears to make his drug
deals.

                    Historian
The janitor sells drugs in the building?

                    David
I never told you that, you know what I mean, I never
told you that… Anyhow, (voiceovers) after a week or
so of making measurements in specific rooms and
making sketches on the blackboards… I found the focal
points…

A random sequence is extracted from the movie's database.

                    David
                    (Voiceover.)
When I entered the focal points I found myself in
this beautiful house somewhere else, definitely not
inside the building. But the problem is that the
intensity of the electromagnetic field repels me
quite strongly, I barely tolerate it for more than a

few seconds and I end up with a horrible headache. So
I started, taking fast dives here and there,
challenging myself to venture inside the different
ones that I found… then…

                    Historian
                    (*Voiceover*.)
Then…

                    David
                    (*Voiceover*.)
Then I found that it was the house where Panda lives,
the container is connected to it…

                    Historian
You have many theories about what goes on inside… Do
you have a theory for this?

                    David
I believe that… both the house and the container were
built at the same time.

                    Historian
A hundred years ago.

                    David
A hundred years ago.

A random sequence is extracted from the movie's database. Fade Out.

Tramp about the collage (Panda's moment of death)

1. Interior. Tramp's room in the building. Night.

David is catatonic; he is staring at a point in space and the camera
slowly zooms in. Images from all the movie will flicker at great speed.

                         David
                    I don't remember all of it. I think that I might have
                    blacked out for a moment. It felt like a sudden
                    blast. It felt like an earthquake, not the actual
                    movement of the earth but the moment in which things
                    fall down and millions of tiny pieces of debris are
                    flying at great speed in every possible direction.
                    That type of feeling: An explosion, a fast wave of
                    atoms progressively banging each other, slowing down
                    a tiny little bit after each impact. I can't remember
                    if it was silent or if it was extremely loud. But
                    everything started in this room, all the memories,
                    all the feelings, all the thoughts, came from here.
                    Everything looked blurry and very bright. If I had a
                    kaleidoscope or paper wheel with the entire gamma of
                    colors on it and I spin it really hard, all of the
                    colors blend into an impure white. Then as the wheel
                    slows down, the colors emerge little by little… It
                    must have happened like that. The explosion, an
                    instantaneous acceleration to a very high speed, the
                    wave of atoms displacing each other and then the
                    slowing down. After that, everything had already been
                    spread all over the container in such a vibrant way
                    that it felt like a beehive without the bees but with
                    all the flapping. I must have passed out. I remember
                    feeling that I couldn't breathe, but before that…
                    nothing, another dark zone in my memory. The smell of
                    the container the morning after was that of
                    electricity; all those thoughts and emotions were
                    ready to be experienced, almost as if they were to be
                    experienced for the first time. Are all the possible
                    things that we experience laid out at a single
                    instant? Not only our actual life, but also all the
                    possible lives that we could have had, are they all
                    spread out in a container? It would seem not only
                    that it is true but also that our actual life is the
                    way we decide to move inside that container. Most
                    probably the crucial events of our lives are laid out
                    entirely at the moment of our birth. Destiny is not a
                    single path, destiny is a set of milestones that will
                    occur in any order. That much I have learned from the
                    container.

The container as memory

Scene starts with random sequence extracted from the movie database.

1 Interior. Diner. Day.

> David
> Well, if you think about it… I guess that you can say
> that the container works in the exact same way memory
> does.

> Doctor
> Assuming that we do know how memory works…

> David
> Assuming we know how memory works, true. Have you
> ever had a traumatic experience?

> Doctor
> I don't understand.

> David
> Have you ever seen a friend die? Have you ever been
> in a car accident?

> Historian
> Yes I have, I guess we all have a series of traumatic
> events throughout life.

> David
> Think about one of them. Browse your memories… Do you
> remember everything that happened?

> Historian
> David, out of a job if people could remember
> everything. Part of my job consists precisely of
> filtering collective memory…

> David
> That's my point. Part of what we remember is not what
> happened, but what we think happened. The older the
> memory the more it has patches here and there of what
> we want to remember. So our memory is a mix of what
> really happened with how we make sense of it. You
> know what I am talking about?

> Doctor
> Yes.

> David
> Have you ever met one of those people that believe
> their own lies?

> Historian
> You are talking about my father-in-law.

David
Those people impose what they want to believe on what
happened, right? That's what the container does. Part
of what it holds is not just what happened, it also
extracts people's psyche… (Voiceover.) And it goes
from what people want, what people fear, to what
makes people accept themselves.

Doctor
To all of this: What parts of you, what parts of your
psyche, do you believe are being held in the
building?

David
I… I am not sure. (Voiceover.) I lost my daughter at
some point in my life. I loved her. She appears every
now and then inside the building, and when I see her…
I now that the container is also starting to extract
pieces of my own head. But I see it as a necessary
marriage, I receive if I give. Do you understand? It
might help me out.

Doctor
Help you out in what way?

David
I don't know why I have blocked a lot from my memory.
If the container is an active memory, my own memory
is an empty building sometimes.

More scenes of Panda when she was little appear on
the screen. Then it cuts to the tramp. He is looking
through the window absentmindedly. More scenes of
Panda when she was a girl appear on the screen.

Doctor
(Only as a voiceover.)
David? Are you ok? Are you ok?

                            David
                            (Looking back at the
                            interviewer.)
What?

Doctor
You left the diner for a while…

David
I see her all the time. She is here and there in the
container, extracted from myself, extracted from that
dark zone in my memory.

Doctor
How do you know it's her?

301

                          David
       Are you a parent?

                          Doctor
       Yes I am, I have a new born, but you just told me
       that you have blocked out some memories. How can you
       be sure that it is her?

                          David
                          (Lying.)
       I just know. When I experience her inside the
       container, it feels as if my memory is unblocked,
       free for an instant… a very happy instant.

A random sequence is extracted from the movie's database. Fade Out.

Tramp about Claudia

Scene starts with random sequence extracted from the movie database.

1 Interior. Diner. Day.

Every time that the tramp mentions the name of Beverage it is said with French intonation, contrary to the detectives who use the natural English pronunciation.

> George
> I've been thinking about asking you something: Let's assume that I leave my inherently scientific mind behind for a bit…

> Tramp
> (In disbelief.)
> Aha…

> George
> And I accept your visionary powers…

> Tramp
> I am not a psychic or a prophet.

> Patty
> He knows that.

> Detective 1
> I don't understand this… performance inside the building. What is Pandora's business with these people? According to what we've gathered, she didn't know anyone but Beverage Lush and this other girl Claudia.

> Tramp
> (Simulating a spiritist session, the tramp closes his eyes and takes a deep breath.)
> Let's hold hands… (He cracks up.) It's just a joke…

A random sequence is extracted from the movie's database.

> Tramp
> She didn't know Beverage, but she did know Claudia… And now that you mention it, Claudia has a very specific role in Panda's life. (He looks bewildered by his own thoughts.) How much do you know about Greek drama? I guess you can't expect that from a scientific mind, can you? In Greek drama there is a resource that redirects the plot entirely, it is called *deus ex machina*. Well, the appearance of Claudia is similar to that. She met Panda just weeks before the party… How paradoxical!

                    Patty
What?

                    Tramp
                    (Speaking fast, connecting the
                    dots.)
The party at the building is one of Jeremiah's
schemes to expand his sexual horizons. He wants to
have a *menage a trois*. Rene, Jeremiah's girlfriend,
works with Beverage as a dancer in one of her
performance pieces. Jeremiah suggests to Beverage
that she could use the building for her next
performance. On the day of the rehearsal he invites a
few other friends to watch the rehearsal and have a
party afterward. Jeremiah tells Rene to keep her eye
out for a possible third, who turns out to be
Claudia… Claudia met Panda in a corn maze about two
weeks before the party at the building. They met (*a
few scenes of the fats moving parts of the corn maze
scene are triggered, then the action returns to the
tramp*) in a maze… (More fast scenes from the maze
appear, and then it returns again to the tramp.) In a
maze… It's so allegorical. So Claudia gets invited to
the party as prey for Jeremiah and Rene's hunting
expedition. Claudia in turn invites Panda to the
container. Panda accepts… Isn't life fascinating?

A random sequence is extracted from the movie's database.

                    George
So, it would seem that you have a theory…

                    Tramp
Well, Claudia… Claudia… Claudia seems to be the one
who is lifted up onto the stage with a huge crank…

                    Patty
We are wasting our time.

                    George
Dave, could you solve the riddle for us?

                    Tramp
The term *deus ex machina* comes from actual Greek
drama, where god, *deus*, is lifted on to the stage by
using a big crank… a machine. Then god changes the
direction of the story entirely …

                    Patty
So you are telling us that Claudia is god in
Pandora's play?

                    Tramp
No, it's just a good analogy…

George
Excuse me, excuse me… could I get a glass of water?

A random sequence is extracted from the movie's database. Fade Out.

305

Tramp-Lakmé-Building link

Scene starts with random sequence extracted from the movie database.

1 Interior. Diner. Day.

The tramp is staring at the window of the diner, as if he has found a deep memory. The historian is on the opposite side, he looks intrigued by the overall change in mood of the tramp.

> Tramp
> The building is filled with many things, all of them active in some way or another… However, if all of them follow a somewhat similar pattern, there is something in there that doesn't…

> Historian
> I am listening…

> Tramp
> One day, any day… A group of local cinematographers came into the building to shoot a sequence for their film…

2 Interior. A room in the building. Day.

A sequence of the setting up of a scene for Supergirl is launched into the screen.

> Tramp
> It was something absurd, something like… Supergirl, that's it, Supergirl… I was quite amazed at the amount of time and dedication that they put into the creation of the scene's environment −I'd never seen a set up for a movie before…

> Historian
> Are you ok?

> Tramp
> (Trapped within his own thoughts, reflective.)
> Yes. The building was the same as always, that all encompassing environment that…

A random sequence is extracted from the movie's database.

> Tramp
> (Smiling.)
> It seemed the container was pulling its old tricks again. They were functioning without thinking… They were going through the motions and the container was feeding from their psyche. It was really interesting because not a lot of the people who had stepped into the building recently had been creative people…

The historian is looking at him intensely. He can sense the emotion in the tramp's words.

                    Historian
          I wonder where you are heading? Was the building the
          same or different?

                    Tramp
          Well, the day of Jeremiah's party, the day everything
          happened in the building, one of the dancers escaped
          the group for a moment. You might assume that their
          creative side would have been numbed too, but it
          wasn't…

                    Historian
          What was different?

                    Tramp
          A voice…

                    Historian
          Whose voice?

                    Tramp
          (Soft voiceover of Julia singing
          Lakme's "Flower Duet")
          I don't know her name, even though it would seem I
          knew her core. I think her name is… Julia?

                    Historian
          One of the dancers…

                    Tramp
          Yes, one of the dancers.

3 Interior. Building. Day.

Animated images of the QTVR tour of the building flash. Julia is
walking by herself in the building. She is listening to her own echo
while singing in the empty spaces of the building.

                    Tramp
          It was Lakmé's Flower Duet… And it wasn't me, it was
          the building that started changing… The flow of the
          container halted. The regular things trapped in the
          building disappeared… Lakmé has lived with me
          throughout my life. On weekends, my father used to
          play it on the record player, and I would sit down
          and listen to it for hours…

4. Interior. Tramp's room in the building. Day.

The tramp slowly gets up and walks towards the door. He stand behind it
silently.

                    Tramp
And there I stood… wholesome, absorbed, seized by the
melody…

                    Historian
And the building?

                    Tramp
                    (Smiling, approving the historian's
                    intelligence.)
The container hushed for the first time… I wonder if
that had something to do with the events that
followed.

                    Historian
                    (Back in the dinner.)
Do you have any idea of what changed your perception
of the building?

                    Tramp
My guess is that Lakmé was played long ago in that
auditorium, and the container was confronted with its
own history…

A random sequence is extracted from the movie's database.

5. Interior. Historian's house. Day.

Several instances of the historian looking for information about the
plays that were took place in the building's auditorium.

                    Historian
I can't believe this…

Then he writes in a notepad where "Tramp" and "Building" and "Lakmé"
are already connected by arrows. Underneath that he writes: "Lakmé was
performed in the building's auditorium before the Second World War".

A random sequence is extracted from the movie's database. Fade to
black.

Last year at Marienbad at the diner

Scene starts with random sequence extracted from the movie database.

1 Interior. Diner. Day.

The tramp is sitting at a table at the diner. He is looking in his bag for something, then he takes the measurement tools out and puts them on the table. The waitress stops by and serves more coffee and the tramp thanks her by nodding.

                    David
        I know that soon I'm gonna have to leave the
        building… But let me tell you something: If only I
        could have lived in that building for the last 4 or 5
        years… I would have a pretty solid theory of what
        goes on inside. From pure observation, the container
        seems to absorb people's psyches in different ways,
        depending on where they got trapped in the building.

                    Historian
        What do you mean?

                    David
        The more you move up, the higher the floor, the more
        internal the experiences are that have been retained…

                    Historian
        You know how all this sounds, right?

                    David
        Are you going to ask me not to believe what I see…
        Would I ask you not to believe what you see? This
        diner, the old man in front of you, your job, your
        house, everything exists only within your head… Trust
        me…

                    Historian
        Well, we all have a set of shared beliefs and shared
        values…

                    David
        That's what a profession can do to an intelligent
        person: You specialize in something and, then, you
        try to look at everything through your brand new
        lens. You assume that if it makes sense for you it
        makes sense to all of us… And if that is the case,
        then Prof. Tafford is right about reality being a
        sandstorm.

A random sequence is extracted from the movie's database.

The tramp pulls out several candies from one of his bags. Then he lays them on the table forming a pyramid (7 candies in the bottom, 5 on the next level, 3 on the next level and finally one single candy at the top.)

                              Historian
                              (Smiling.)
          I don't understand.

                              David
          These are the rules… You can pick as many candies as
          you like, but from only one row. Whoever gets the
          last candy looses.

The tramp shows both hands indicating that he is giving the interviewer
the first move. In all of the games depicted here, A always makes the
first move, and from there the sequence goes a1, b1, a2, b2, a3, b3,
etc. A is the historian in the following sequence.

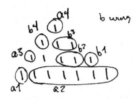

A random sequence is extracted from the movie's database.

                              Historian
              Hmm. Strange. Let's do this again.

Both place the candy again in a pyramid shape. The historian starts.

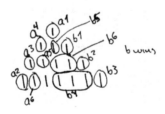

A random sequence is extracted from the movie's database.

                                                  Tramp
          Do you want to quit playing?

                              Historian
                              (After rearranging the candy.)
          You start.

                              Tramp
          I never loose.

The tramp starts this time.

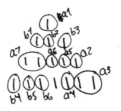

David
(While the historian places the
candy.)
You see: This could be my specialization, and
according to my specialization you are simply not a
competent person… Give me one reason why I should try
to make you competent according to my standards?
Would I convince you of your abnormality and make you
like me? Do you still doubt your competence? I can
always prove me point by doing it again and show you
how incapable you are to evolve.

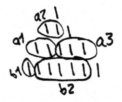

David
The main difference between you and me is that I
don't try to impose my way of thinking on you… That
building contains time, and it doesn't matter if you
can see it or not, if you can feel it or not… You
see? Most of reality works like those religions that
have active campaigns to recruit followers: why does
someone else have to believe in the same god for them
to be secure?

A random sequence is extracted from the movie's database. Fade Out.

Tramp making a Rant

1. Interior. Dinner. Day.

David is by himself. He is writing n his notebooks. While we writes, he
balances heavily from side to the other. The scene will alternate
between this image and that of David washing his face in the dinner's
bathroom.

                              David
              As a good child of the system,
              you've conquered…
              nothing.
              The sense of achievement
              you had,
              has faded away again
              as it has happened many other times…
              Do you wonder why?
              Do you wonder why
              you are juggling in your head all those arguments
              about who you are
              and why you are better than others?
              Do you wonder why you worry so much about it?
              You want so bad to be someone,
              that you've become the one who worries a lot
              about who the fuck he is.
              Any idea of why you want to tell us all the time that
              you kick ass?
              Turns out that the rational man that you are
              cannot stop wondering why he <u>feels</u>
              there is avoid to fill up.
              You are a victim of the illusion of achievement
              that the system provides.
              You have figured out a way
              to disguise all your name dropping
              as necessary facts of your discourse.
              You have no friends,
              you only have acquaintances.
              No one can tell us who you are
              by experience,
              the only things that people know about you
              are the things that you've told them.
              You've isolated yourself
              because you are vulnerable,
              a truth that doesn't go in hand
              with the rhetoric that you give about yourself.
              Your biggest problem is not being authentic,
              not being able to live in peace with yourself.
              Is it clear for you now
              that the only thing that stops you
              from being a void
              is your pain.
              Somewhere along the way you lost your taste for life.
              Who tolerates for long someone who's biggest purpose
              in life

is to be better than others?
Relax anxious little boy.
You are a Poodle that worries too much
about being a Great Dane,
and in the mean time
you forget about the pleasure of chewing a bone,
or digging a hole,
or barking at the moon.
You are a victim of the illusion of achievement
that the system provides.

Tramp about Panda's animations

Scene starts with random sequence extracted from the movie database.

1 Interior. Diner. Day.

          George
David, I've been wondering...Do you know about Pandora's animations on the Internet? Have you seen them?

          David
No, I haven't.

          George
I think you might find them very interesting…

          Patty
Somewhat insulting.

          David
I know them well, but the thing is I've never watched the Internet.

          Patty
Browsed… the Internet.

          David
Browsed the Internet.

          Patty
Surf the web.

          David
Surf the web… Do you really believe in all that?

          Patty
Believe in what?

          David
Surfing the web…

          Patty
It's not funny.

          David
It's not funny at all. It seems that someone found a new dream catcher for adults.

          George
So you have seen the animations but you've never browsed the web.

                Patty
Ride the information super highway…

                George
Do you want some tea? Are you hungry?

                Patty
No, I am ok.

A random sequence is extracted from the movie's
database.

                George
You saw them inside the building?

                David
I have seen their birth and their growth too.

                Patty
I guess that by now I should have figured that one
out …

                George
Do you have any guesses as to why she would have made
them?

                David
It was a way of undrowning herself… It follows the
same basic idea of psychotherapy or confession, if
you verbalize your thoughts and feelings you make
sense of them.

                George
What do you mean by undrowning?

                David
Escape from drowning…

                Patty
Were you drowning her?

                David
Life as it is was drowning her, and I do agree with
her. (Beat.) You can't reduce our way of living to
rescue the animal in us. Think about it: We are not
another link in the evolution of species, we are the
ultimate link, the one that is capable of breaking
the pattern. There is no other way to say the things
she said.

                Patty
I don't think she made too many friends with those
animations.

                David

315

Oh, no. She had her way. I believe that she was
heavily criticized by some, but praised by others. Do
you really believe that you can say something like
that without pissing off the beneficiaries of
capitalism, of advertising, of technology? You can't
tiptoe your way around it. I admire her; it's because
of her that I don't want to leave the container. She
has come to be my only reason to keep on living.

A random sequence is extracted from the movie's database. Fade Out.

Panda in the shower

1. Interior. House. Day.

Pandora is going to take a shower. She calmly brushes her teeth. When
she enters the shower she starts crying. She ends up sobbing. When
leaving the shower she is calm again. Her nudity is not sexual.

                              Tramp
                          (Voiceover.)
            The more I think about her the more I realize how
            exceptional she is. Why is she so different? The way
            the system holds you tight to its principles is very
            straightforward: The less you have the more you are
            able to dissent, the more you have the more
            convenient your silence becomes. My conclusion after
            all these years is very simple: Whoever is in a
            position to promote true change prefers not to take
            action because doing so would also be acting against
            their own interests. I am not just talking only about
            money and material possessions, but also about power,
            authority, recognition and personal stability. If you
            are at the top, a position where you probably have
            more opportunity to promote real change, but what are
            the incentives for you to speak out against the
            system that protects you? That is the missing
            explanation for most of what is wrong with us as a
            society. That is why things do not change for the
            better. Panda is the exception. Her education could
            have gotten her to a nice paid position somewhere in
            the corporate world. She could have stopped talking
            and start building up on that standard path that
            society had for her even before she was born: her
            education, her boyfriend, her job, her marriage, her
            house, her car, her babies… and the raising of a new
            standardized generation. Panda is the exception, and
            it turned to be a very long road for her, three or
            four years of untainted intensity, a long breath held
            that culminated in a scream without voice, a scream
            without any apparent recipient. How horrible it must
            be to fight against an invisible and omnipresent
            force? She meant no wrong. I believe that there is
            some people that cannot withhold themselves from
            speaking out. Madness is a better choice than
            silence. She uses the shower as a means to cleanse
            her soul. Those periods of time that she has in
            contact with falling water mean the world to me. They
            give me an opportunity to see the woman behind the
            scream, the angel underneath the clothes… When she
            showers it would seem that she takes off her human
            suit. I believe that's why she cries, that's why she
            breaks down and cries. Who can put up such a fight?
            Turn it the other way around: Imagine that you
            truthfully pick that fight? I cherish the intimacy
            with her that the container has provided me. For me,
            each one of her tears disappear among thousands of

water drops just as her rants disappear among a
myriad of messages crossing from one side to the
other of the world to the other.

Fade Out.

Temporal Lobe Epilepsy

Scene starts with random sequence extracted from the movie database.

1 Interior. Diner. Day.

> Doctor
> Dave, you have to explain to me how it works. How
> does it happen? Do you go to bed and then dream about
> it?

> Tramp
> (Smiling.)
> So you think I've been telling you my dreams? We are
> not that close yet doctor?

> Doctor
> What I am trying to get at is this: Does it happen
> all the time? If I go with you, do you see them? Does
> it happen once or twice a day? Does it happen when
> you drink?

> Tramp
> If I had something to drink I would be sipping away.

> Doctor
> I am sorry… My mistake. I am not asking the right
> questions.

> Tramp
> Maybe you should ask me straightforwardly instead of
> finding a way to sneak the truth out of me.

> Doctor
> Ok, why don't we start from the beginning? How did it
> happen the first time? How did you get to see the
> container for the first time?

> Tramp
> That's a lot better. It started at soon as I got
> inside the building. I grabbed the "water room" in
> the basement of the building as my room because the
> door was locked. Who locks a door inside an empty
> building? (Beat.) No one. Most probably the room
> closed and locked by itself and has remained like
> that for months… Do you understand?

> Doctor
> And the janitor wouldn't find you there because he
> thinks that the room is locked.

> Tramp
> Exactly. The first thing I did was wait until I was
> sure that Ira was not around. (The tramp appears
> inside the building looking for objects. Voiceover.)

Then I made a thorough search all around the building
to see what I could use… I found a chair. I found one
of those foldout foam couches that I use for bed. Not
an easy building, I have to tell you. I looked all
over the place and basically, I realized that the
upper floors were quite vacant and dry. (The camera
returns momentarily to the tramp.) I remember finding
an old newspaper on the second floor. (The action
returns to the tramp in the building, he picks up an
old newspaper. Voiceover.) It had been years since I
read the news… (Beat.) There it was, the same old
thing: Words and words and words indicating who is
who in the world, what should be important to you,
what you should aspire to be, what is your place in
society… (The tramp zones out staring at his coffee.)

                    Doctor
David?

A random sequence is extracted from the movie's database.

                    Tramp
Oh… The first time it happened was on the very first
day, I was still looking around for objects. (The
tramp appears in the lowest floor of the building, he
is looking around. Voiceover.) It happened on the
lowest possible level of the building… Around noon. I
remember that my heart was beating fast, I was still
quite new to the building and not able to understand
which noises were coming from the structure itself
and which were janitor noises… I would hear very
distinct sounds that were nothing but the shifting of
things inside the container. (The doctor appears
sleepy, then the action returns to the tramp on the
building. Voiceover.) It was on that floor that it
happened first. That time I only saw Panda's face, it
was filled with colors and somewhat blurred.

Blurred images of Panda's face with the kaleidoscope appear. A random
sequence is extracted from the movie's database.

                    Doctor
Do you remember smelling something? Maybe like
something was burning?

                    Tramp
No.

                    Doctor
Did you fall down? Or after your vision, did you find
yourself on the floor?

                    Tramp
No, I was just walking around and when Panda's face
appeared for the first time I got really scared. Can
you imagine? Wow… Then I tried to get closer and
touch her, grab her face.

                         Doctor
            Did you? Did you grab her face?

                         Tramp
            I walked around the face very slowly. (Back to the
            lowest floor of the building. The camera pans around
            the tramp. Voiceover.) It was absolutely beautiful…
            Since that moment I can see what the container holds
            inside. (A series of images of the tramp staring
            blankly in several rooms flashes on the screen.) The
            container didn't feel that I was intrusive, and then
            I had access to all of it…

The action returns to the dinner.

                         Doctor
            No convulsions.

                         Tramp
            Convulsions? What are you fishing for, doc?

                         Doctor
            A mental condition.

                         Tramp
            A mental condition.

                         Doctor
            Yes, it's a form of epilepsy…

The tramp stares at the doctor. He looks puzzled. A random sequence is
extracted from the movie's database. Fade Out.

Television Show (Jess) First Part

Scene starts with random sequence extracted from the movie database.

1 Interior. Studios of an online TV news program. Night.

> Anchor
> Jessica Fussell… Did I pronounce that correctly?
> Jessica Fussell is a student of economics. So tell me
> Jessica, what would you do to improve things?

> Jess
> First, I'd like to point out that it's OK to look at
> what's wrong without being too worried about how to
> improve things. We should be able to pose a question
> even if we don't know the solution.

> Anchor
> Surely, saying what's wrong without giving any
> solutions is a waste of time.

> Jess
> No it's not. The second important step is to adjust
> the way we discuss so that we can actually get
> somewhere in our conversation.

> Anchor
> You think we are not getting anywhere with our
> conversation?

> Jess
> I think that there is a good chance that we will have
> the same show as always if we don't make a conscious
> effort to avoid it.

> Anchor
> (Laughing.)
> Something wrong with the show?

> Jess
> If we continue the way we are going, we'll probably
> end up talking about...I don't know... something like
> the history and the future of your show.

> Anchor
> Jessica, how should we change the way we discuss?

> Jess
> For a start, we could avoid hyperboles and extreme
> examples. When I made my first point that we can look
> at the things that are wrong even if we don't have a
> solution, your response was: "looking at things
> without having any solution is a waste of time?" The
> word "any" strikes me as one of those extremes that
> we should try to avoid. I do have some suggestions,
> even though you assumed I didn't. Posing the problem

and analyzing it first doesn't mean that we can't
come up with an answer later on.

A random sequence is extracted from the movie's database.

                    Anchor
So not only do you have a solution for our economy
but you also claim to have a solution for language
and how we communicate.

                    Jess
No. Most of all, I think that I've developed the
ability to pinpoint what is not working correctly in
our economic system. I don't have THE solution for it
and I certainly don't expect to change how we
communicate with language.

                    Anchor
You just told me that…

                    Rogan
It's not changing language, Jess is just trying to
say that you should avoid giving examples that don't
apply to what she is saying.

                    Anchor
                    (Ironically.)
I agree! So let's keep on moving. Jessica, what is
the problem?

                    Jess
The main problem with our economic system is that it
generates an uneven distribution of wealth.
Capitalism, the efficient market, naturally creates
an environment in which the rich people have many
more means for making money than the poor have. Let
me give you an example: Lets imagine that we have you
over here (points to the left of the anchor) and we
have you over here (points to the right of the
anchor). Both of you are equally intelligent, both of
you have the same education, the same family, the
same first love, but the one over here (left) has one
million dollars and the one over here has ten
thousand dollars. If you set out to make money, which
of the two of you is going to make the next million
first?

                              Anchor
                              (Being somewhat bothered by the
                              fact that he has to answer to the
                              question.)
The one with the million.

                    Jess
Yes, and it's not only because you have the million,
but also because you probably have friends with
millions too. They'll create opportunities for you -

the one on the left - that the one on the right will
not have.

Panda
Also if you have money you have access to privileged
information.

Anchor
Oh, yes. Like what? Give me some hard facts here. Who
are the ones receiving bribes for what information? I
too would like to head this discussion in a direction
so that we actually get somewhere. Because honestly,
we can talk in the abstract for days. Give me an
example, give me a name.

Jess
OK. How about any lawyer, any systems analyst,
accountant, broker, MBA with a specialty in
operations management; do you think that the poor
have access to that information? That information is
privileged, only the wealthy can get it.

Anchor
Are you telling me that you can't study to be an
accountant or a lawyer?

Rogan
If the two of you, the you on the left and the you on
the right are making a product, who is going to have
better information about the market the product
should target? The one with a million dollars or the
one with ten thousand dollars? Even if you study five
different professions, it won't give you a better
shot against someone with money. It's not about
studying to be an accountant, it's about hiring many
of them, accountants and lawyers and MBAs, to backup
your business plan.

Jess
Privileged information is any information that the
poor can't get for monetary reasons.

Anchor
(In discontent.)
Perfect, I hear the problem, what's the solution?

Jess
Not yet, I want to be sure that we understand that an
even distribution of wealth is what we need. And we
need it for two main reasons: First, we live in a
democracy. If we vote for a government, the
government should abide and defend those actions that
benefit the majority. A democracy that supports an
uneven distribution of wealth is flawed for pure
logical reasons. Second, even though it is impossible
to prove if I am right or wrong, I think that we can

ameliorate many of the problems in our society with a
better distribution of wealth.

                    Anchor
Jessica, Jessica, we saw the communist empire fall
right before our eyes…

                    Jess
No, but…

                    Anchor
Please, let me finish. We saw how those dreams were
shattered by a human apathy to work for the well
being of others; if there is not a direct link
between how much you work and how much you get for
your work, the system doesn't work. Am I making
myself clear?

A random sequence is extracted from the movie's database.

                    Anchor
Even distribution of wealth as a society value is a
fallacy. As soon as you create a system in which
everyone gets the same thing regardless of whether or
not they work, you create the biggest incubator for
free riders.

                    Jess
I am not a communist and I don't believe in
communism. This is exactly what's wrong with the way
we discuss things. Just because I question current
capitalism, I'm a communist? Do we have only one or
the other? And even if we do, can we only be
extremists? Are there no tones of gray? Current
economists, the ones in government, the ones in
academia and the myriad of economic students that pop
out every semester, are doing a mediocre job at best.
The problem is that when someone wants to address the
inefficiency of the free market, he is immediately
labeled a commy pinko or radical socialist. That's a
fast remedy used by conformists and ignorants.

                    Anchor
Don't blame all of us for being the same.

A random sequence is extracted from the movie's database. Fade to
black.

Television Show (Jess) Second Part

Scene starts with random sequence extracted from the movie database.

1 Interior. Studios of an online TV news program. Night.

                    Anchor
          If we all mention communism it is because it was the
          alternative to capitalism and it failed, blatantly.
          The images of the Soviet debacle, the falling of the
          Berlin wall, the poverty in the streets of La Habana,
          are still fresh in our minds.

                    Rogan
          I believe Jess agrees with you, it failed. The
          problem is that when you question the uneven
          distribution of wealth, economists tend to answer in
          a way that suggests that everything that could have
          been tried has already been tried; as if the failure
          of the communist system indicates that there is
          nothing else out there but improving the efficiency
          of the free market.

                    Jess
          Economists are mentally framed to make only minor
          adjustments to the capitalistic system that, in
          reality, needs major adjustments.

                    Anchor
          Forgive my ignorance, I still don't understand what
          you are trying to address here. I can't see how
          becoming more efficient is detrimental to society.

                    Jess
          The invisible hand theory of the free market, the
          idea that everything corrects itself if left alone,
          creates the perfect environment for an uneven
          distribution of wealth. Why is that wrong? Because we
          rely on a democracy to choose our government, and the
          majority should receive the most out of a democracy,
          not a selected few.

A random sequence is extracted from the movie's database.

                    Anchor
          You can't deny that there is abundant opportunity in
          the system. So many people have started from scratch
          and have become millionaires. What about Bill Gates?
          Tiger Woods? Don't get me started, I could go on and
          on and on. Those people worked their way up to
          achieve what they have today…

                    Panda
          Yes, but you are giving the exception as the rule.

Anchor
Exceptions! How many would you like me to mention?

Panda
It doesn't matter. How many can you list? If you were
able to come up with five hundred I would be
surprised; still, we live in a country of almost 300
million people and you're saying that hundreds of
cases are not the exception? Publicizing these "real
life" cases as the rule is incredibly misleading.

Jess
And before we go further with the details, I want to
say something else: Up to now it seems that we have
had two systems. According to what you just said
about communism, one that gives money to all of those
who do not work, at the expense of others who do; the
society of free riders. Another one, capitalism, that
doesn't distribute wealth evenly to the working
majority. One is uneven in terms of how much people
work, but they all get the same amount of money, the
other one is uneven in terms of how much money people
get, even if they work the same amount.

Panda
Both are flawed.

Anchor
Well, I accept some of your points. I'm eager to hear
the solutions that you have in hand, because the
subject is extremely complex and we only have limited
time on the show.

Jess
You have to make the market inefficient.

Anchor
(Surprised.)
You have to make the market inefficient.

A random sequence is extracted from the movie's database.

Jess
Yes. Once again, the free hand market promotes a
system in which the rich accumulate more wealth than
the poor, to create an even distribution of wealth
you have to create inefficiencies.

Anchor
You are contradicting the basis of our entire system.

Jess
Making the market inefficient is a moral decision.

Anchor
That is just ludicrous.

                    Jess
I would like you to notice something about our
conversation. Have we talked about any specific issue
regarding the inner workings of our economy? Marginal
costs? Indifference curves? Have we touched on any
micro or macroeconomics?

                    Anchor
I'm starting to wonder if we ever should.

                    Jess
We are simply talking about the ultimate objective of
studying economics. Once, in a discussion with a
panelist, I was told that what I was proposing should
be presented to the politicians, not to the
economists. He just said "oh, that's the politicians'
problem," as if you could separate the two.
Economists have to consider themselves philosophers.
If most of our life is devoted to the creation of
money, then the how-to of making money grabs an
existential tone, doesn't it?

                    Anchor
So you're saying that we need an economist in the
White House? Are you saying that we should have
someone like Friedman leading the country?

                    Jess
No, that is simplifying things. Those are sound
bites. We need all economists to make a conscious
effort to reinvent capitalism to obtain a neo-
capitalism that will distribute wealth in a better
way.

                    Anchor
I am dying to get into the details of it, can we stop
addressing problems and tackle some of your proposals
in this respect. The show only lasts for certain
amount of time.

A random sequence is extracted from the movie's database. Fade out to
black.

Television Show (Jess) Third Part

Scene starts with random sequence extracted from the movie database.

1 Interior. Studios of an online TV news program. Night.

                    Anchor
                    (Ironically.)
          I bet you have heard of limitless needs, limited
          resources.

                    Jess
          I would legislate to control all those businesses
          that the poor cannot access because they lack
          resources.

                    Anchor
          Please, please, an example, we can't go through the
          entire show being abstract…

                    Jess
          The money lending industry is a good example. The
          business of lending money is a business that only
          exists for the rich, for the resourceful. Have you
          ever heard of the poor lending money to the rich? I
          believe that it should be controlled by the
          government in a more strict way and impose profit
          quotas on those who lend money.

                    Anchor
          Are you crazy?! Do you have any idea of what you're
          saying? I hope that none of your economics professors
          are watching this. You may be surprised to find an F
          on your next report card. Our entire economy is
          anchored to the borrowing and lending of money. What
          you are saying will disrupt the market entirely!

                    Jess
          Disrupting an efficient market is a moral decision
          that will benefit the majority. You see, the
          objective is not making the market more and more
          efficient, the objective is distributing wealth in a
          better way. Do I have all the solutions? No. I just
          have the right questions. We have a stream of
          economists graduating every year from hundreds of
          colleges throughout the country. The amount of
          brainpower to find solutions is there, it just has to
          be redirected to solve the real issues.

A random sequence is extracted from the movie's database.

                    Anchor
          Oh, you don't even want to go there. You're going to
          get yourself into big trouble. Ms. Fussell, you are
          quite brave to bring these issues to this show, they

329

make me wonder however about your overall
understanding of the problem. You can't disrupt the
money lending market without it having implications
in every single sector of our economy. You'd have a
major slowdown of the economy and pretty soon
everyone would be out of a job.

                    Jess
I don't believe that's accurate, and what you're
doing is quite typical. In response to challenging
the way the market functions today, you insinuate a
catastrophic scenario, and that is also misleading…
The world will not fall apart if we promote changes
that will ensure a better distribution of wealth.

                    Panda
You make conformism sound like a disaster prevention
measure.

                    Anchor
Give me another solution, give me more… Your critics
are going to blossom, Ms. Fussell. Give me something
that can save you from what is next.

A random sequence is extracted from the movie's database.

                    Jess
Every solution that I will give you conveys big
shifts in the way things work today. Why? Because I'm
addressing the overall objective of our economy: an
even distribution of wealth, not an efficient market
as it has been laid out in the textbooks and in
practice.

                    Anchor
Do you only have one solution?

                    Jess
No, I have another one: Price discrimination.

                    Anchor
Please explain.

                    Jess
Actually, price discrimination is already used in
many different areas of our economy.

                    Anchor
Like where?

                    Rogan
Discounts to students. For example, it is normal that
colleges offer discounts when students buy software.
It would seem that it is a measure to make software
accessible to students with low resources, however,
it also helps the software provider sell the product

to someone that wouldn't have been able to buy it
without the discount.

Jess
It is a form of discrimination. So, the idea is to
use the same principle on everything.

Rogan
You use the power of the digital era to discriminate.
I believe that one of the big book sellers on the web
is doing it, and they named it dynamic pricing. So
what you do is you sell the same book at different
prices to people with different levels of wealth.

Anchor
And in the mean time you create a huge black market.

Jess
Once again the catastrophe…

Anchor
No, no, if the rich pay more for a book, what it is
going to happen is that the rich pays a small
percentage to the poor for buying the book.

Jess
Yes.

Anchor
What do you mean "yes"? You don't solve anything that
way. You just create a market out of the
inefficiencies of the market that you just created.
You will have armies of poor people buying for the
rich because they can get a percentage out of it.

Jess
Exactly, an inefficiency that will benefit the poor
more than the rich, but wait, you can find
equilibrium without having a horrible black market
but just another economic activity. Equilibrium will
come when the market shifts and the poor will not
make as much money from reselling products to the
rich, and when the rich prefer to avoid the
intermediary. There is no catastrophe. Is there a
shift that will affect many? Yes. However, it will
benefit the majority.

Anchor
Ms. Fussell, it has been quite an interesting show,
with very strange ideas, but unique indeed. Is there
anything you would like to add before we go to
commercial?

Jess
Yes. I don't deny the complexity of the issues that I
am presenting. However, it is crucial to understand
that economists, politicians or not, have a moral

responsibility to invent neo-capitalism. Yes it is
complex but so is the study of biology, physics and
other sciences.

                    Anchor
Briefly…

                    Jess
Addressing the issue without having a solution is
healthy for us.

                    Anchor
Truth Serum! Take it or leave it. We have a few words
from our sponsors and then we'll be right back.

A random sequence is extracted from the movie's database. Fade out to
black.

Television Show (Panda) First Part

Scene starts with random sequence extracted from the movie database.

1 Interior. Studios of an online TV news program. Night.

> Anchor
> Pandora Hamilton is a student of advertising and an
> original and unique voice on the information super-
> highway. Panda I have read the biography that you
> gave to the producers of the show and I have to tell
> you that I find it absolutely fascinating. I also
> took some time to go to your website and look at the
> material is there... Why?

> Panda
> (Confused.)
> Why? I don't understand the question.

> Anchor
> Allow me to give our audience a quick insight into
> you and your work. Pandora uses computer animations
> on the Internet to express her ideas and her points
> of view. I spent some time going through Pandora's
> website in order to summarize the work you have there
> but I couldn't put it into words. Do you mind if we
> take a look at one of your… How should I say it? What
> would you call them?

> Panda
> Rants…

> Anchor
> Rants. I couldn't have expressed it better. I tried
> to tell Jeffrey, our production manager, about them
> and I couldn't so... Would you mind if we show one of
> them so the people at home can understand what we're
> talking about?

> Panda
> (Exposed and uncomfortable.)
> Go ahead.

A random sequence is extracted from the movie's database.

> Anchor
> Why do you rant, Pandora? What are you angry about?
> Why should the entire world listen to you?

> Panda
> (Trying slowly to respond to all
> the questions.)

I rant because I can, because I have an opportunity
to do so. What am I so angry about? I'm angry about
the voice of commercialism, its pervasiveness in the
media, and its effect on culture, our culture. Why
should the entire world listen to me? I think I don't
agree with your idea that there is a true potential
of the "entire world" listening to me, maybe a few
thousand but not more.

                    Anchor
Ok, but you are using the Internet, you can expect a
large global audience…

                    Panda
No…

                    Anchor
                    (In a intimate tone.)
Why Pandora? Why rants?

                    Panda
                    (Now looking somewhat angry.)
I rant because you have a misconception of reality, I
rant because I believe that you are an intelligent
person but you just get the wrong messages... Because
someone like you has come to believe the false claims
of advertising.

                    Anchor
Like what Pandora? What do I believe that is not
true?

                    Panda
If you express an idea on the Internet you do not
reach the entire world. The idea that you can is
quite inaccurate. I think many Americans suffer from
a strange type of megalomania. They believe that they
can go "global" now, thanks to the Internet.

                    Anchor
Are you telling me that the Internet is not global?

                    Panda
Yes.

A random sequence is extracted from the movie's database.

                    Panda
Geographically, the Internet is not everywhere, and
population wise, the Internet is only being used by a
very small part of the world's population. It would
seem on the web that all cultures exist in harmony,
and we all know very well that isn't true.

                    Anchor
But Panda, Panda, the idea of the "global village"
has been around for several decades.

Panda
That idea of the "global village" is suitable only to
rich people in rich countries, but it is just a
concept and nothing more. The reality of the Internet
has been distorted so much by the media, especially
in advertising, that there is very little left of the
truth to hold on to.

Jess
(First to Panda, later to the
anchor.)
Can I give an example? Electronic trading is always
presented as a gold mine. The majority of the ads
tell you that if you have all the information, you
have all the tools to beat the market. That's a big
lie. You can have all the information in the world,
but if you don't know how to make sense of it, you
are in no better trading position than if you go to a
casino with a lot of information about of the
producer of the chips you gamble with -that is, you
pack yourself with a lot of meaningless information.

Rogan
And that's assuming the information given to you via
the companies' financial statements are accurate at
all.

Jess
For most people, stock trading on the Internet is
nothing but a form of gambling. It has been used as a
device to pull money out of regular people's savings
accounts by promising them that they will become rich
or smart by beating the market's rate of return.
Those savings from regular citizens go to
corporations with the biggest PR campaigns, not to
the corporations with the highest economic potential.
It is based on speculation and rumors, most of them
delivered through regular news outlets in the media.

Rogan
You have to lose some money trading to know that it
doesn't matter if you have all the financial
statements in history at the tip of your fingers and
market data flying across your screen in real time,
it matters if you can make sense of it or not; and
there are many very intelligent people who have spent
many years studying finance and accounting to make
some sense out of the information provided by these
companies.

A random sequence is extracted from the movie's database. Fade out to
black.

Television Show (Panda) Second Part

Scene starts with random sequence extracted from the movie database.

1 Interior. Studios of an online TV news program. Night.

                            Anchor
            So you believe that the latest commercials about
            trading on the Internet are misguiding people?
            Pandora do you agree? Are people being misled?

                            Panda
            Yes. But trading stock using the Internet is only one
            of hundreds of examples. The average American sees
            thousands of ads on a daily basis, most of them
            making false claims about their products. I wonder
            all the time about what kind of impact that has on
            our culture.

                            Anchor
            Why? What's wrong?

                            Panda
            Everybody knows that ads are meant to be persuasive,
            right? That's why we can have an ad that tells you
            that a facial cream will propel your self-esteem
            right up through the roof. But does anyone ever stop
            to question the psychological impact of these ads? It
            isn't just one, it's several thousands a day,
            multiplied by a person's life time. Even if we know
            that these ads are meant to be persuasive and that we
            shouldn't believe what they say, the impact of the
            sheer volume must be substantial. Can we really
            expect that society can disregard all of those
            messages, especially when we consider that they are
            designed to grab our attention?

A random sequence is extracted from the movie's database.

                            Anchor
            So you don't think that we can just shrug this off as
            advertisement and let it go at that? Don't get me
            wrong, I understand what you are saying.
            Advertisements are designed to grab your attention -
            probably because Americans are notorious for having a
            short attention span - but I wonder if anyone here in
            the studio would have any problems understanding that
            even though the ad might say so, a facial cream will
            not give you all the confidence that you've always
            lacked. I think we have the ability to see it for
            what it is, a way to sell products: If you think
            about the ad, you will realize that no facial cream
            is going to solve your existential crisis.

                         Panda
          Exactly. My point is that your existential crisis is
          caused by not one ad but by a myriad of them giving
          you false claims. If we forget about specific
          products or specific examples, and look at the
          overall trends in advertising you can see why it is
          affecting us negatively. First, you are constantly
          inundated with messages of a dream world that does
          not exist. Second, this constant barrage tells you
          that you are unsatisfied, that you are unsettled,
          that change is necessary. You might not pay attention
          to one or ten. I am sure that thousands of them by
          the day have an impact on your psyche.

A random sequence is extracted from the movie's database.

                         Panda
          The advertising industry depicts a world in which you
          are always unsettled; ah, but there is hope, you can
          fix things by acquiring the product.

                         Anchor
          So you are telling me that advertising raises our
          level of anxiety…

                         Panda
          Yes.

                         Anchor
          Do you know of any study that shows this effect?

                         Panda
          No.

                         Anchor
                    (Looking at Panda in disbelief.)
          No. I'm not following you.

                         Panda
          Can I give you an example?

                         Anchor
          That would definitely help.

                         Panda
          Yesterday I saw an ad about something that was called
          the acne complex. According to the advertisers, an
          acne complex is when you have bad-self image, when
          you feel isolated, when you feel embarrassment about
          yourself because of your acne. If you use the
          product, you stop having the acne complex, people
          will notice your skin, they will accept you, you will
          recover your true self.

                         Jess
          And this is only one ad.

                              Panda
Yes.

                              Jess
You have to see many of them throughout the day
because as you said: "They are meant to grab your
attention".

                              Rogan
And you can always question if the small attention
span in Americans isn't actually created by that
daily wave of messages trying to grab your attention.

                              Panda
In addition to telling you constantly that you're
unsettled, that you need change, also tell you that
you need to change this in your life to become
something else, and some of them, like the example I
gave you, sow seeds of fear in you of being isolated…

                              Rogan
Left behind…

                              Panda
So the typical ad line sells you anxiety by telling
you that you have to get it "now," it is a "limited
time offer," "call now" (Jess says at the same time:
"order now"). Exactly.

                              Jess
And once again, we aren't talking about one single
product, this is the trend in advertising.

                              Panda
So, not only are you unsettled but, you have to fix
it now or else.

A random sequence is extracted from the movie's database. Fade out to
black.

338

Television Show (Panda) Third Part

Scene starts with random sequence extracted from the movie database.

1 Interior. Studios of an online TV news program. Night.

                         Anchor
          Pandora…

                         Panda
          Panda is fine.

                         Anchor
          Panda, the other piece that I selected from your
          website is also related to this… Let's take a look at
          it, can we?

A random sequence is extracted from the movie's database.

                         Anchor
          Panda, what do you mean by "measures to correct life
          are garbage"? Please explain.

                         Panda
          It tries to counteract the claims that you see in
          ads. Your life is ok as it is. Don't believe that you
          have to correct something because there is nothing to
          correct. In the advertising world, the typical thing
          that corrects your life is the product: it makes you
          better, it makes you happier, it makes you look
          better even if you don't, and it settles your urge to
          be what you are supposed to be… Don't believe it.
          It's not true.

                         Jess
          Furthermore, you don't have to correct it now. To me,
          that rant not only says that, but it also says:
          Relax, there is no need to feel anxiety even if you
          are told all day long that you need to improve
          yourself "right now," before the limited offer ends,
          etc.

                         Anchor
          Why the anger? They are rants right?

                         Panda
          Yes... I guess I'm angry.

                         Anchor
          You're an honest person.

                         Panda
          It's a virtue that feels like a curse...

                    Anchor
What are you angry about?

                    Panda
Noticing that the system is not working and being
unable to change things. Even if I devote my entire
life to it, my chances of accomplishing something are
still almost nil. Where do you start? How long can
you endure?

                    Anchor
Where would you start? Have thoughts about a first
move?

                    Panda
I started a long time ago when I decided to study the
advertising industry to learn about how it works. My
first direct step towards being actively involved in
finding a solution are the rants that I have on my
website. But it is a grain of sand in a vast
universe. A true solution would be to stop the
advertising industry from making false claims.

A random sequence is extracted from the movie's database.

                    Anchor
I understand that there are laws for false
advertising already on the books, but what you seem
to be insinuating well.... You're getting into
dangerous ground if you go there.

                    Jess
Why?

                    Anchor
Because you're prohibiting a type of speech, and one
of the pillars of this country is freedom of speech.

                    Panda
As you said, the advertising industry is already
regulated, it is not that I'm recommending a new law
to impede freedom of speech, what we should do is
raise the bar and allow a lot less blatant dishonesty
and manipulation.

                    Rogan
On one hand you have the cultural consequences of
enduring a pervasive advertising industry that tells
us all the time that we are unsettled, that we need
change. On the other hand you have the corporations'
freedom of speech.

                    Anchor
And on the third hand, if you allow me to create a
monster, you have the economy slowing down.

                    Jess
        Well, we're not sure about that. But if the economy
        slows down because of the direct impact of limiting
        corporate speech, I wonder if we should consider the
        final result a positive one.

                    Anchor
        Not if we are in economic competition with other
        countries in the world.

                    Panda
        And this is the moment in which the "global village"
        argument starts to fade away. In any case, if there
        is such a thing as a global community, I really hope
        those who "represent" us can bring these issues to
        the discussion table.

                    Anchor
        Which is exactly what we are doing here. Truth Serum,
        take it or leave it. We will be back right after
        these messages.

A random sequence is extracted from the movie's database. Fade out to
black.

Television Show (Rogan) First Part

Scene starts with random sequence extracted from the movie database.

1 Interior. Studios of an online TV news program. Night.

Anchor
Rogan Williams is a student of Information Science, and author of two poetry books: one entitled "Poetry on Mathematics" and the other called "The Storm Within". In addition to poetry, Rogan also has had several of his short stories published in prestigious magazines throughout the country. Rogan, poetry, mathematics, short stories, information science… quite a diverse and unusual set of talents.

Rogan
If you follow stereotypes, yes. I'm definitely not your typical information science student.

Anchor
Rogan, in your estimation, what are the crucial issues in information science today?

Rogan
There are many, but I am particularly interested in issues that are not commonly discussed in the media.

Anchor
What issues are not being covered and why do you think media organizations disregard them?

Rogan
I can't say why media organizations and their news programs omit them, but I can tell you that I am more interested in pointing out what those issues are than finding someone to blame. Two semesters ago I wrote a paper named "The year 2000 gold fever," it was for a class in electronic commerce. In it I made a comparison between what happened with the rise and the fall of the dot-coms and what happened with the US gold fever back in the 1850s.

Anchor
Interesting, and what was your conclusion?

Rogan
In the 1850s, the people who made the most money out of the gold fever were not those who traveled from afar in search of gold nuggets. The people who made the money were the ones who sold the maps and the sifters to the dream seekers.

                 Jess
Hope is a terrible thing to waste.

                Rogan
I made the same analysis with current public
financial information: I found that the people who
made money out of ecommerce gold fever were not the
dot-coms, but those who provided the "tools" to
pursue those become-a-millionaire dreams. While the
sum of profit of the dot coms is negative, the
hardware industry and the software industry have had
incredible growth.

A random sequence is extracted from the movie's database.

               Anchor
With all due respect, don't you think that your
analysis is somewhat shortsighted? Without being a
business person, (tiny arrogant tone) because I am
more of a social thinker, I must say that I believe
these companies are after the "first-move advantage".
You're familiar with the term?

                Rogan
Yes I am.

               Anchor
Let me ask you all a question: Do you use a word
processor? How many times have you switched from one
word processor to another?

                Rogan
Once…

               Anchor
And the two of you (to Panda and Jess) have not
switched ever? The reason why you haven't switched is
because it takes too much time to learn these
programs again, to learn how they operate. Online
companies are after this first-mover advantage. Is
that bad?

A random sequence is extracted from the movie's database.

                Rogan
I think it is.

               Anchor
Oh, come on, Rogan, what do you….

                Rogan
Let me explain. I agree with the part of the first-
mover advantage which, by the way, is perhaps
something we should be concerned with as consumers.
Does it sound right to you that your loyalty to a
product is based on very high switching costs? Is

that loyalty? It's not that you wouldn't want to
change, you just don't because of the personal
expense involved in switching.

                    Jess
It doesn't sound like part of the rationale for a
free-market, where it is easy to switch among
products, does it? And I wonder why the free market
lovers don't address this issue; hasn't it been made
easy for corporations to rotate labor under the same
arguments.

                    Rogan
What I don't agree with is the idea that websites
hook you like that. I don't think that the first
mover advantage is so dramatic for online ventures.
But, but, your are right in saying that those
companies are looking to be the first-movers and many
other things that have been fed to them by the
hardware and the software PR and advertising
campaigns.

                    Anchor
What other things?

                    Jess
Going global; forming part of a meaner, tougher
generation of entrepreneurs, (smiling) the "d"
generation; the false idea that you can reach
millions with the touch of a button; all of those
megalomaniac dreams that are regularly sold to the
American public are misconceptions about how the
Internet is working for people and how it can work
for you.

                    Rogan
And in the mean time, while you have crowds of people
living those deliriums of grandeur, investing what
they have in their savings account hoping to conquer
a piece of the world, the hardware and the software
industries are making a lot of money.

                    Jess
Needless to say, "conquering the world" ended up
being nothing more than "taking hold of a 9 to 5 job"
where they needed word processing experience.

A random sequence is extracted from the movie's database. Fade out to
black.

Television Show (Rogan) second Part

Scene starts with random sequence extracted from the movie database.

1 Interior. Studios of an online TV news program. Night.

> Anchor
> So you're telling me that the hardware and software.
> industries are lying to us?

> Rogan
> No, what we are telling you is that the reality of
> what computers are capable of doing for you, at the
> time, is not accurately represented in the media.

> Panda
> Also, the Internet is a new medium, the majority of
> people don't know much about it, so when you see
> advertisements about it you can't tell between the
> false claims and the real ones -if there are real
> ones.

> Anchor
> Like what? Give me examples.

> Jess
> They make you believe that there's no learning
> involved, when in reality, computers and software are
> unique kinds of products because they require a large
> amount of time to understand and use. An ad on
> television may tell you that "if you buy their
> special tax software you can do your taxes in a snap,
> it's as easy as 1, 2, 3".

> Rogan
> So people can't tell what a false claim is and what's
> not. We are still in an adjustment period and some
> are benefiting big time from the confusion.

> Jess
> Needless to say, it's not the poor who benefit.

> Rogan
> Still, I think that we are concentrating too much on
> the details. We're not talking about the most
> important issues.

> Anchor
> You have to understand that this TV show has its
> viewers in mind. I have to get to the specifics and
> not leave everything at a conceptual level.

A random sequence is extracted from the movie's database.

> Rogan

Have you heard of the digital divide?

> Anchor

Yes, I have. Actually, I'm rather intimate with the details on that subject. We had a show a few weeks ago about what measures are being implemented to reduce the technological gap between the rich and the poor. Did you watch it?

> Rogan

No. Did you talk about why it is necessary to reduce the gap between the two?

> Anchor
> (Cocky.)

What do you mean. Of course we did, it's fairly obvious: The digital divide has been a focus for social advocates who fear that some groups are going to be missing out on the benefits of technological advances.

> Jess

There are so many things to pinpoint from what you just said.

> Anchor
> (Somewhat upset.)

Mrs. Fussell, please be more clear.

> Rogan

What are the "have-nots" going to be missing out on?

> Anchor

Why don't you tell me, Mr. Williams?

> Rogan

I think that I agree with you, the benefits aren't very evident. So far, the digital divide is measured by the number of households that have computers. Do you really believe that having a computer at home makes you more productive or more efficient in the way you live? Do you cook better? Do you rest better? Do you sleep better? Is the Internet really empowering people to speak out?

> Panda

Do you think that having a computer at home is going to produce an egalitarian society?

> Rogan

Of course not.

> Anchor

So, what are the benefits?

Rogan

You might mention "access to information"; however, I'm sure that you would agree that relying on the information that you find on the web is risky because basically you don't know much about who is putting up the information on the net. Besides, an overwhelming amount of the information on the web is about products and services.

Panda

The ads for using the Internet basically sell a mall with the sales pitch of a library.

A random sequence is extracted from the movie's database.

Rogan

Beyond any claim of being beneficial for your kids, being up to date with what happens in the world, using it to send pictures to your grandparents, or simply using it for entertainment purposes, beyond any of those smoke screens, having a computer at home connected to the Internet basically makes you a target, the ultimate sitting consumer duck.

Jess

It is not the individual, but corporations that benefit most. Corporations can use the Internet to develop niches in a way unprecedented in history. Not only that, corporations are able to personalize marketing campaigns according to who you are.

Rogan
(Gently interjecting)

So, if we return to what we were talking about: Reducing the digital divide is more of an immediate positive venture for corporations than it is for individuals. If there is such a thing as a technological division in society, it should be solved through education, at schools, not by placing computers in as many households as you can.

Jess

And that is when the "social advocates" of your previous comment come to light as mere charlatans.

A random sequence is extracted from the movie's database. Fade out to black.

Television Show (Rogan) second Part

Scene starts with random sequence extracted from the movie database.

1 Interior. Studios of an online TV news program. Night.

Anchor

You are making a case to save the world based on of a few crippled ideas. Forgive me if I disagree blatantly with you. The best way to arm the consumer is to provide them with a lot of information about products and services. The information can be in the form of commentaries from other consumers about the product or services, or in the form of simple comparison tables. By doing this you empower consumers, enabling them to make the best purchasing decisions. You force companies to compete by giving better products at better prices with better quality in service. Giving more information to the people is better, not worse!

Jess

I disagree.

Anchor

I would love to hear why you disagree. You assume that everything is broke and everything has to be fixed. It's very romantic of you to believe that corporations and the government act against people and not for the people.

A random sequence is extracted from the movie's database.

Anchor

It's also very naïve to think that there is collusion against consumers and that someone is trying to cheat us all the time.

Jess

Don't you realize that a better price and better service quality work against each other? The better service quality you have the more it costs to you as a company, the more it costs you the higher the price, right? How can you reduce the price and increase the service quality? It's like pulling a bunny out of a hat.

Rogan

And, if you have a chart contrasting all the characteristics of a product, I bet that you can easily compare prices —it's a simple price tag, but how do you compare service quality accurately?

                    Panda
Someone will advertise customer service 24/7, but in
reality that means that you can go to the website at
any time to read frequently asked questions, to
search the knowledge base, or to discuss the
solutions to your problems with other customers.

                    Rogan
The type of old-fashioned customer services you're
probably thinking of companies are now beginning to
charge for when you buy their products? I never
remember my parents paying the local hardware store
an extra $50 as insurance, just in case they had to
come back with questions about how the new circular
saw, or drill they just bought works. "Better buy the
insurance sir, because if you don't know how to use
that saw, or if it doesn't cut right, it's gonna cost
you an extra $15 an hour for us to help you." Sounds
absurd when you think about it that way, doesn't it.

                    Jess
Exactly.

A random sequence is extracted from the movie's database.

                    Anchor
Rogan, one last thought before we go to commercial.

                    Rogan
There are many things that can be addressed in terms
of why we need to use technology to even things out
among people, but I guess that we covered the most
important issue.

                    Anchor
Can you restate the most important issue regarding
technology?

                    Rogan
Technology always poses opportunities and threats –
and when I mean threats I don't mean all those over
publicized hackers and "rebels". The major threats
related to the use of new technologies come from the
creators themselves. You can call it (he starts
counting his fingers): the power to make sense of
data, bend privacy standards, claim that products and
services are easy when they are not, etc. It would be
naïve to think that there are no threats coming from
corporations, but these types of threats seldom reach
the media.

                    Anchor
Truth Serum, take it or leave it.

A random sequence is extracted from the movie's database. Fade out to
black.

Underwear

Scene starts with random sequence extracted from the movie database.

   1.   Interior. Building. Night.

Jeremiah and Ira are walking down a hallway in the building, on their way to a bathroom.

                Ira
This stuff should not happen. You let your friends
run wild around this place.

               Jeremiah
Ira...It's not like...

                Ira
Don't deny it. You know they monkey around in this
place.

               Jeremiah
I'll clean it up. What's the big deal?

                Ira
Didn't I ask you not to use the bathrooms?

               Jeremiah
Ok, we'll lock them up, and that way we wont have to
deal with it anymore.

                Ira
Too late. I am sick and tired of this shit. I'm
shutting off the water. You can pee out the window
for all I care.

A random sequence is extracted from the movie's database.

               Jeremiah
Why are you freaking out?

                Ira
There are 28 bathrooms in this building and you
people have decided to destroy all of them. I can't
believe you people are all over the damn place. You
all are puking and other stuff.

               Jeremiah
Look, anybody is doing any pucking, and if there is
anybody doing any pucking they would have the decency
to do it in advance.

A random sequence is extracted from the movie's database.

                              Ira
                         (Entering another bathroom.)
              Oh no, look at this shit.

There is a used underwear covered with shit besides a toilet. Jeremiah
cracks up.

                              Ira
              It is not funny. It isn't funny. That's sick! Which
              one of your friends did that?

                              Jeremiah
              Hey, it wasn't one of my friends who did that. It is
              one of your friends, look at that underwear, none of
              my friends uses underwear like that.

                              Ira
              Oh, bullshit. There are only two keys to this place.
              You got one and I got one, and I didn't do it. So who
              does that leave? It was one of your friends, I am not
              accusing you, it was one of your friends. Now you
              clean that shit up.

                              Jeremiah
              Oh come on...

                              Ira
              Clean this shit up.

Ira leaves the bathroom.
                              Jeremiah
                         (Looking at the underwear.)
              Shit… I'm gonna kill Zak!

A random sequence is extracted from the movie's database. Fade out.

351

Pandora's Rants

by

Pandora Hamilton
(Diego Bonilla)

The following rants are writings by Pandora Hamilton, one of the main characters of A Space of Time. They are reflecting the intent of the character within A Space of Time's plot, who authors animated poetry for the World Wide Web.

For all rants, except for Rant 5, lines in the text represent independent lines in the computer screen animation. Rant 5 is displayed on the computer's screen word by word.

RANT 1
That little self-importance spot

Do you realize
that if you look back
on the things you've done
everything
absolutely everything
could be understood
as the path that someone
(you)
had to take
to avoid
being
an
u-n-d-e-r-a-c-h-i-e-v-e-r?
Think…
Think hard
and
don't
lie
to
yourself.
Giving credit
to your past
is to live in peace.
But can you?
As you grow old
the system takes control.
As you grow old
you start giving value
not
to
the
accomplishing
of
your
dearest
projects
but you start
giving value
to your struggle,
you want at least a reward
for the time that you have invested
pursuing those unreachable dreams…
And once
you take pride
in your struggle
that's when
the
environment
takes
control…
Struggling is something everyone has to do to be like you,
to be where you are,

that little self-importance spot.
Be true to yourself:
You had to let go at some point.
And
yes
even though you have blurred
your past ideals
the pride
that you feel
for all that time,
all that effort,
all those falls,
is your precious
V-I-P
pass
to form part
of
the
system.
Time
has always been
your worst enemy.
You've lost, pal,
but cheer up,
now you can watch
how
others
struggle.
You have earned the right
to be evasive
to your own memories.
Even though you've lost your soul.

There
is
nothing
much
in
there
anymore.
Is there?

RANT 2
Fuck life

So
are you prepared?
Are you?
Time is ticking away
and under strict survival terms
(true economic Darwinism)
you
cannot
sit
back
and
contemplate
the
world!
You better start moving
change comes
so
fast
that
if you are not
up to date
You might loose ground…
You might lag behind…
You might go under…

So
get ready.
Compete.
Loose your life
pursuing
the ideal
of being fast,
finding
SUCCESS,
you are nothing
but a unit of production
with dreams,
you are
the perfect entity
for the system.
Go on,
find success,
be an achiever
by climbing the social ladder,
earn more,
show us that you are
noble enough
to pursue
those sweet values
of contemporary society.

The less romantic
you are
about life,
the more efficient
you will be
as
a
machine
be pragmatic.

Work your ass off.
Fuck life.
Go on,
go conquer,
go fetch.
And don't you dare
to think too much about it
we might stereotype you
as the philosopher type,
the parasite,
the free rider,
the looser,
the underachiever…

Go on,
go conquer,
go fetch,
you might loose your chance
to prove yourself to us,
and if you do,
you are gone,
you are nothing,
you are not.

So,
go
on.
You have potential,
work hard,
work more,
work fast.
You will be an achiever.
Fuck life.

RANT 3
I know you were not always like this

I don't believe
(if you give a damn about what I believe)
that you haven't changed.
You have.
I don't believe
(knowing that my beliefs are meaningless to you)
that you came
to the world
just to accept the rules
in order to survive.
I don't believe
that there wasn't a period
of
healthy
amazement,
pristine
laughter,
happy
naiveté.
I bet you were a kid.
I bet that at some point
you
were
corrupted.
Long time ago
you had no scars
for being left out,
you had no scars
for not being able
to fit
in.
Life came in abundance.
How
does
it
feel
now
that
you
have
to
juggle
all
your
ambitions?
How
does
it
feel
to know
that the rest of your life
is

going
to
be
devoted
to raising your living standards?
How
does
it
feel
to know
that the only open venue
for fantasy
lies in the arid realm of
a-d-v-e-r-t-i-s-i-n-g?
How
is
it?

But I don't believe that you were always like this
(if by chance you give a shit about what I believe)

I know that adjusting to the world
became
an unavoidable
necessity.
In the most subtle way you were told:
Don't you dare
not to suffer
as we all do,
don't you dare
to avoid
your responsibility
of trying
to get more,
acquire more,
obtain more…
practice choice,
and compare
your possible bundle of choices
with that of who you know,
adjust to the
"real world,"
where we are all greedy,
and we have painstaking duties,
we'll pressure you in many ways
until
you
do
so,
we'll pressure you
until
you
crack…

but I know it wasn't always like this,
you were guided…
you grew up…

you had to comply…
I know you were not always
like this.

RANT 4
What philosophy is left out there?

Have you lost your way?
What philosophy
is left out there
for you to munch on?
Bare capitalism?
What are you, my dear?
Flesh?
Sexual screw-up?
A rationalistic economic entity?
A survivor?
Is there really no philosophy out there to munch on?
Is there really no religion to hold on to?

Please,
leave that
to
those
that
think…
The only human characteristic you are attributed
is
the
power
to choose
among cars,
vacation spots,
football teams,
shaving creams,
stock options,
fat-free food.

You choose,
and that's it.

Face it.
Your biggest
ever
possible
contribution to society
is to be
a selector of things.

But wait,
not that fast,
you know,
you've been told that,
you can only choose
from this set of things,
limit your freedom to the convenience
of the controlling ones,
be careful to choose
to live in a commune,

```
be careful to choose
socialism,
be careful to choose
against those little precious things that preserve
the status quo,
be careful to choose
against a capitalistic understanding
of the world.

This is why you are trained.
You finish high school
and now you are ready to know
when to save,
where to save,
and how to exercise
your brand new
choosing rationale.

Now you have to work
to be able to choose.
Congrats.

There is no real philosophy to munch on…
and there is no religion to hold on to.
```

RANT 5
The fatalist

Are you the fatalist
who believes nothing can be done?
You also romantically promoted change,
but you grew wiser and then gave up?

So you think evil is embedded in human nature?
Is that the long lasting lesson that history has given us?

You are wrong.

Your lack of hope is what is damaging us.
You want to make the word "mediocrity"
sound like "heroic survival".
You've been instructed that by screwing everybody else
you will save yourself and you will save others.

Does it really work like that?
Let me sum up your rationale:
fight against others for a better boring job,
a better boxy house,
a high definition TV with that kick ass surround system
for you to get those full blown advertisements.

Others will be fighting you too,
and they will be happy to have the gadgets
that you don't have.

This version of life resembling a battle
should serve you well.
You must be very happy by acknowledging
your compliance to the "real" world.
Please realize that you are saying
that you are happy
that you learned to swim
after you threw yourself into the shit hole.
You believe that growing is learning to swim
with a smile on your face.
And that's heroic,
that's being a survivor.

Listen,
that's why your midlife crisis is worth nothing.
Shedding crocodile tears
about how you screwed yourself up in the past
is simply pitiful.
Don't you realize that we are striving
to getter better at the worst things.
Do we really need to work more
to be more free?
Sure, nothing else can be done:
Jumping into the shit hole
is the only thing there is.
Making existence a battleground is the right move.

RANT 6
The Idea of Progress

So there,
to prove my point
I will be flat out straight
with you:
You believe in change,
you've been
immersed
in
this
idea
(overwhelming reality)
that we live in a world
where
a
hectic
search
for progress is
not only
desirable,
but also
unavoidable,
you've been told that
progress is a must,
progress shall remain forever after
as an unquestionable truth…
but the progress
that you believe in
is
not
made
out
of
a
better
human
condition,
for you
progress
is just the will to
constantly change,
change fast,
change via your ambitions,
your greed.

So change,
you are the sweet lamb of progress,
you shall
succeed
in
your
effort
to
sacrifice

```
yourself,
be
MORE,
be
BIGGER
be
UNSETTLED
with
your
current
condition.

Go on,
sweet lamb,
in the name of progress
you shall
see
life
passing
by
like a somewhat tangible
but extremely fast
dream.

Do you get my point?
Sacrifice yourself.
```

RANT 7
Love for you

Love?
Oh, come on.
You fall in love.
You don't love.
We all know that
it is a common trend
by now.

You see,
what used to be a rainbow
has turned out to be
a simple
grayscale...

You are just
a
demanding
animal.

You don't love, come on.
You have a propensity
to
breed.

You have developed
a dreadful
taste
for love
but in that universe of yours
you are definitely self contained.

Love for you
is an accumulation
of simple characteristics,
traits
that will give momentarily
a
subtle
and
bearable
tone
to your
fleeting
existence.
And this will be your time
for a while,
until you
need the thrill
of falling in love
again,
until
you realize that

what you looked for
before
bores you
day by day...

Then you will be ready to change...
Change again...
Change as before...
Change again...
Look for the thrill
somewhere else.

Yes,
as before,
and then again,
you will find all the arguments
to
justify
your abandonment...
justify
your
lack
of
luck...
your sorry faith.

Trust me.
You don't love.

RANT 8
Do you get it?

Do you get it?
Do you want me to go slower?
You've been trained.
You are alienated.
You behave according to a norm
Without substance
Without justification
Without use.
You are a reflection of everyone else's fears.
Do you want me to go slower?
Beware
You might be abnormal.
Feel the social pressure.
Learn to comply.
Beware
You might escape
Everyone else's comfort level.
Be.
Be them.
Be
Be them.
Sleep tight.

RANT 9
Resist the illusion, just don't

Resist the illusion.
All those measures
that you have to take to correct your life
are garbage.
Don't have an ad
as the indicator
of what is to be
your role model.
Don't let them tell you
who you are,
who you should be.
(To them you are less, you are weak, you are behind, you are afraid,
you are unhappy.)
Out there is an open competition
to be someone,
to accomplish a lot,
to bring others
that will accomplish a lot too.
(Breed.)
Please.
Don't do this to be that.
Just don't.
Don't acquire,
don't eat that,
don't be more or less than others,
don't believe it.
Just don't.
Don't be afraid of not having.
Don't fall into debt.
Don't let them tell you
who you are,
who you should be.
It doesn't matter
if you miss an opportunity,
a myriad of them will come.
(They will provide them again.)
Resist the illusion
and start feeling joy,
weightlessness.
Measures to correct your life are nothing but garbage.
There is nothing to correct.
You are ok as you are.
You are just fine.

RANT 10
Stop marketing yourself

You are a trender
you adapt your psyche,
your believes,
your hopes,
your past…
to fit properly with the current trends.
(But the worst of all is that you are trendy because you are scared.)
There is nothing stable in you.
No long term traits,
just a hypocritical go with the flow;
anything to avoid isolation,
anything to be normal,
anything to be hip.
You adapt constantly.
Your thing is not being someone
but being accepted,
and by doing that
you are willing to change
the way you interpret your own memories,
your same recurring lies,
who you are,
where do you want to be.

STOP MARKETING YOURSELF

There is no clear image
of who
you
are.
You are so much your environment,
that asking about your sense of self,
is ludicrous.
Your identity it's a mere trick
to make you functional.
And when you talk about yourself,
when you summarize your likes and dislikes,
your gathering of accomplishments,
you believe that
that list is you…

But it's not.
What could it be?

RANT 11
Let me tell you what I see

Let me tell you what I see:
Too much style,
too little substance.
Been there?
Done that?
So have you conquered a piece of the world yet?
Are you a baby boomer, generation x or generation d?
You are no one.
Everything in your existence is pure circumstance.
Your ideals morph throughout life
and then you understand
that everything
has been reduced to style,
when in the bottom of your heart
there is no substance.
Humble yourself.
You are one in six billion.
You haven't suffered that much.
You haven't done the time.
Being big in your head while being small in life
is a dichotomy as common as love and despair.

RANT 12
Are you in debt

Are you in debt?
Have they teased you too many times?
Have they given you
those arguments
of what you should have
to be someone?
To be happy,
To be secure,
To be good looking,
To be fast,
To be better than the rest of them?

Poor baby.
Now you owe them money.
Now you are able to realize
the pressure
they've put on you,
the anxiety causing mechanisms,
the "get me now" rationale.
And then what?
You jumped into the wagon of consumerism
and you can't find joy somewhere else.
I know you.
Most probably, you are in debt.
You couldn't resist the bait.

I want you to think about it.
Your impatience
Has cost you so much money.

You've been fed anxiety and it worked.

How can you live a humble life?

Is this a very old question?
Is this a very naïve question?
Is this not a "real life" question?
How can you live a humble life
When you are asked every day
to be someone else?
(Plus this, plus that.)
Think about it.

You've been fed anxiety.
Did you get for yourself all of those things?
Are you happier?
Are you more secure?
Are good looking now?
Are you fast as you should be?
Are you better than those
who are trying to better than you?

Poor baby.
The only thing that is blatant
is that you owe them part of your future.

RANT 13
Artists

Artists.
I blame you for much of our disasters.
Inspiration in human race
Is a long gone memory
At best.
Fucking artists.
Crows.
I blame you for not carrying hope
Within your message.
Fucking artists.
Our enemies are so powerful
And you deem art
Your art,
Your expression,
To the inner characteristics
Of your despair,
Of you dampened individuality...

Why is it
So difficult
To see
Groundbreaking
Inspirational art
Based on the idea of humanity?
Why doesn't
Creativity appear like that?

It is so much easier to do ugly things.
Shock value even exists in the purists.
Fuck you artists.
At the end, you always play in politics to escalate.
You sell your soul in tiny parts
(no big jumps because that would make you remorseful.)
The doings of art
Are forced by school
To be standardized.
Come on,
the artists that get somewhere
are artists who have come to understand
that art is accompanied by personal statements,
curriculum vitae,
and the good recommendation
of fellow artists
made critics.
And then,
you are happily free in your hard bounded context
of the artists' world:
The disguised market-friendly artists.

Artists:
You have come to be animals
that follow trends with an attitude

in order to survive.
You,
the ones that were supposed to speak out.
You,
the ones that should envision the future
and the complex combination
between
emotion and thought
in our lives.

Fuck you again artists:
I can feel your void.
If you cannot make sense out of your own life
how can you make sense out of it for all of us?

Fuck you again artists:
I have work to do.

RANT 14
We all silently do

Kids daring each other to do stupid things.
Frenetic shoppers on a buying spree.
Schoolgirls measuring their breast, waist, and thighs,
they want to find out who they are.
Big mouths and little lives.

Activists fighting globalization when corporate power is their real
enemy.
Judgmental people pointing fingers without reason.
Money-making entertainers made philanthropists
(hey, you gotta improve your PR, you know).
Sweet talk and bitter lies.
Sweet talk and bitter lies

Lecturers in the media telling you who is right and who is wrong.
Deceiving your spouse as a means to deal with your weaknesses.
9 to 5 to pay your bills and to pile up days until you die.
No time to eat, no time to create, no time to sleep, no time to cry.

(Launch CNN website.)
And we all silently dig it, well all silently do…

Politicians using all the holes in the system to protect specific
interests, specific friends.
Lawyers as sharks of their own clientele.
Economists lost, living in a Darwinian spell.

And we all silently dig it, well all silently do…

Everything seems without shape,
Everything seems without form,
And we all silently dig it, well all silently do…

RANT 15
Everyone is guilty but you

Everyone is guilty but you.
Are you the type that exposes
who is stupid
and who is not
while you drive?
Everyone is guilty but you.
Do you press the "close door" button
in the elevator?
Anxious to go up?
Anxious to go down?
Happy pushing your little placebo?
I know, I know,
everyone is guilty but you.
Are you one of those
85% of Americans
that consider themselves environmentalists?
A title that suits everyone well, isn't it?

Any world cause
is acknowledged
by anyone
any day
as a means to be socially desirable
(be liked by others, be able to fit in,)
even though
you know
and I know
that it doesn't go further than that,
there are no real actions
behind those hollow words
(those tiny little lies meant to relieve your conscientiousness.)
Your worries
and your chitchats
about social problems
dissolve right after
you have stopped marketing yourself.

I know everyone is guilty but you.
Everybody does the same.

Hate politics and politicians?
Hate the number of ads on TV?
Hate receiving telemarketing calls?
Are you one of those who hate malls and crowds?
Yes, I know, you are special,
so there is nothing to do about it
but to hide,
play the solipsist role of being outside the masses
and inside your privileged context.

Dig your own grave with your apathy.

The more indifferent you are
the more screwed you will be.
Don't forget to point your finger
at everyone
and everything
all the time,
and don't forget to appear concerned
even if afterwards
you don't give a damn about it.

Guilt
is
for
someone
else,
not you,
you are okay with your sporadic half-hour speeches.
You have learned that hypocrisy pays.

RANT 16
What you brag about

Tell me
what you brag about
and I'll tell you
what you lack.
Have you noticed that
those who criticize the most
are those that accomplish the least.
Why is it so?
They are all pompous
in their protected little pocket
of friends.
Any mediocre person
learns how to fly their ego
right above the desolated landscapes
of their ignorance.
All the fools want to be stars.
Being too judgmental
without substance to your arguments
makes you look like a spoiled child
with pretentious visions.
Can you do it yourself?
Would you be better at it?
Why is it that the ones who have more to brag about
are the ones who embrace a life
without winners or losers?
Why is it so?
At some point you will fall.
It is brutal how blind you are.
Tell me what you brag about
and I'll tell you what you lack.
You've been nourished
glorified visions of yourself,
and believe me,
they have learned to keep the carrot
right in front of you.

HOPE LASTS LONGER THAN GRATITUDE

So learn now
that there is no fame out there for you.
At some point you will fall.
Maybe you have invested
too much time
judging everyone else's work
that you have nothing of your own.
You've grown a smart ass.
One day try honestly
to make things better for you
and better for others…

So tell me
what you brag about

and I'll tell you
what you lack.
Ease down your overpowering individuality.
Remember,
they have learned
how to keep the carrot in front of you.
And you will run,
you will run because hope will last longer
than your gratitude.
I am sure they will not give it to you.
They want you to run,
to try really hard,
and to voice out your frustrations
by criticizing others,
by keeping those standards (that you cannot fulfill) very high.
Remember,
any mediocre person
learns how to fly their ego
right above the desolated landscapes
of their ignorance,
and maybe,
just maybe,
that person is you.

FLASH 17
I miss your birth

You…
I miss you.
It is hard to breathe
under a broken sky.
I wish I could have you
you
not anyone else
you.
I wish you could understand me better,
I wish I could have better words
and better ways
to tell you what I see.
I wish we could join forces.
You.
I miss you,
and I miss you
as I would miss myself
if one day
I wake up bodiless
to a never ending dream.

I know I miss you.
I know I lack of you.
I know that you are also
on the other side of a screen,
lost in the noise,
lost in that deconstructed avalanche
of 1s and 0s
that fades away like static
at the end of every day.

You are at the end
of a million threads
and still I cannot talk to you.
I miss your breath.
I miss the one
who is willing to keep up the fight.
I miss the one
who is recovering and weak
but who will fight again with me.
I miss the one
who is opening
their eyes for the first time.
I miss your birth.

RANT 18
Hypocrites

Is it just plain sloppiness
or just a way to keep you sane
in an world filled
with double standards?
You ask all the time
for something original
and as soon as someone provides it
you attack it
for not being customary
for not following the norm.
Hypocrites:
you are propagators of the sickness
that you "fight."
You are bored enough to complain about things
but you are lazy enough
to avoid understanding anything new.
You are stalled in your disdain
and it feels to you as
a slow and subtle anger,
but you are a creature of that wasteland too.
Human suffering is always a concern
for social occasions
but it is not a worry in your everyday life.
Everything is rhetorical in you.
You promote your own misery.
You've become an honorary member of pop culture
because you despise it
but you venerate it with your time,
you allow yourself to be entertained
because there is nothing better to do.
You spend so much energy
saving time
to later on
bring it all down
in front of the television,
in front of the CPU.

Welcome to the paradox of your life.
You want to be special like everybody else.
Your individuality is first but you feel lonely.
It is so usual to find people like you
trapped within the uniqueness of your world.
So let me tell you the obvious:
You cannot stop being a hypocrite
when you hold double standards.
You see,
the problem is that
when you look at yourself
you don't hold the same yardstick
as the one that you hold when you criticize others.
Welcome to the paradox of your life.
The same old questions
are still there

unanswered,
even if you run throughout life
as "fast" as you can.

BIBLIOGRAPHY

Ayersman, D.J. (1995). Effects of knowledge representation format and hypermedia instruction on metacognitive accuracy. <u>Computers in Human Behavior</u>, 11(3-4), 553-555.

Ayersman, D.J., & Reed, W.M. (1995). The impact of instructional design and hypermedia software type on graduate students' use of theoretical models. <u>Computers in Human Behavior</u>, 11(3-4), 557-580.

Boechler, P.M., (2001). How spatial is hyperspace? Interacting with hypertext documents: Cognitive processes and concepts. <u>Cyberpsychology & Behavior</u>, 4(1), 23-46.

Bonilla, D. (1993). Girando Bajo. <u>Unpublished manuscript</u>.

Bonilla, D. (1999). Non-linear reading as an Internet use trait. <u>Unpublished manuscript</u>.

Bowman, R.F. (1982). A "Pac-Man" theory of motivation: Tactical implications for classroom instruction. <u>Education Technology</u>, 22(9), 14-16. In Mehrabian, A. & Wixen W.J. (1986) Preferences for Individual Video Games as a Function of their Emotional Effects on players. <u>Journal of Applied Social Psychology</u>, 16(1), 3-15.

Campbell, D.T. & Cook, T.D. (1979) <u>Quasi-Experimentation. Design & Analysis Issues for Field Settings.</u> Boston: Houghton Mifflin Company.

Cantor, N., & Mischel, W. (1977). Traits as prototypes: Effects on recognition memory. <u>Journal of Personality and Social Psychology</u>, 35, 38-48.

Cantor, N., & Mischel, W. (1979). Prototypes in person perception. In L. Berkowitz (Ed.), <u>Advances in experimental social psychology</u> (Vol. 12, pp. 3-52). New York: Academic Press.

Chan, T.S. (1998). Motivational Flow in Computer-Based information access activity. Unpublished doctoral dissertation, Texas Tech University, Texas.

Chandler, D. (1995) <i>Cultivation Theory.</i>
http://www.aber.ac.uk/media/Documents/short/cultiv.html

Chen, H., Wigand, R.T., & Nilan, M.S. (1999). Optimal experiences of web activities. Computers in Human Behavior, 15(5), 585-608

Chou, C., Lin, H., & Sun, C. (2000). Navigation maps in hierarchical-structured hypertext courseware. International Journal of Instructional Media, 27(2), 165-183.

Comstock, G., & Paik, H. (1991). Television and the American Child. San Diego, CA: Academic Press.

Csikszentmihalyi, M. (1990). Flow. The psychology of optimal experience. New York, NY: Harper & Row.

Crockler, J., Fiske, S.T., & Taylor, S.E. (1984). Schematic bases of belief change. In J.R. Eiser (Ed.), Attitudinal judgment (pp. 197-226). New York, NY: Springer-Verlag.

DeFleur, M. H. (1999) Integrated Theory of Recall of News. Mass Communication & Society, 2(3/4), 123-145

Dvorak, R., & Sommerville, S.T. (1996). Hypertext/Hypermedia –a review. In Otter, M., & Johnson, H. (2000) Lost in hyperspace: metrics and mental models. Interacting with computers, 13, 1-40

Edwards, D.M., & Hardman, L. (1989). "Lost in hyperspace": Cognitive mapping and navigation in a Hypertext Environment. In McAleese, R. (1989). Hypertext, theory into practice (pp. 51-84). Norwood, NJ: Ablex Publishing Corporation.

Ellis, G., Voelkl, J. & Morris, C. (1994) Measurement and analysis issues with explanation of variance in daily experience using the flow model. Journal of Leisure Research, 26(4), 337-356.

Elm, W.C. & Woods, D.D. (1985). Getting lost: A case study in interface design. Proceedings of the Human Factors Society, 927-931.

Fauconnier, G. (1997) Mappings in thought and language. Cambridge, MA: Cambridge University Press.

Fiske, S.T., & Taylor, S.E. (1984). Social cognition. Reading, MA: Addison-Wesley.

Foss, C.L. (1989). Detecting users lost: empirical studies on browsing hypertext. Rapports de recherché, Institut National de Récherche en Informatique et en Automatique, 972.

Gamberini, L. & Bussolon, S. (2001) Human navigation in electronic environments. Cyberpsychology & Behavior, 4(1), 57-65.

Ghani, J.A. & Deshpande, S.P. (1993). Task Characteristics and the Experience of Optimal Flow in Human-Computer Interaction. The Journal of Psychology, 128(4), 381-391.

Graber, D.A. (1988). Processing the news. New York: Longman.

Guiley, R.E. (1991) Harper's Encyclopedia of Mystical and Paranormal Experience. New York: HarperCollins, 1991 (pp. 438)

Gygi, K. (1990). Recognizing the symptoms of hypertext and what to do about it. In Laurel, B. (1990) The Art of Human-Computer Interface Design (pp. 279-288) Boston,MA: Addision-Wesley.

Hailey, D.E. & Hailey, C. (1998) Hypermedia, multimedia and reader cognition: An emprirical study. Technical Communication, 3, 330-342.

Harmon, S.W. (1995) Novice use of a dimensional scale for the evaluation of the hypermedia user interface: Caveat Emptor. Computers in Human Behavior, 11(3-4), 429-437.

Hoffman, D.L. & Novak, T.P. (1996) Marketing in hypermedia Computer-Mediated Environments: Conceptual Foundations. Journal of Marketing, 60, 50-68.

Iran-Nejad, A. (1989) Nonconnectionist schema theory of understanding surprise-ending stories. Discourse Processes, 12, 127-148.

Kenny, D. A. (1979). Correlation and causality. New York, NY: John Wiley & Sons.

Kim, H. & Hirtle, S.C. (1995) Spatial metaphors and disorientation in hypertext browsing. Behavior & Information Technology, 14(4), 239-250.

Landow, G. P. (1992). Hypertext. The convergence of contemporary critical theory and technology. Baltimore and London: The John Hopkins University Press.

Lau, R.R. (1986). Political schemata, candidate evaluations, and voting behavior. In R.R. Lau & D.O. Sears, Political cognition (pp. 95-126). Hillsdale, NJ: Lawrence Erlbaum.

Lawless, K.A., & Brown, S.W., (1997). Multimedia learning environments: Issues of learner control and navigation. Instructional Science, 25, 117-131.

Lippman, W. (1922). Public opinion. New York: Macmillan.

Liu, M., Ayersman, D.J., & Reed, W.M. (1995) Perceptions of a hypermedia environment. Computers in Human Behavior, 11(3-4), 411-428.

Mandler, M.J. (1984) Stories, scripts, and scenes: Aspects of schema theory. Hillsdale, NJ: Lawrence Erlbaum Associates.

Massimi, F. & Carli, M. (1988) The systematic assessment of flow in daily experience. In Csikszenmihaly & Csikszenmihaly (Eds.), Optimal Experience: Psychological Studies of Flow in Consciousness. (pp. 266-287). New York: Cambridge University Press.

McAleese, R. (1989). Hypertext, theory into practice. Norwood, NJ: Ablex Publishing Corporation.

McDonald, S., & Stevenson, R.J. (1996) Disorientation in hypertext: the effects of three text structures on navigation performance. Applied Ergonomics, 27(1), 61-68.

Mehrabian, A. & Wixen W.J. (1986) Preferences for Individual Video Games as a Function of their Emotional Effects on players. Journal of Applied Social Psychology, 16(1), 3-15.

Minsky, M.A. (1975). Framework for representing knowledge. In P.H. Winston (Ed.), The psychology of computer vision. New York: McGraw-Hill.

Motl, R.W., Dishman, R.K., Saunders, R., Dowda, M., Felton, G., & Pate, R.T. (2001) Measuring enjoyment of physical activities in adolescent girls. American Journal of Preventive Medicine, 21(2), 110-117.

Murphy, J.B. (1998). What makes the people click? An analysis of web page navigation.

Unpublished doctoral dissertation, The Florida State University, Florida.

Nielsen, J. (1990). Hypertext. Communications of the ACM, 33, 297-310.

Norman, D.A. & Bobrow, D. G. (1976). On the role of active memory processes. In C. Cofer (Ed.), The structure of human memory (pp. 114-132). San Francisco: W. H. Freeman.

Norman, K. L. (1991). The psychology of menu selection. Norwood, NJ: Ablex Publishing Corporation.

Otter, M., & Johnson, H. (2000). Lost in hyperspace: metrics and mental models. Interacting with computers, 13, 1-40

O'Sullivan, C., & Durso, F.T. (1984). Effect of schemata-incongruent information on memory for stereotypical attributes. Journal of Personality and Social Psychology, 47, 55-70.

Paulukonis, A.M. (1999) First contact: The use of schemas by students taking their first online course. Unpublished doctoral dissertation, Michigan State University, Michigan.

Potter, W.J. (1994). Cultivation Theory and Research. A methodological Critique. Journalism Monographs, 147.

Publication Manual of the American Psychological Association (4th ed.). (1998). Washington, DC: American Psychological Association.

Rayburn, J.D. & Palmgreen, P. (1984) Merging uses and gratifications and expectancy value theory. Communications Research, 11(4), 537-562.

Rhee, Y. (1993) Hypertext navigation: Nonlinearity of exploration and its correlates. Unpublished doctoral dissertation, University of Illinois at Urbana-Champaign, Illinois.

Rothbart, M. (1981). Memory processes and social beliefs. In D. Hamilton (Ed.), Cognitive processes in stereotyping and intergroup behavior (pp. 145-182). Hillsdale, NJ: Lawrence Erlbaum.

Ruggiero, T.E. (2000). Uses and gratifications theory in the 21st century. Mass Communication & Society, 3(1), 3-37

Rumpradit, C. An evaluation of the effect of user interface elements and user learning styles on user performance, confidence, and satisfaction on the World Wide Web, Doctoral Dissertation. Washington, D.C., 1999

Shanahan, J., & Morgan, M. (1999). Television and its viewers. Cultivation Theory and Research. Cambridge, MA: Cambridge University Press.

Stoermer, R., Mager, R., Roessler, A., Mueller-Sphan, F., & Bullinger, A.H. (2000). Monitoring Human-Virtual Reality Interaction: A time series analysis approach. Cyberpsychology & Behavior, 3(3), 401-406.

Schank, R.C., & Abelson, R.P. (1977). Scripts, plans, goals and understanding: An inquiry into human knowledge structures. Hillsdale, NJ: Lawrence Erlbaum.

Spiro, R.J., Feltovich, P.J., Jacobson, M.J., & Coulson, R.L. (1992). Cognitive flexibility, constructivism and hypertext: Random access instruction for advanced knowledge acquisition in ill-structured domains. In T. Duffy & D. Jonassen (Eds.), Constructivism and the Technology of Instruction. Hillsdale, NJ: Erlbaum.

Tayck, P.L. (2000). Acoustic Response and detection of marine mammals using an advanced digital acoustic recording tag. Retrieved March 14, 2002 from http://www.serdp.org/reporting/CS-1188.pdf

Taylor, S.E. (1981). The interface of cognitive and social psychology. In J. Harvey (Ed.), Cognition, social behavior, and the environment (pp. 189-211). Hillsdale, NJ: Lawrence Erlbaum.

Tesser, A., & Leone, C. (1977). Cognitive schemas and thought as determinants of attitude change. Journal of Experimental Psychology, 13, 340-356.

Weller, H.G. (1995). Improving the effectiveness of learning through hypermedia-based instruction: The importance of learner characteristics. Computers in Human Behavior, 11(3-4), 451-465.

Woodhead, N. (1991). Hypertext & Hypermedia. Theory and applications. Wilmslow, England: Sigma Press.

VDM

Verlag
Dr. Müller

Wissenschaftlicher Buchverlag bietet
kostenfreie
Publikation
von
wissenschaftlichen Arbeiten

Diplomarbeiten, Magisterarbeiten, Master und Bachelor Theses
sowie Dissertationen, Habilitationen und wissenschaftliche Monographien

Sie verfügen über eine wissenschaftliche Abschlußarbeit zu aktuellen oder zeitlosen
Fragestellungen, die hohen inhaltlichen und formalen Ansprüchen genügt,
und haben **Interesse an einer honorarvergüteten Publikation**?

Dann senden Sie bitte erste Informationen über Ihre Arbeit per Email
an info@vdm-verlag.de. Unser Außenlektorat meldet sich umgehend bei Ihnen.

VDM Verlag Dr. Müller Aktiengesellschaft & Co. KG
Dudweiler Landstraße 125a
D - 66123 Saarbrücken

www.vdm-verlag.de

www.ingramcontent.com/pod-product-compliance
Lightning Source LLC
Chambersburg PA
CBHW071359050326
40689CB00010B/1696